An Independent Mind

'Juliet Hopkins has quietly encouraged and inspired generations of colleagues and students' – Dilys Daws, from the Foreword.

An Independent Mind: Collected papers of Juliet Hopkins follows the professional journey and influence of an innovative figure in the history of child psychotherapy. Juliet Hopkins spans Kleinian and Independent psychoanalytic traditions and brings a critical scientific mind to these theories. Amongst her main influences were Winnicott and Bowlby – both of whom her work addresses. This book contains her most important papers, bringing together psychoanalytic theory, family and individual approaches, attachment theory and infant-parent work. With a writing style that is clear, straightforward and readily accessible, Juliet Hopkins promotes a scholarly integrative way of thinking about psychotherapy without compromising the basic psychoanalytic principles that inform her work.

The papers have been gathered chronologically into four sections, each given context by the Editors with a brief introduction:

Trauma and child psychotherapy
Attachment and child psychotherapy
Infant-parent psychotherapy
Integrating and exploring Winnicott

An Independent Mind: Collected papers of Juliet Hopkins is a collection of classic papers whose relevance today is undiminished. It will be essential reading for established and trainee child and adult psychotherapists and psychoanalysts; counsellors, psychologists, psychiatrists interested in psychoanalytic approaches; and social workers, nursery workers and those who work with children in voluntary organisations.

Ann Horne was head of the Independent child psychotherapy training and post-graduate development at the BAP (now IPCAPA). She is co-editor of *The Handbook of Child and Adolescent Psychotherapy* and of the three earlier books in this series. Now retired, she gives talks and writes, retaining a special interest in children who act with the body rather than reflect.

Monica Lanyado was founding Course Organising Tutor of the Child and Adolescent Psychotherapy Training at the Scottish Institute of Human Relations (now Human Development Scotland). She is author of *The Presence of the Therapist*, co-editor of *The Handbook of Child and Adolescent Psychotherapy* and of the three earlier books in this series. Retired from clinical practice, she supervises (at IPCAPA and privately), and enjoys teaching and writing.

Independent Psychoanalytic Approaches with Children and Adolescents series
Series Editors: Ann Horne and Monica Lanyado

Titles in the series

An Independent Mind

Collected papers of Juliet Hopkins

**Edited by Ann Horne and
Monica Lanyado**

Routledge
Taylor & Francis Group

LONDON AND NEW YORK

First published 2015
by Routledge
27 Church Road, Hove, East Sussex, BN3 2FA

And by Routledge
711 Third Avenue, New York, NY 10017

Routledge is an imprint of the Taylor & Francis Group, an informa business

British Library Cataloguing in Publication Data
A catalogue record for this book is available from the British Library

Library of Congress Cataloging-in-Publication Data
Hopkins, Juliet.
  [Works. Selections]
  An independent mind : collected papers of Juliet Hopkins / edited by
Ann Horne and Monica Lanyado.
      pages cm. — (Independent psychoanalytic approaches with children
and adolescents series)
  1. Child psychotherapy.   2. Child psychotherapists   3. Hopkins,
Juliet.   I. Horne, Ann, 1944–   II. Lanyado, Monica, 1949–   III. Title.

  RJ504.H67 2015
  618.92'8914—dc23
  2014048874

ISBN: 978-1-138-01531-9 (hbk)
ISBN: 978-1-138-01532-6 (pbk)
ISBN: 978-1-315-76414-6 (ebk)

Typeset in Times New Roman
by Apex CoVantage, LLC
Printed in Great Britain by Ashford Colour Press Ltd

MIX
Paper from
responsible sources
FSC® C011748

Contents

Contributors

Dilys Daws has written many papers on child psychotherapy and particularly parent-infant psychotherapy, including the volume *Through the Night: helping parents and sleepless infants*. Formerly Chair of the Association of Child Psychotherapists and the Child Psychotherapy Trust, she was the founding Chair of the Association for Infant Mental Health, UK. She is an honorary Consultant Child Psychotherapist at the Tavistock and Portman NHS Foundation Trust.

Juliet Hopkins trained as a child and adolescent psychotherapist at the Tavistock Clinic and worked on the staff of the Child Guidance Training Centre and the Tavistock Clinic until her retirement from the National Health Service. She has continued to teach at the Tavistock where she is an honorary consultant child psychotherapist. Juliet also trained as an adult psychotherapist at the British Association of Psychotherapists (now an association of the British Psychotherapy Federation) and works in private practice. In 1980 she was one of the across-training-schools group assembled by Anne Hurry to develop the first Independent training in psychoanalytic child and adolescent psychotherapy at the BAP (now IPCAPA), and has been engaged with this since its inception. Her interests and publications include attachment theory and psychotherapy, parent-infant psychotherapy and psychoanalytic child psychotherapy.

Ann Horne trained as a child and adolescent psychotherapist at the British Association of Psychotherapists (now IPCAPA) and is a Fellow of that organisation and an Honorary member of ČSPAP, the Czech Society for Psychoanalytic Psychotherapy. She served terms of office at the BAP as head of training and later of post-graduate development. A previous joint editor of the *Journal of Child Psychotherapy*, she is co-editor with Monica Lanyado of *The Handbook of Child and Adolescent Psychotherapy* (1999; 2nd edition 2009) and of three earlier books in this series. Now retired from the Portman Clinic, London, she gives talks, writes and teaches, retaining a special interest in children who act with the body rather than reflect.

Monica Lanyado trained at the Tavistock Clinic, and was the founding Course Organising Tutor of the Child and Adolescent Psychotherapy Training at the Scottish Institute of Human Relations (now Human Development Scotland). A previous joint editor of the *Journal of Child Psychotherapy*, she is joint editor with Ann Horne of the *Handbook of Child and Adolescent Psychotherapy* (1999; 2nd edition 2009) and the Independent Psychoanalytic Approaches with Children and Adolescents Series of which this book is the fourth. The first three books, *A Question of Technique*, *Through Assessment to Consultation* and *Winnicott's Children*, were also co-edited with Ann Horne. She is author of *The Presence of the Therapist* (2004). Now retired from clinical practice she is a training supervisor at the British Psychotherapy Foundation (of which the former British Association of Psychotherapy is a part) and teaches, gives talks and is published widely in the UK and in Europe.

Acknowledgements

During the 50 years of my professional life I have received a wealth of inspiration and encouragement from a multitude of colleagues and friends. In particular, it will be apparent from my writings that my indebtedness to my uncle, John Bowlby, and supervisor, Donald Winnicott, is immense. Equally so is my gratitude for the great benefit I have received from the resources, first of the Child Guidance Training Centre, and then of the Tavistock Clinic where Margaret Rustin and colleagues provided an analytic setting, both protective and stimulating, in which to thrive. In addition I have enjoyed the support of the superb Tavistock library.

Especially warm thanks are due to two friends who read all my drafts. Dilys Daws's wisdom and friendship saved me from a variety of errors and overcame my recurrent despondency, and Mary Sue Moore generously shared her many original and prescient ideas while helping me to clarify my own.

Finally, I owe much to my present editors who recognised that my papers were worth collecting and who have looked after me and my writings with great thought and care.

JH

These editors are grateful for the following permissions to reprint the papers by Juliet Hopkins included in this volume:

'Solving the mystery of monsters: steps towards the recovery from trauma' *Journal of Child Psychotherapy* 1986 copyright © Association of Child Psychotherapists, reprinted by permission of Taylor and Francis Ltd, www. tandfonline.com on behalf of the Association of Child Psychotherapists;

'Living under the threat of death: the impact of a congenital illness on an eight-year-old boy' *Journal of Child Psychotherapy* 1977 copyright © Association of Child Psychotherapists, reprinted by permission of Taylor and Francis Ltd, www.tandfonline.com on behalf of the Association of Child Psychotherapists;

'The probable role of trauma in a case of foot and shoe fetishism: aspects of the psychotherapy of a six-year-old girl' *International Review of Psycho-Analysis* 1984 © John Wiley and Sons;

'The observed infant of attachment theory' *British Journal of Psychotherapy* 1990 © John Wiley and Sons;

'Failure of the holding relationship: some effects of physical rejection on the child's attachment and on his inner experience' *Journal of Child Psychotherapy* 1987 copyright © Association of Child Psychotherapists, reprinted by permission of Taylor and Francis Ltd, www.tandfonline.com on behalf of the Association of Child Psychotherapists;

'Facilitating the development of intimacy between nurses and infants in day nurseries' *Early Child Development and Care* 1988, reprinted by permission of Taylor and Francis Ltd, www.tandf.co.uk/journals;

'Overcoming a child's resistance to late adoption: how one new attachment can facilitate another' *Journal of Child Psychotherapy* 2000 copyright © Association of Child Psychotherapists, reprinted by permission of Taylor and Francis Ltd, www.tandfonline.com on behalf of the Association of Child Psychotherapists;

'Infant-parent psychotherapy: Selma Fraiberg's contribution to understanding the past in the present' *What Can the Matter Be? Therapeutic Interventions with Parents, Infants and Young Children* edited by L. Emanuel and E. Bradley 2008 Karnac Books reprinted with kind permission of Karnac Books; and 'Infant-parent psychotherapy' *Journal of Child Psychotherapy* 1992 copyright © Association of Child Psychotherapists, reprinted by permission of Taylor and Francis Ltd, www.tandfonline.com on behalf of the Association of Child Psychotherapists;

'Therapeutic interventions in infancy: two contrasting cases of persistent crying' *Psychoanalytic Psychotherapy* 1994 copyright © Association for Psychoanalytic Psychotherapy in the NHS, reprinted by permission of Taylor and Francis Ltd, www.tandfonline.com on behalf of the Association for Psychoanalytic Psychotherapy in the NHS;

'The dangers and deprivations of too-good mothering' *Journal of Child Psychotherapy* 1996 copyright © Association of Child Psychotherapists, reprinted by permission of Taylor and Francis Ltd, www.tandfonline.com on behalf of the Association of Child Psychotherapists;

'Narcissistic illusions in late adolescence: the role of defensive and gratifying object-relationships and generative opportunities' *Psychoanalytic Inquiry* 1999 reprinted by permission of the publisher Taylor and Francis Ltd, www.tandf.co.uk/journals.

Chapter 11 appeared as 'From baby games to let's pretend: the achievement of playing' *Journal of the British Association of Psychotherapists* 1996 31: 20–28. This was the in-house journal of the BAP and ceased publication when the BAP took over the *British Journal of Psychotherapy*. The BAP recently merged with other psychoanalytic organisations to form the BPF. We have therefore been unable to seek permission for reprinting this chapter but remain grateful to the BAP for encouraging its initial publication.

Foreword

Einstein said, 'Make things as simple as possible, but no simpler.' He must have been thinking of Juliet!

Juliet's style is always simple, and direct. It is succinct, knowledgeable and challenging, but never sarcastic or throwaway.

Juliet and I trained together, qualifying more than 50 years ago. She has been encouraging to me personally in the years since of friendship and working together. I would never have dared write without her gentle persuasion. And it has been a creative on-going discussion and cross-fertilisation of ideas over these decades of work and writing. She has also encouraged and inspired generations of colleagues and students. Juliet, and what she says, is quietly memorable. In every teaching event I find myself quoting her. One of the most striking sayings that comes to mind is: 'You are never alone with a grievance.' Those of us doing parent-infant work listen to many tales of childhood grievance, often serious, but also tales of many rather nebulous parental ill-doings. With a new baby at home, these complaints can be reconsidered and 'good-enough' mothering discovered.

Recently I was with Simon Cregeen, a Tavistock-trained child psychotherapist working in Manchester and Leeds; he asked after Juliet and spontaneously told me how valuable her teaching had been. I asked him to write a note on it, and think it conveys beautifully one of Juliet's main contributions:

> When training as a child psychotherapist at the Tavistock many years ago, for two years I attended the 'Work with Families' seminar led by Juliet. This was clinically engaging and stimulating. Juliet was a clear and subtle teacher and facilitator of the group process. One thing I took from the seminar was this: when a child is referred with an idea of having individual psychotherapy, rather than immediately and solely focus on this as a possibility, we might rather ask the question 'what might be usefully offered to the family as a whole?' This could be work prior to, or instead of, individual therapy. The question was not a response to scarce resources but was based on sound clinical principles.
>
> Juliet's model of meeting with families, briefly or over time, was not systemic family therapy, though there is undoubtedly some shared ground and interests. What distinguished it was its employment of core psychoanalytic

principles and techniques, including anxieties and defences, splitting and projection, transference and counter-transference. A developmental model, incorporating both individuals and the family grouping, was also important. Attachment concepts, particularly those relating to the intergenerational transmission of troubled attachment styles and relationships, also informed her clinical thinking. What Juliet seemed to be saying about the experience of seeing families together was something like this: seeing the family allowed the therapist to experience 'live' the family relationships; the child could observe how the therapist managed and communicated with the (troubled) parents; the parents could observe the therapist with their (troubled) child, and how she communicated with that child; the parental couple relationship can be observed and perhaps commented on; family projective processes could be observed by the therapist and interventions made directly. Families where scapegoating is taking place may be helped, as individual psychotherapy is unlikely to be useful when a scapegoated child is living in the family where this continues. A final point – the family culture and collective identity can be experienced by the therapist, something which I think is very difficult to grasp through individual work and reviews.

Juliet has widened our view of what child psychotherapy can encompass, and she does it without attacking the basic concepts of individual work. She shows that diametrically different approaches can co-exist and nourish each other. It takes away the worry some therapists have that embracing, for example, attachment or family therapy might be disloyal to psychotherapy.

In her way of helping us think outside fixed ways of responding to patients, she has shown how sometimes a low-key comment is enough. She knows that people can be disturbed, that malevolence exists, but her simple thought of saying to a patient 'that must have been disappointing for you' might enable that patient to keep a betrayal in proportion.

Juliet herself is a prime example of inter-generational influence. Her parents were both ground-breaking in their fields, and were modest in their self-perception. Her father, the economist Professor Henry Phelps Brown, wrote *Egalitarianism and the Generation of Inequality* (Oxford University Press 1988), which foreshadowed today's writings on social and economic responsibility. Her mother, Evelyn Phelps Brown, helped start the Pre-School Play Groups Association which brought many young children and their mothers out of isolation and into a social world.

The integrity of their work is continued in Juliet's and also in her own three children's work in medicine, economics and film. You can see elements of Juliet's love of theory, social responsibility and creativity in what they all bring to their professions. She has also kept alive John Bowlby's legacy that theory needs to be translated into social action.

Juliet's influence on the mental health of infants and young children has certainly been considerable, and the Tavistock owes part of its high profile for parent-infant psychotherapy, and the principles of child care, to her. She has taught and mentored those trying to improve the experience of children in day-care. More than 20 years ago at the Tavistock she started a Course in Infant Mental Health that I worked on with her. This led on to the creating of the Post-Graduate Diploma/ MA in Infant Mental Health. Students from this Course have raised the profile of IMH round the country, have set up trainings and services, have inspired colleagues. These were the years that I worked most closely with Juliet and we have had much fun together. I also learned from her that you gain as much from the students as they do from you.

Her generosity towards other people's work is legendary. Mary Sue Moore once pointed out that if you wanted to have some positive criticism after giving a talk, you should make sure Juliet was in the audience. Not many of us bother to reassure or give constructive feedback to the speaker, or indeed the writer of a paper!

It took a scientist like Einstein to point out the value and beauty of simplicity, and Juliet is also a scientist; her first degree was in Natural Sciences. Her scientific mind underpins her natural insight and empathy.

This is a very welcome book, one that should have come out a long time ago! It is good that there is now an opportunity to make Juliet's thoughts available to a wider professional readership.

Dilys Daws

Introduction

This volume of her papers went to press in the year in which Juliet Hopkins turned 80. We have been the beneficiaries of her writing, teaching and thinking for over 50 years. It is timely that the papers are now collected and made available to many more readers and it has been a great pleasure to work with her to accomplish this.

The influence of Juliet Hopkins's thinking has been wide – although as a resolutely unassuming woman she would try to demur. One mark of this lies in her papers being used for teaching on five continents and speaking requests being as widely sourced; and her work has been published in English, German, French and Dutch. Those who have been taught and supervised by her recall the process with continuing warm affection. Her audience, moreover, has been a broad and international one – not simply the psychoanalytic child psychotherapists whom she has taught during and beyond training but a large number of front-line professionals working in child care, child psychology and development, education and others with concern over troubling families, as well as parents interested in the growth and development of their children. Three reasons lie behind this:

a) her commitment to infant and child development, improving practice and disseminating understanding of the processes at work in families, and basing this on observational research;
b) an ability to integrate a range of approaches – psychoanalytic, family, attachment, infant-parent – and demonstrate how one can use these together to enhance work with the child and family;
c) her capacity to communicate the scholarly and complex in a clear and accessible way. Her own summary: 'My desire has always been to write in plain English' (Hopkins 1998:7) does not quite cover it – this is a desire to communicate and a signal (and, in psychoanalysis, often unusual) ability to succeed.

Biographical information

The eldest of three children, and only daughter, of the economist Henry Phelps Brown and Evelyn Bowlby, younger sister of John Bowlby, Juliet Hopkins took degrees in biology and psychology at Cambridge. That scientific attitude was one that was to imbue her approach to method, theory and the testing of theory throughout her work. As important was a Darwinian outlook and the influence of the new science of ethology:

> I left Cambridge aware that infant mortality was a selective factor, not only for the race but also within the family. In order to survive the risks of accident, illness and infanticide, babies depended upon winning the devoted protection of their parents. In previous centuries their survival depended in part upon their capacity for relatedness, upon what has since become known as the capacity to form 'secure attachments'.
>
> (Hopkins 1998:1)

From Cambridge, in 1956 she began her training in clinical psychology at the Tavistock Clinic, then located in Beaumont Street near London's Maryle-bone Road. Her uncle, John Bowlby, had joined the staff there as part of the hugely influential inflow of Army psychoanalysts after the 1939–45 war, initially as deputy medical director to Jock Sutherland, and had for some time been engaged in attachment research. The psychoanalytic ethos of the Tavistock and the emphasis on the theories of Melanie Klein offered important clinical insight and illumination, if not always gaining automatic acceptance: the biologist valued the more scientific approach that Bowlby was taking in reframing psychoanalysis to open it to research. Juliet Hopkins worked on Michael Balint's research unit on short-term psychotherapy and explored projective testing – which she still holds in good regard. Her first published paper (with the psychologist Herbert Phillipson) would arise from a research study comparing anxieties and defences in patients as revealed by projective testing and as uncovered by psychiatric interview. The agreement between them, she noted, was 'striking' (Hopkins 1998:2).

This training was followed by two years at Yale University Child Study Center. Yale was in some ways familiar ground, as she had spent several wartime years there as a child with her mother and brother and there attended school. Now, she could not but perceive the difference in analytical stance between classical/Anna Freudian Yale and the Kleinian Tavistock:

> This experience left me with a healthy scepticism for theory which I have always been careful to treat as hypothesis, not as the fact it is so liable to become assumed to be. It also assured my future allegiance to the Middle or Independent Group of British Psychoanalysis, the group most open to learning from sources other than the couch.
>
> (Hopkins 1998:2)

Work at Yale included paediatric settings, assessing the development of infants and pre-school children, and offered opportunity to observe babies at home and in 'an extremely depriving orphanage'. It was this last experience that stimulated what would become a life-long interest in deficit in development; and an ambition to influence procedures in institutions for children and to promulgate education and good practice in such places.

Long intent on training to be a child psychotherapist – not uninfluenced by her uncle – she returned to the UK to the Tavistock. The Anna Freud training at the Hampstead Clinic had appealed by reason of its greater emphasis on the role of parents in child development; but there might be less room for disagreement on that training, she thought! She sought an Independent analyst, there being some flexibility in this matter in 1960, and Enid Balint became her training analyst. She has since reflected that at a far earlier stage of life she had perhaps been subject to an unconventional Kleinian analysis:

> It was Uncle John who introduced my mother to psychoanalysis and so my own introduction began in the womb as I lay inside my mother on the couch of Joan Rivière, a close friend and colleague of Melanie Klein. (Mrs Rivière was also Uncle John's own analyst at the same time as far as I can ascertain.) My mother reared me on interpretations of sibling rivalry, death wishes and penis envy which aroused my curiosity and contributed to my decision to study psychology.
>
> (Hopkins 2010:1)

The child psychotherapy training offered a grounding that remained indispensable, despite the ever-questioning observing attitude:

> Although I was always sceptical of much Kleinian theory I am grateful that in my twenties I learned from Kleinians the significance of the here-and-now relationship, the reality of destructiveness and the value of conceptualizing all behaviour and perception in terms of underlying object relationships, anxieties and defences.
>
> (Hopkins 2010:2)

Her unique experience of supervision with Winnicott (see chapter 11) – and Winnicottian ideas – was influential. This was not, either, in conflict with attachment thinking. As Bowlby commented in interview:

> In many ways my viewpoint and that of Winnicott are highly consistent. He was no theoretician; he was an intuitive therapist with great gifts. I try to put the whole thing in systematic form. But we're singing the same song.
>
> (Bowlby, Figlio, & Young 1986: 55)

Juliet Hopkins notes, 'The song that they sang was about the significance of real life experiences in early childhood' (Hopkins 2010:2).

Marriage, family and two years in Hong Kong consequent on her husband's university secondment followed. There, working part-time in the Paediatric Department of the University of Hong Kong where she taught Chinese medical students, she encountered the impasse that unreflecting constancy to a theory can cause. With parents only allowed to visit for an hour a day, children on the wards were patently distressed; observations to the contrary were dismissed. The solution was creative:

> I realised that only observations made by Chinese observers could influence practice so I required each medical student in my seminars to befriend a young patient from admission until discharge and to record the child's reactions. The resulting paper (Hopkins 1969) was presented to the Paediatric Department and led to more liberal visiting policies at first in the University hospital and then throughout the Colony.
>
> (Hopkins 1998:3)

The use of observation to challenge and influence practice was to continue as a strategy.

The Child Guidance Training Centre had been established in Canonbury, London, in 1929, the second Child Guidance Clinic in the country. When the Tavistock Clinic moved in to its purpose-built building in Swiss Cottage in 1967, the CGTC was subsumed into the building where, until 1985, it carried on a separate existence in a wing away from the Child and Family Department. Juliet Hopkins worked there as a child psychotherapist from 1972, through the merger in 1985 with the Child and Family Department of the Tavistock, retiring in 2000. She continued teaching, supervision and consultation work as an honorary member of staff for the following decade.

Influence and influences

Family work and the place of parents

It was a pleasing coincidence that John Bowlby had also experienced the CGTC – indeed, it had been his first child psychiatry work setting:

> . . . it was in the period '36–'39, when my viewpoint on aetiology, having been influenced initially in 1928 towards real life experiences, was greatly amplified by my experience at the Child Guidance Training Centre; where we were as a matter of course seeing children's problems in terms of family dynamics, and very frequently, of the emotional problems the parents had, stemming from their own childhoods. I was working with two analytically oriented psychiatric social workers who were very capable people doing very good work. I learned a great deal from them. So you see my emphasis was on the real life experiences within the family.
>
> (Bowlby et al. 1986: 37)

With a remit for training psychologists, child psychiatrists and psychiatric social workers, the CGTC had a firmly multi-professional philosophy and outlook. In line with the child guidance ethos in the UK, its approach was family and child based, beginning with the family and moving into individual child psychotherapy if there was, nevertheless, a 'stuck' child. Assessment began with the family. Although Bowlby had joined the Tavistock in 1946 to develop the service for children (he renamed the Children's Department the Department for Children and Parents), the conflict he faced between his emphasis on the real-life experience of children and the classic psychoanalytic stress on the internal world (as articulated by Ernest Jones and by Mrs Klein and her followers) led him in 1977 to reflect: 'In certain respects I have been a stranger in my own department' (Senn 2007). It was perhaps advantageous for his niece to have first worked in the CGTC with mainly like-minded Independents and an eclectic mix of colleagues. All child psychotherapy schools at that time focused on the uniquely internal: a few Kleinians, writes Hopkins, 'were particularly dedicated to understanding how the child created his own internal world from his life and death instincts and his unconscious fantasies and were seemingly blind to the influence of parents and even of trauma' (2010: 3). But this, although perhaps at times dogmatic at the Tavistock, was really the case in all trainings. When the Independent child and adolescent psychotherapy training was established at the BAP[1] in 1982 – one in which Juliet Hopkins was involved from the planning stage – the shocking cohabitation of family therapy and individual work in our Child Guidance Units and in our individual practice was an on-going subject of very lively discussion between staff and trainees, and an introduction to Family Therapy did become part of the BAP course from the early years. Her influence must have been at work. She notes the contrast with today's practice:

> Overall, the increased significance of the interpersonal approach has given much more weight to the role of parents whose contribution to their child's development was liable to be minimized by extremes of the intrapsychic stance.
>
> (Hopkins 2010: 11)

Placing weight on the importance of child *and* family stemmed in part, of course, from Bowlby and Winnicott. It led Juliet Hopkins, when in 1972 the family moved to Princeton for a year and her children were all in school, to enrol on a family therapy course. Here she covered the basic reading and engaged in a more formal manner with a systemic approach. On her return to the Tavistock, she was given one session a week to train in family therapy and was supervised by John Byng-Hall, whose approach was psychodynamic and who was developing an attachment-oriented approach to family therapy (Byng-Hall 1995). For several years she ran a very popular family therapy workshop for child psychotherapists – one attendee's memories are quoted by Dilys Daws in her Foreword to this volume.

One particular consequence of reminding the psychoanalytic professions of the role of parents was outlined by Bowlby in 'On knowing what you are not supposed to know and feeling what you are not supposed to feel' (Bowlby 1979), where he suggested a link between parental prohibition of acknowledging trauma and subsequent borderline development. This paper quotes freely from Juliet Hopkins's work of 1982, itself published in the *International Review of Psycho-Analysis* in 1984 and reprinted here as chapter 3. In 1984, she was addressing issues of intra-familial trauma and abuse and subsequent dissociation – a paper very much ahead of its time. The child patient's initial position of gender dysphoria and her delusion of possessing a penis, it was proposed, 'served as a defence against a terror of violation' – a hugely important finding.

Theory and technique

It is impossible to separate the influence of changes in theoretical position from the technical modification that follows: when theory is reassessed, practice may alter. Juliet Hopkins has been important here, both in expounding alterations and developments in theory and in engaging with the importance of the relational aspects of the therapist's stance:

> The change of emphasis from the focus on int*ra*personal pathology to a focus on disturbances in relationships has been widespread. Psychoanalysis has become more relational and int*er*personal, transference and counter-transference are widely seen as co-constructed, and it seems likely that the findings of attachment research have helped to facilitate this change. Ainsworth et al.'s demonstration (1978) of the interpersonal origin of infant defensive strategies and Main's demonstration of the way in which parents' representations of their own childhood experiences are transmitted to the next generation have been transformative.
>
> (Hopkins 2010:10)

> Attachment brought an unfamiliar dimension to psychoanalysis, a dimension ranging from security and safety to danger and fear. I think that its implications for therapy, particularly with children, were easily assimilated in this new climate of awareness of the ubiquity of trauma. The need to help the child feel safe in therapy has become a central aim whereas the Kleinian aim at the time of my training was always to keep the child's anxiety high in order to maximize the relief offered by interpretation. Clearly the art of the clinician is to achieve a balance between "too scary" and "too cosy". In therapy feelings of security are invited by the therapist's sensitivity and empathy and are disrupted by the limitations and separations built-in to the relationship. This creates a necessary instability that provokes change.
>
> (Hopkins 2010: 5–6)

It is a very interesting consideration that the concept of an axis of safety and danger in the child's experience – and hence in the nature of his attachments – would be incorporated by psychotherapy where, in turn, it would aid the recognition of trauma and the prevalence of traumatisation in childhood. Parallel developments – also stemming from psychoanalysis – in family therapy and group analysis (Foulkes and Skynner were undoubted influences) also had an impact on a professional environment that was to become able, but really only by the mid-1980s, to recognise child abuse and the role of family, and that would later learn to make use of attachment theory in this work. Psychotherapy thus reassessed Freud's retreat from understanding hysteria as stemming from trauma to his identifying it as the consequence of fantasy. It was a profound change – for those who could accept it – in psychoanalytic theory.

Her writing has placed the findings of attachment research in particular before a previously disbelieving audience and ensured that the audience paid attention. In this, she has helped knit together psychoanalytic theory – especially that of Winnicott but also, critically, of Fraiberg – with developments in infant mental health research, attachment research and the implications for practice. She reflected on the technical consequence of greater recognition of the role of parenting in child mental health:

> I wonder if this change of emphasis has contributed to child therapists becoming, as it is generally agreed, kinder and more empathetic to their patients than when I trained. For example, children who were once seen as making "attacks on linking" may now be seen as "victims of dissociation", while children who felt themselves to be bad and dangerous need no longer be supposed to harbour unconscious murderous intent but might be supposed to have been persistently misperceived as evil by their parents. Child psychotherapists today are freer to be friends to their patients and less focused on being an observing other.
>
> (Hopkins 2010: 11)

Where the symptoms are viewed as constructed between child and adult environment, and the activity of therapy seen as a joint enterprise in the transitional space created by therapist and child, then therapy can address process even with children who are driven to act. The injunction always to follow the child, too, may not always be the most creative response when the real world distorts reality:

> My Kleinian training taught me always to follow the child's material and not to raise external relationships with the child unless the child initiated this. The Anna Freud training on the other hand was actively prepared to provide children with help in understanding family problems like parental mental illness or scapegoating (Hurry and Sandler 1971).
>
> (Hopkins 2010: 13)

Describing her thinking about the case of eight-year-old Adam, who suffered a life-threatening illness from birth (chapter 2), she comments:

> The paper also aimed to modify the rigour of Kleinian technique, as then taught, by accepting the therapeutic value of play in its own right and by suggesting that it was not always necessary to challenge the child's defences with

interpretation. I intended in this way to integrate the value of some of Anna
Freud's and Winnicott's thinking with the benefits of my Kleinian training.

(Hopkins 1998: 3)

This freedom to learn from all theoretical thinkers, and to encourage such learning, has been a mark of her practice and teaching.

Observation and theory

Psychoanalysis has long suffered problems with the idealisation of its key progen-
itors. As the profession fought its own internal wars, the development of curiosity
and theoretical challenge outside the boundaries of each orthodoxy was greatly
hindered. Institutionalisation, after all, frequently curtails criticism. Juliet Hopkins has always valued a scientific approach that questions what it sees, that does
not shoehorn what it thinks it sees into one particular theoretical construct. She
could be said to advocate matters of science rather than matters of belief. In this
she is certainly the successor of John Bowlby and of Winnicott, who frequently
advocated observation and privileged it over theory: 'if the theory doesn't fit it,
it's just got to adjust itself' (Winnicott 1967a). But she is also her clear-thinking
own person. Her introduction to 'Ways of seeing 4' – a paper given at an ACP
conference where child psychotherapists from four different theoretical schools
commented on a video recording of a mother and baby – comments on the tribal
nature of and safety in adherence to theoretical positions but also on the necessity
of seeking theory that can develop, incorporate and adapt:

> . . . when we venture to explore new territory, in our role as scientists, we
> have to be prepared to welcome novelty. And we do need novel develop-
> ments. Whatever my prejudices about the abuse of theories, good theories are
> essential. They facilitate observation, understanding and research. Theories
> of pathology are necessary for therapy and theories of aetiology are necessary
> for prevention.

(Hopkins 1989: 33)

She was much sought-after as a teacher of parent-infant observation, not least
because of an ability to enable her students to *see*, to record and report what they
saw and to reflect on it, whatever theory might have been assumed to indicate.
(One recalls her impact on the medical students in Hong Kong.) A generation
of IPCAPA parent-infant observation tutors, taught by co-working with her, has
continued this method of examining the real relationship and what it means for the
development of the infant's external and internal worlds.

Finally: Education and change

'I've always felt that the ultimate solution to these schisms is better science' – so
said John Bowlby, reflecting on the polarisation of perspectives in psychoanalysis (Bowlby et al. 1986). Juliet Hopkins in 1998 noted the 'breaking-down of

doctrinal barriers within psychoanalysis' and a shift from intrapersonal development to interpersonal relationships as the focus of the child psychotherapist's work in the UK. It is certainly easier to have cross-border conversations than it was 50 years ago and one feels we now engage with children in ways that show they do not bear responsibility for the insults and unkindnesses that they have encountered. Much of the credit for this must go to the Juliet Hopkinses of the profession who have rejected the institutionalisation of theory (and thence practice) and insisted on observation, hypothesis and theoretical development; and who have made their knowledge (garnered from experience and from within and without the professions of psychoanalysis) available to those who might influence practice and policy for children:

> . . . the stimulus to write most of these papers was a sense of mission: to improve the well-being of children in hospital and of babies in day-care; to encourage early preventive or therapeutic intervention in infancy; and to alert Kleinian colleagues to significant developments concerning trauma, abuse, attachment and the role of play . . .
>
> Present thinking is at last in tune with the biological orientation of my student days.

> (Hopkins 1998:7)

Ann Horne
July/August 2014

Note

1 British Association of Psychotherapists – now the Independent Psychoanalytic Child and Adolescent Psychotherapy Association (IPCAPA), part of the British Psychotherapy Foundation.

Trauma and child psychotherapy

Introduction

When Juliet Hopkins was writing her earliest papers on trauma in the late 1970s and early 1980s, the world was a very different place. It seems extraordinary now, but the impact of external real life traumatic events on a child's emotional, family and behavioural life was not at that time an obvious consideration in clinical or theoretical psychoanalytic psychotherapy.

Even in Anna Freudian and Winnicottian thinking and clinical practice, where the importance of child care and the facilitating environment within which the child developed were core ideas, the impact of traumatic real life events only played a small part in clinical papers and theoretical thinking. And when Boston and Szur (1983) wrote about psychotherapy with children who had been removed by social services from their birth families, they attributed the children's difficulties solely to severe deprivation. John Bowlby also began his work with a focus on the ill effects of deprivation (Bowlby 1951) but found himself almost alone among psychoanalysts when he attributed much childhood psychopathology to a wide range of real life family trauma, including parental violence (Bowlby 1969/1982). Juliet Hopkins valued the development of his ideas and also benefited from his personal interest and encouragement.

It is intriguing to wonder why, in the post Second World War years, when there had been so much traumatic loss, separation and physical devastation, trauma remained in the background. And this was after the clinical recognition of shell shock and post-traumatic stress, which was so carefully documented during and after the First World War. Maybe, in itself, this is an example of the powerful psychological and social defences that are needed to protect the individual and society at large from the full-on impact of trauma; defences that are vital for the beginnings of recovery and healing of whatever can be recovered and healed after such devastating trauma (Menzies Lyth 1959). It may only become possible to look the trauma in the face after 'time has done its work' and there is a firm enough new structure in society, or the individual's internal world, to cope with the blast that comes from recognizing trauma that has become dormant in the meanwhile.

It is from within this context that Juliet Hopkins's papers on trauma need to be read. They are relevant to clinicians working with trauma of any kind. One of the two child patients discussed suffered life-threatening illness from birth which involved many medical and surgical interventions. The other child came from a violent home and was probably sexually abused by her father. When they were written, these papers were highly individual and illustrated the need to think independently about clinical experience when it did not fit contemporary theories. Juliet Hopkins comments that her undergraduate degree in Science trained her '*not to see* what she thought she *ought* to be seeing'! She presents an example of allowing clinical experience and observation to inform the clinician's working theoretical model, rather than the other way round.

The opening paper to this section of the book, 'Solving the mystery of monsters: steps towards the recovery from trauma', has become a classic paper. It is based on material from the psychotherapy of two children whose detailed treatment is separately presented in the two following chapters. It discusses the key issues in the therapeutic process where traumatic experience is recognised as the central problem and, in the title of the paper itself, expresses the idea that recovery is a long process made up of many *steps*. In her conclusion Juliet Hopkins is clear that, in her view, recovery can never be complete. There is substantial discussion of the interaction between the patients' internal and external reality experience and the importance of very cautious reconstruction of events, carefully timed according to the child's ability to know and face both psychic and corroborated external truth. The treatment of the parents of both patients is described as vital to the children's recovery.

In a postscript to the paper when it was re-published in a collection of child psychotherapy papers in 2004, Hopkins noted how she had previously underestimated the role of containment in enabling reconstruction and healing to take place (Barrows 2004). We have included this 2004 postscript to the original paper in this volume.

Chapter 2, 'Living under the threat of death', brings details of the therapy of Adam, the child with a life-threatening illness and medical trauma. The importance of trying to help the child patient to acknowledge the unfairness of life in dishing up such awful experiences, and being able to face squarely the anger and pain that belongs to this recognition, is movingly described. The clinical material shows how the child's enhanced capacity to express anger about his life-threatening illness and many painful medical interventions and hospital admissions, and in time to mourn and accept the cruelty of fate rather than manically deny it, enabled him to become more loving and less defended in his relationships with his parents.

Chapter 3 describes the challenging therapy of Sylvia, a 6-year-old girl with a foot and shoe fetish. Salient details of Sylvia's trauma were long withheld by her mother and had to be deduced from the child's material. The therapy brings confirmation of the colloquial saying that traumatic experience can "drive you mad" since its most significant contribution is to illustrate how a near-psychotic condition can result when a child takes flight from knowing the reality of a traumatic experience. This is particularly liable to happen, as in Sylvia's case, when significant adults in a child's life have put a taboo 'On knowing what you are not supposed to know and feeling what you are not supposed to feel' (Bowlby 1988). John Bowlby was working on drafts of this ground-breaking paper while Juliet Hopkins was working with Sylvia. He encouraged her to publish her work and quoted details from it in the final version of his paper. When her paper was accepted for publication in 1984 the etiological importance of trauma was still so strongly denied that she had to appease the editor by amending her title from 'The role of trauma . . .' to 'The probable role of trauma'. We are pleased that in this volume we can revert to the original title.

These papers, particularly when read as a group, provide a valuable insight into the treatment of childhood trauma in which the reality of the external traumatic events and their impact on the child's internal world are considered as a whole. This integration is a hallmark of the Independent psychoanalytic approach to the treatment of trauma.

ML

1 Solving the mystery of monsters

Steps towards the recovery from trauma[1]

Freud wrote in 1909 that "a thing which has not been understood inevitably reappears; like an unlaid ghost it cannot rest until the mystery has been solved and the spell broken."

This paper is concerned with solving the mystery and breaking the spell which binds children who have become the victims of trauma. It illustrates how psychotherapy can free children from the worst effects of trauma by enabling them to accept both the reality of the traumatic event and of the feelings which it aroused. In this way both these elements of the traumatic experience can be integrated and a start made in the process of recovery. I give examples from the psychotherapy of two children and consider the stages by which recovery from trauma takes place, and discuss the role of the child psychotherapist in facilitating it.

In defining trauma I follow Freud's statement of 1926: "The essence of a traumatic situation is an experience of helplessness on the part of the ego in the face of accumulation of excitation, whether of external or internal origin." This definition links the specific external event with internal psychic conditions and indicates the shattering, devastating and generally overwhelming effect of a trauma. Spontaneous recovery from such an event is possible, though commonly subsequent development is altered and takes a pathological course, as it did in the case of the two children whose clinical material I want to present. These children had both been subjected to recurrent traumas from their earliest years. They both had serious learning difficulties, and they were both preoccupied with monsters to the exclusion of all other interests. But I have selected them mainly because of the different response to trauma which each represents: one child retained detailed knowledge of the traumas but had no awareness that these events had been the cause of any suffering; the other child had retained no conscious knowledge of the traumas but remained overwhelmed by the distressing emotions which these events had aroused.

Psychotherapy with Adam

Adam was referred to our clinic at the age of eight years because he could not read in spite of good intelligence (Hopkins 1977). He had an encyclopaedic knowledge of dinosaurs and monsters, but otherwise was uninterested in learning. He was unhappy and bullied at school. At home he spent his time playing with models of dinosaurs and drawing endless pictures of imaginary monsters. His parents, who were concerned and caring people, complained of his apathy and felt there was "a certain meanness" about his emotions.

Adam had been born with a hereditary blood disease which made him pale, weak and anaemic and which required transfusions every few months. His parents were told he might not survive. As an infant he found weekly blood tests and regular transfusions extremely distressing, and his mother always stayed with him in hospital. However, when he was just four years old, he responded to reassuring explanations about his treatment by becoming completely confident, and he no longer appeared to need his mother in hospital. From this time onward he rejected physical cuddling and became very independent and self-reliant. His parents proudly reported that he had been very brave about a major abdominal operation at the age of seven years. When I met Adam at the age of eight years he described hospital as his favourite place. He knew all about his unusual illness and its treatment and was devoted to the doctors who had saved his life.

In the first of his once-weekly psychotherapy sessions, Adam told me about his eager co-operation in medical research and his "best Christmas ever", spent in hospital. At the same time he was modelling a dinosaur which fell into a cave-man's trap, and was eaten alive slowly, starting at the tail. He said that luckily the dinosaur didn't feel much because it was very insensitive. I acknowledged Adam's eager wish to co-operate with me too, but I thought his play revealed fears that I would deceive and attack him, just as he must have felt the kind doctors had done with their horrible treatment. I also compared the dinosaur's insensitivity to the way Adam appeared to have become insensitive to the distress which he could have been expected to feel about a chronic illness and its treatment.

Adam was interested in my ideas and showed me in drawings what his imaginary monsters were like. Each one aimed to deceive its prey. For example, if you protected yourself from its dangerous mouth it would be its tail which hid a lethal sting. Some monsters had snouts like drills which penetrated underground and tapped veins of gold which they stole. I thought that these monsters transparently disguised Adam's fears of treacherous attack and his dread of doctor's needles which penetrated his veins and stole his precious blood. Adam had apparently become a perfect patient at the cost of losing conscious awareness of his feelings about his treatment. His dread of doctors had been displaced on to monsters.

In the course of Adam's therapy with me which lasted nearly two years, he gradually re-experienced his anxiety, anger and distress about his illness and its treatment. This occurred first in the transference when Adam broke into violent rebellion against his psychotherapy, claiming that it was very unfair and unkind that he should have been picked on to have this sort of treatment, and begging instead for more physical treatment at the hospital.

It was in the second year of Adam's therapy that he gradually became painfully aware that cruel fate had picked on him to suffer a chronic illness and to endure endless physical treatment for it. He became intensely persecuted about it and also very depressed. His realisation of the trauma was so distressing for him it was hard for me to believe that it could be of any benefit for him to face such a stark reality. I felt as though I myself had been responsible for traumatising him. Gradually he changed from feeling crushed by the realisation to lamenting his fate and to becoming angry about it. In his play he openly identified with savage monsters seeking revenge. He was very frightened of expressing his anger openly to me or at home, but little by little he took courage to do so with his parents, and finally exploded into violent tantrums which he hadn't had since he was very small.

When Adam rediscovered his anger he also rediscovered his early love for his parents which he hadn't expressed since he was four years old. He became cuddly and affectionate, lost his preoccupation with monsters, developed other interests, and began to learn well in school. His emotional "meanness" had gone, and he had become able, to a limited extent, to think about his illness and its implications as a chronic misfortune and handicap in his life. For example, he groaned at the prospect of always being seen to be different from other children because he couldn't play games, and he resented the need to explain his condition, in contrast to the way in which he used to be proud to be special.

Psychotherapy with Sylvia

Sylvia was referred to our clinic at the age of six years because she was hyperactive, unmanageable and unable to learn, in spite of receiving special education at a school for children with emotional and behavioural difficulties. She had been previously assessed as borderline psychotic (Hopkins 1984). Sylvia, like Adam, was obsessed with monsters. She constantly talked of them and dramatized attacks both on them and by them. Much of the detail of her monster play derived from the TV series *Dr. Who*.

Sylvia's history was related by her widowed mother, a defensive young Italian woman who supplied only the barest details and made no mention of the traumas which she later confessed. She said that Sylvia had screamed endlessly as a baby and had thrown violent tantrums as a toddler. She was so backward when she started nursery school that she was thought to have learning difficulties. Her father had died in a car crash shortly before her fourth birthday and her behaviour had become increasingly unmanageable after this event.

In therapy, Sylvia quickly became extremely messy and aggressive, attacking me constantly in the role of a monster and enacting fantasies in which she herself was attacked by a variety of monsters too. She called the furniture "Daleks" and seemed convinced that chairs moved across the room to strike her, causing her to duck and cower in terror. As treatment progressed Sylvia increasingly demanded that I should act the part of terrifying monsters who pursued her with roars and threatened to eat her up. "Be a Dalek," "Be a carpet monster" or "Be a light switch monster," she said. By making me enact the monsters I thought she was trying to localize and control her terror of being attacked. But this stratagem was never wholly successful for she often screamed out in terror that a chair, a light or an unseen monster was attacking her; at such moments she seemed to be hallucinated.

I first interpreted one of her dramas as an attempt to communicate the past when she told me, "Be a cross dream!" She made herself a bed and hid under the blanket.

"Roar" she shouted. When I did, she asked, "Are you a real Mummy? Are you a Daddy too?" "Yes," I said. "Speak Italian then!" said Sylvia. "I'm Never-Mind-Boy in bed. I'm not Sylvia. Sylvia was too frightened." I said she was trying to remember what it was like when she was little and her mummy and daddy had terrible rows in Italian and she had been too frightened to bear it. Sylvia was moved by my reconstruction and wanted me to tell her more about what had happened in the past. At this stage of her treatment, during part of each session she would repeatedly enact a drama in a particularly urgent manner. I understood this as a request for me to reconstruct past events, which were at first more rows between her fighting patents. Sylvia now claimed to remember their fights. "Dad beat my mummy up," she said with conviction.

Soon Sylvia voiced more memories of her own. One session when she asked me, "Be a fierce daddy monster and frighten me very much," I said I thought she was trying to remember how she had been frightened of her own fierce daddy. Sylvia suddenly looked at me with great amazement and said, "My Dad broke up our house! It was another house. He threw all the furniture." She was perplexed about where this event had happened, and I told her I knew she had lived with her dad in a different house which her family left just before he died.

Sylvia's vivid recollection of her father throwing furniture helped me to understand her terrors of flying Dalek furniture and her own need to fling the furniture herself. She quickly responded to interpretation about her wish to throw furniture in order to terrify me, so that I would know how she had felt when her father did it. As a result, she lost her terror of being attacked by furniture and also stopped throwing it.

In her role of Never-Mind-Boy Sylvia then began to think increasingly about the past. Just as her recollection of her father throwing furniture had laid the Dalek monsters to rest, so her recollection that her father had died in a car accident, collecting a carpet, led to the disappearance of her need to make me attack her dressed as a "carpet monster." Sylvia's attacks on the lights in my room and her terror of the "light-switch monster" seemed related to her intense fear of the dark and her almost equal fear of turning on the light to reveal her monster parents fighting together. Discussion of these fears stopped Sylvia's attacks on the lights, and the light-switch monster also disappeared. She no longer seemed to be hallucinated.

In 1937 Freud reached the conclusion that there is "not only method in madness but also a fragment of historical truth." He wrote: "Perhaps it may be a general characteristic of hallucinations, to which sufficient attention has not hitherto been paid, that in them something that has been experienced in infancy and then forgotten returns" (Freud 1937: 267).

After I had reconstructed some of the forgotten events which had kept returning to Sylvia in the disguise of monsters, she began to bring happier memories about her father. She liked to sit on top of my cupboard because it was "just like riding on my daddy's back." She told me with delight how she could now remember going to the park with her daddy and paddling with him in the pool. Sylvia was then in touch with her love for her friendly father as well as with her hatred and fear of her fierce and angry father. Following this she grew openly depressed and cried recurrently as she genuinely mourned the dad she had loved as well as feared and hated. Before this she had dealt with his death by disavowal.

It was a whole year after Sylvia had shared her memories of her father's violence with me, that her mother at last confirmed these memories by confessing that her husband had thrown furniture in his rages and had broken the arms off the chairs. She also confessed that he had beaten Sylvia frequently and had thrown her across the room. When Sylvia was a screaming baby he had kicked both mother and daughter out of the house, or else he would have killed Sylvia. His violence outside the home had led him into serious trouble with the police.

The effect on Sylvia of recalling her traumatic experiences with her father was dramatic. She became much more manageable and was able to talk about what angered her. She was no longer possessed by preoccupation with monsters but began to develop other play themes, to draw pictures and to talk about them. At school she became sufficiently in touch with reality to learn, and after completing two years of twice weekly psychotherapy she was able to transfer to a school for normal children.

The meaning of monsters

The course of each of these children's psychotherapy illustrates Freud's idea (1920) that compulsive repetition in children's play is a means of mastering anxieties associated with trauma. It also illustrates a possible meaning of monsters.

For both Adam and Sylvia, monsters appeared to represent a compromise between their terrors of real aggressive assaults and terrors related to their own aggressive impulses. This is likely to be the case whenever a repetitive preoccupation with monsters is concerned. In practice it means that details of monsters can often give us clues to the people or events which have aroused the terror and rage which the monsters represent.

Stages in the recovery from trauma

Adam and Sylvia were both freed from their repetitive pre-occupation with monsters by recognising the traumas which the monsters had disguised. The analytic work had provided the understanding which solved the mystery, laid the ghosts and broke the spell. But revealing the monster's disguise was only a step in the children's recognition of the underlying traumas. Such recognition involves both a cognitive and an emotional awareness, it proceeds slowly and it is hard to say at what stage, if ever, it is complete.

Adam was interested, during his very first session, in my idea that his monsters might be doctors; he soon brought more material to amplify this view which he easily came to accept. However, it was not until the second year of his therapy, after he had re-lived the persecutory aspect of his medical treatment with me in the transference, that he could get in touch with his feelings about the suffering which he had undergone. He had of course known about the fact of his illness and his need for medical treatment as long as he could remember, but it now came as a terrible shock to him to realise that cruel fate had discriminated against him and had not simply made him uniquely special as he had supposed.

The shocking realisation that a congenital illness or a disability is a catastrophe is an occurrence in the lives of many disabled children. For example, Anna Freud (1967) has described how traumatic the discovery of blindness can be to a congenitally blind child. For Adam, the shock of acknowledging his handicap was followed by a retreat to bed for more than two weeks with flu, but it was after his recovery from this apparent set-back that he gained the freedom to express both his love and his anger and started to learn in school.

Sylvia's first acknowledgement of the reality of the traumas which she had endured was achieved through my reconstructions of the violence in her past. Reconstruction effectively gave her permission, in a safe setting, to recall and share what she already knew but was not supposed to know. The analytic literature (e.g. Bowlby 1985; Khan 1972; Rosen 1955; Tonnesmann 1980) suggests that the therapist's ability to construct external events is of particular importance when the patient has taken psychotic flight from reality, or when important adults in the patient's life have put a tabu on knowing. In both these conditions, which applied to Sylvia, the therapist risks colluding with the patient's defences if he treats the traumatic events only as fantasies. He may also risk repeating the behaviour of the original traumatogenic adult, for, as Balint (1969) points out, it is common for an adult who has traumatised a child to behave afterwards as though nothing had happened.

For both children, the intellectual and emotional acknowledgement of trauma achieved during therapy resulted in the significant improvements in their development already reported. However, in many respects the improvements were very limited. When therapy ended, Adam remained a passive, subdued boy, no longer bullied at school, but still without friends. Sylvia was still a borderline psychotic child, preoccupied with violence. A further limitation to their improvement was shown by both children's continuing propensity to repeat their traumas, a tendency which has been considered to be diagnostic of a traumatised child.

Adam's need to repeat his traumas was demonstrated by his voluntary submission to experimental medical procedures. Although he became very resentful of his illness and recognized his fear of doctors, he remained devoted to the medical team at the hospital where he was treated. He willingly continued to volunteer as a guinea pig in medical research and to submit himself to further painful investigations. The manner in which he described his collaboration suggested that he took a masochistic pleasure in his submission to experiments. It seemed likely that masochism might remain a significant feature in his pathology, as it has been found to be in some victims of medical and surgical assault in early childhood (Glenn 1984). However there were also other motives in Adam's participation as guinea-pig. His willing co-operation allowed him a sense of mastery and control over the inevitable, he was proud of his courage, won the admiration of doctors and nurses and aimed to help to discover a cure for his disease.

Sylvia's continuing propensity to repeat her traumas was manifest in her persistent provocation of violence. She did this recurrently in her treatment with me where her assaults taxed my patience to the limits and made it extremely hard to resist retaliation. She also provoked her mother repeatedly at home. Her mother confessed that she was driven to being brutal to her, and no doubt this meant that she was colluding in recreating Sylvia's early traumatic experiences. However, at school Sylvia gave up her provocative behaviour. She stopped attacking her teacher and the other children and ceased to be constantly involved in fights.

Neither Adam nor Sylvia was successfully freed from the aftermath of trauma. In order to recover more fully than they were able to do, children need to accept not only the reality of the traumatic events and the feelings which they engendered, but to become able to grieve about the damage done to them and to express appropriate anger about this. Adam was able to do this to some extent as far as his congenital illness was concerned, but not with regard to his medical treatment. Sylvia's initial acknowledgement of her trauma was followed by a phase of active mourning, but this was due to her new capacity to recognise the death of her father and to weep for him. She never reached the point of recognising what harm her father had done to her and she never became able to grieve for her misfortune in having had a father who had battered her and a mother who had failed to protect her. By the time that treatment ended she had reached the point of recognising that she felt psychologically damaged and in danger of becoming mad, but she blamed me for it. "You broke me. You tore me apart," she said, and she took revenge on me by threatening suicide and by making renewed assaults.

At this stage of psychotherapy, Sylvia had moved beyond the initial feelings of terror and rage evoked by the trauma to an emotional recognition of the damage which had been done to her. In the transference, she attributed the cause of the damage to me, because I had put her in touch with it. Much further work would have been needed to enable her to recognise where the blame belonged, to grieve for her terrible misfortune, to achieve some detachment from it and to relinquish the past sufficiently to prevent the need to re-enact it in the present. The initial intellectual and emotional recognition of trauma is only the beginning of a very long and painful process of working through. Only if this process is successful can a patient finally experience grief and anger for what has happened, and then detachment and relinquishment.

Both Adam's and Sylvia's psychotherapy had ended prematurely, after about two years, at their parents' insistence. More treatment would probably have helped them further, but it remains debatable whether recovery from severe infantile traumas, like Adam's and Sylvia's, can ever be complete. Greenacre (1953a) maintains that no truly traumatic event is ever wholly assimilated and that increased vulnerability inevitably remains, predisposing the individual to break down at some later date if faced with some repetition or near repetition of the original injury. In the case of an ongoing trauma, like Adam's illness and its treatment, from which there is no escape, the question of a complete recovery cannot exist. After the traumatic impact of the initial realization of the chronic catastrophe, there can be a period of assimilation and recovery, as Adam demonstrated, but he was bound to have to experience further traumatic crises as he faced the implications of his handicap for each new developmental stage. Although the social implications of his chronic illness were likely to become increasingly distressing, his medical treatment should have lost the monstrous qualities which it had for him as a very young child.

The role of parents

Parents frequently contribute to the original trauma and always influence the course of their child's recovery.

In a review of the psychoanalytic literature of trauma, Balint (1969) concluded that not one of the childhood traumas reported had occurred according to the model of a railway accident. On the contrary, "there existed a close and intimate relationship between the child and the adult who inflicted the trauma upon him," so violating the child's love and trust.

Even when parents are not the direct psychological cause of a trauma, as Adam's parents were not, probably they never escape blame in the child's mind. At the most basic level they have failed to protect the child from harm and have violated his trust in their omnipotence. Often, and probably always in the case of very young children, the trauma becomes attributed to the parents in the child's fantasies. For example, Adam went through a long period in therapy in which the monster doctors had clearly become monster parents who cruelly attacked him or else abandoned him while they fought each other. Another example is provided in Anny Katan's account (1973) of the analysis of six women who had been raped in childhood. All but one of these women in fantasy attributed the rapes to their innocent fathers.

Whereas children may *feel* their parents to have been responsible for the occurrence of traumas, there is no doubt that parents *are* at least partly responsible for determining the outcome of their children's reactions to these overwhelming events. Several authors have pointed out that many children do recover from truly traumatic experiences, given adequate environmental support. However, Adam's parents had inadvertently encouraged the repression of his distress about his hospitalization and treatment by their appeals to him to be calm and reasonable. Sylvia's mother had encouraged her flight from reality by her refusal to mention Sylvia's father or to acknowledge his violence. Regular casework at the clinic helped Adam's parents to feel less guilty about his hereditary illness and so to be more tolerant of his distress about it as this emerged during therapy. Similar help for Sylvia's mother freed her to lift the tabu on speaking to Sylvia about her father and his violence. Changes in their parents' attitudes were beneficial to both children, although the crucial changes in the children's own attitudes were independently achieved by them in their psychotherapy. It was their own understanding of the meaning of monsters which solved the mystery and broke the spell of repetition.

The therapist's role in helping children to understand external reality

The remainder of this paper focuses on the technical issue of the therapist's role in enabling children to recognise traumatic or adverse aspects of external reality, when these adverse aspects are contributed by their parents. I am not thinking only of the blatantly traumatic effects of physical or sexual abuse, but also of the less dramatic but damaging influences of, for example, parental mental illness or of rejection and scape-goating of the child. Evidently the first step in giving a child a minimum of protection or of autonomy from these adverse influences is for him to recognise what is happening to him.

Children have strong inclinations not to notice their parents' deficiencies. Their loyalty to the parents they love and their wishes for perfect parents are both very strong, and so is their susceptibility to pressure from their parents to be seen in a favourable light. In addition, young children have not achieved the experience or objectivity necessary to know that relationships could be different, let alone to be able to see their parents as people with their own problems. All this means that it is significantly harder for children than for adolescents to become aware of parental pathology or neglect, and the younger the child the harder the task.

The central aim of the work of child psychotherapists has always been to ana-lyse the transference so that children are enabled to discriminate between their own projections, their introjection of their parents' projections and their parents' actual contributions. Melanie Klein clearly illustrated how effective this can be, particularly when, as can be the case, children's internal parents are more sadistic and severe than their actual parents are. Adam provides an obvious example of a child who became able to express and enjoy affection with his parents, only after therapy had helped him to discriminate between his cruel internal monster parents and his real parents who had always done their best to help him. It can prove harder to help children to give up idealised versions of their internal parents in order to recognize monstrous behaviour in their actual parents.

I have found in my clinical experience that therapy may often get stuck at the point where a child clings to his internal, subjective, egocentric view of an external problem and steadily resists a more objective appraisal. This impasse can occur because the child prefers to feel responsible for, even guilty about, an external situation which he can control within the ambit of his omnipotence, rather than to admit his helplessness in the face of an intolerable reality. Looking back, I now wonder whether I have sometimes colluded with a child in turning a blind eye to painful aspects of external reality, while hoping that the issues could be sufficiently disentangled within the transference to enable the child to make the necessary changes in perception himself. This process of disentanglement can be extremely slow, even in adolescents.

A typical example of the length of this process concerns my work with a child, Alison, who needed three years of three times weekly psychotherapy before she at last recognized that her mother was in some respects mad. Alison was by then 9 years old. Before this she had clung to her mother's view that she herself was crazy and so was entirely responsible for provoking her mother's unpredictable and impossible behaviour. Alison's new capacity to conceptualise her relationship with her mother in a more objective manner freed her from feeling enslaved by her mother and enabled her to contemplate going to boarding school with some relief.

The question arises whether child psychotherapists can accelerate the slow course of their work by providing children with help in understanding their families. It is part of the tradition of work at the Anna Freud Clinic to give children such explanations if necessary, in conjunction with traditional analytic work. A good example of this approach is presented in a paper by Hurry and Sandler (1971) in which they described how a four year old boy was helped to understand some aspects of his mother's rejection of him and of her mental illness. They emphasized the importance of very careful timing in this work, in order not to provide the child with "a magical defensive formula" but to free him to achieve some autonomy. The same paper also described the work of helping an 11 year old girl to disentangle herself from her parents' projections and to resist being cast in the role of family scapegoat.

More recently, and working within a different tradition, using concepts derived from the work of Bion, Emanuel (1984) has described his work with a three year old boy who had suffered from "the primary disappointment" of having parents who had failed to meet "his innate expectations." He talked with the boy about his real parents' incapacity and felt that it was essential to have acknowledged how they had failed him in infancy in order to show that as therapist he could bear the pain of knowing about it and therefore that it was bearable and could be understood.

Such interventions can do more than indicate that the unbearable is both knowable and bearable. When well timed they make sense to the child and enable previously unrelated data to be integrated in a new conceptual framework. They can free children from unnecessary feelings of guilt and responsibility and make it more possible to cope with external reality. All these factors help to mitigate the pain and shock with which the child's new perception of his parents may be associated. They also help to mitigate the pain for the child's therapist. Exposing a child to starkly distressing aspects of reality can easily make the therapist feel guilty and responsible. There were certainly many moments in the treatment of both Adam and Sylvia when I wondered if I should have left well alone. It seems that helping a child to recover from trauma is liable to involve the therapist not only in sharing the pain but in suffering grave doubts about whether facing pain so starkly is necessary, and whether the self-protection of turning a blind eye may be preferable. Recognition that suffering such doubts is a feature of the psychotherapeutic work with traumatised children may help to make the work more tolerable.

Postscript – added in 2003 for the paper's being reprinted in Barrows, P. (2004) *Key papers from the Journal of Child Psychotherapy*, London & New York: Routledge

In retrospect, this paper gave too much significance to the role of insight and understanding in the resolution of trauma. Although I had to tolerate and contain much negative emotion as my two child patients worked through their traumas, I failed to realise how much this containment itself must have contributed to their recovery. At the time that I wrote the paper, Boston and Szur (1983) had already recently reported that containment reduced the compulsion for repetition in very deprived children. Since then clinical evidence in support of this view has become overwhelming.

Many traumatised children entering psychotherapy are unready and unable to confront their past. They may benefit from spending long periods in which they communicate their inchoate and unprocessed experience through compulsive repetition in the here-and-now. It is the therapist's capacity to tolerate, contain and process these negative experiences without joining the dance of rejection, retaliation, humiliation and helplessness that enables children to move beyond the need for re-enactment and to discover that relationships with adults are less frightening than they had believed. Perhaps Freud (1909) was right to suppose that ghosts of the past can never fully rest until they have been understood, but meanwhile the therapist's capacity for containment can reduce the pressure to repeat the past and so allow new relationships to develop.

Note

1 *Journal of Child Psychotherapy* 1986 Vol. 12 No.1. This paper was first presented at the A.C.P. Study Week-End in March 1986.

2 Living under the threat of death

The impact of a congenital illness on an eight-year-old boy[1]

Introduction

This paper is about a child's concern with life and death.

I present material from the psychotherapy of Adam, a boy of eight years, whose first five years had been severely affected by a debilitating congenital illness which endangered his life. He required repeated treatment in hospital and his parents were told that he might not survive. Between the ages of five and eight years his health gradually improved, but the medical prognosis was that he would probably die before adulthood.

I briefly outline Adam's referral to our clinic and his history and family background, before I describe his expectations and anxieties as I encountered them in the early months of treatment. I then bring material which focuses on Adam's concern with the preservation and resuscitation of life and the evasion of death.

Referral and history

Adam was referred to our clinic at the age of eight years four months because he was failing at school. He was the first child of successful Jewish parents; his father was a writer and his mother a potter. He was born after a pregnancy fraught with anxiety on account of three prior miscarriages. At birth he was severely jaundiced and required a complete exchange transfusion. After a week in an incubator he returned to his mother who managed to breastfeed him until he was twelve weeks old, although his sucking made her nipples sore. He gained weight but was very pale and lacking in energy. Further investigations revealed him to be the victim of a severe anaemia, associated with mild jaundice, and caused by an enzyme deficiency. Treatment was by drugs, supplemented from the age of nine months by regular blood transfusions, at first needed every five months but increasing in frequency until by the age of four years they were given at two monthly intervals. These transfusions required Adam to spend only a day in hospital but on at least three occasions during his first two years he was admitted for longer periods while research investigations were done. After each blood transfusion Adam emerged well from the hospital, only to follow a downhill course of increasing fatigue and irritability until his parents recognised the exhausted fretful state which indicated the need for another transfusion. In between transfusions weekly blood samples were taken for assessment. Throughout Adam's first five years his blood haemoglobin averaged about 45% of normal which meant he was markedly lacking in vitality.

At some point in Adam's development his feelings about hospital underwent a striking change. Although in infancy his mother reported that he was always very distressed by admission to hospital and found transfusions traumatic, by the age of five years, or maybe earlier, he had grown to love his visits to hospital and to enjoy co-operating in medical research. He became the pet of the ward and of the research laboratory.

After the age of five years improvements in Adam's medical treatment resulted in less frequent transfusions but at the age of seven-and-a-half years he required a major abdominal operation to correct some side-effects of his condition. Following the operation his health improved further and by the time of his referral to our clinic his haemoglobin had stabilised at 80% normal, a level associated with breathlessness and fatigue, but in itself only a minor handicap. He no longer needed transfusions but continued to rely on drugs.

Adam's general development had been slow and his parents felt that he had not made use of the abilities he had. For example, they were sure he could have walked alone six months before he actually did so just before his second birthday. His first single words were spoken at nineteen months. He started attending a small playgroup at the age of two-and-a-half years and was said to have enjoyed it. His sister, Susie, was born when he was just three and he was apparently delighted by her arrival, though quickly disillusioned. Mother began part-time work when Susie was a year old, and at the time of referral both parents shared equally in the care of their children.

Clinical assessment

When they were seen at our clinic Adam's parents impressed us as concerned, articulate people who had created a good home for their children. Mother, in particular, was very honest in her attempts to express her feelings about Adam. She was a rather boyish woman who might well have found the transition to motherhood difficult, even in happy circumstances, and she freely admitted that her anxieties about Adam's health had stopped her making the most of his infancy. She said she had vacillated between over-protecting him and trying to treat him as though his illness did not exist. As he grew older Adam had been helped to understand the cause of his anaemia but had been given less support for his feelings about it. Both parents attached importance to sensible, independent behaviour and had been much relieved when Adam began to enjoy hospital. They were very reluctant to admit that he had emotional problems as well as medical ones. However, mother confessed that what worried her most about Adam was not his learning difficulty, but his undemonstrative nature. She felt there was "a certain meanness" about his lack of feelings. She described him as charming to adults and eager to please, but very tense at bed-time and liable to terrifying nightmares. He was passive, unadventurous and babyish, and could not stick at anything or stand up for himself. He had been preoccupied with monsters for years but had few other interests except fishing. There were only twelve different foods he would eat and he devoured them as if he were starving.

Psychological testing revealed Adam to have a reading age of only six years five months. His score on the intelligence test gave a wide scatter compatible with minor brain damage, probably due to anoxia caused by the anaemia. His vocabulary was very superior and he possessed all the skills necessary for reading. Psychotherapy was recommended and was arranged on a once weekly basis for practical reasons. Adam had a total of sixty six sessions with me spread over twenty months. His parents accepted the offer of regular casework interviews with an experienced social worker. They used their time with her to overcome their defensive denial of Adam's problems and to face their guilt about them; and they became much more accepting of his limitations.

Behaviour in treatment

My first glimpse of Adam was of a boy with a plain, pallid face sitting listlessly in the waiting room. He greeted me with a faintly apologetic expression and accompanied me to my room with a shuffling gait. After his session I wrote, "He is a slow-moving, slow-spoken child who carries himself like an old man or an invalid." I supposed that his lack of vitality stemmed from his anaemia and I did not imagine that his detachment from his body would become a theme in treatment. I was more struck at that time with his detachment from his emotions. Whatever we discussed he remained emotionally blank and completely unmoved. He aimed to be politely and pleasantly co-operative, and it was only when his co-operation broke down and he gently retreated behind a vacant facade, that I knew our conversation had become disturbing to him and that he was not as uninvolved as he seemed. As treatment progressed I was sometimes aware that his numbness had given way to feelings which he was struggling to suppress. Although he became increasingly aware of feelings, throughout the twenty months of his treatment he was unable to express affection, dependency or hostility to me directly.

Adam began each session as he felt a good patient should, co-operatively talking while drawing or playing. His communication had a very placating quality but he also showed wishes to be understood and he seemed to listen to my interpretations, however painful. At some point in almost every session the scene changed. Adam withdrew from interaction with me and became deeply absorbed in his own play. I was allowed to be a friendly onlooker as long as I did not intrude. If I insisted on giving him interpretations he retreated inside himself, behind the blankest of faces, and appeared unaware of my presence altogether. When the session ended he tidied up carefully and was slow to go.

Early treatment

I shall now describe some of the themes which claimed my attention early in treatment and which illustrate clearly the devastating impact which Adam's illness and its treatment had had upon him. Before I go further I should say that

Adam's material in early treatment showed that he had reached the Oedipal level of development, though very tentatively. Some work was done on Oedipal themes but the major work of treatment focused on the more primitive material which is presented here.

Unconscious preoccupation with doctors and medical treatment

Adam started treatment with the preconscious expectation that our clinic was really a hospital where something terrifying would be done to him. While he chatted in his first session about his willing co-operation in medical research and his "best Christmas ever" spent in hospital, he was modelling a plasticine dinosaur which set out to kill cavemen but fell into a trap and so was eaten by cavemen instead. "Did you know," he asked, "that dinosaurs are not very sensitive and can have half of their selves eaten without feeling much?" I suggested that his lively talk was intended to please and interest me and to distract us both from the terrifying feelings dramatised by the dinosaur play. I thought this play might represent his recent operation when the anaesthetic had stopped his feeling pain while bits of him were eaten up; he might be afraid that I would set a trap for him in my clinic in order to get my teeth into him before he could get his into me. Although Adam gained a clear understanding of the work of our clinic, his expectation of physical assault never wholly disappeared and he continued to anticipate betrayal. One way he dealt with this was to set a series of small traps for himself, apparently practising minor self deceptions as a defence against the terrifying traps he really dreaded. For example, he hid his toy cars in the wrong boxes in order to surprise himself in the next session when he discovered that the one he wanted was replaced by another.

Adam's preoccupation with monsters and traps featured in all the early sessions and transparently disguised his fantasies about doctors and the treatment they gave. Monsters were drawn with hard shells and spikey armour and were often reminiscent of lobsters with pincer claws. Some had protuberances like drills which bored deep into the ground to tap seams of coal and rich veins of gold, a vivid representation of the needles which had tapped Adam's veins and stolen his precious blood.

In his play monsters were sometimes the victims of traps and sometimes were themselves the trappers. The traps took the form of deep pits, suffocating bags or hidden mouths. Some monsters had false heads with secret mouths, or their heads and tails were interchanged for purposes of deception. For Adam, the trap of traps undoubtedly was the mouth. At this stage in treatment all relationships seemed experienced in unconscious phantasy as devouring or being devoured. He began to bring vast quantities of sweets to treatment, in order, I thought, to keep his voracious desires for me at bay. He would have been reassured if I had accepted his repeated offers and eaten some too.

At its simplest level I interpreted the monster material in terms of the cruel way in which Adam felt the kindest adults had monstrously betrayed and trapped him into undergoing painful and terrifying medical procedures which had in turn led him to experience monstrous feelings of revenge. These feelings were re-experienced in the transference with regard to the treatment which I was giving him. Because the savagery of the monster material was horrifying to me but unaffecting to Adam I suggested that he needed me to experience the horror for him because it was too frightening to be aware of it himself.

Adam lost his preoccupation with monsters early in treatment but he remained devoted to the doctors whom the monsters had represented. He still insisted "My illness is very valuable because I can go to hospital and I love that best of all." Anna Freud (1952) gives us some understanding of this. She writes: "It is the psychological meaning of pain which explains why doctors, and other inflictors of pain, are not merely feared but in many cases highly regarded and loved by the child. The infliction of pain calls forth passive masochistic responses which hold an important place in the child's love life. Frequently the devotion of the child to doctor or nurse becomes very marked on the days after the distress caused by a painful medical procedure has been experienced." Adam also appreciated that he was dependent on doctors to keep him alive. He could not afford to turn against them.

Being an exception

At first sight Adam's lack of any conscious sense of injustice about his illness conflicts with Freud's observations reported in his essay on "Some Character Types met with in Psychoanalytic Work" (1915b). In it he describes patients with either a congenital injury or an illness acquired in early childhood who considered themselves to be exceptions. They felt they had already suffered enough on account of their unjust injury and so rebelled against the reality principle and the frustrations of analysis. They claimed instead the right to special privilege.

Although Adam appeared to have passively submitted to his fate, like one of Freud's patients who changed suddenly from acceptance of her illness to violent rebellion when she learned that her illness was congenital, Adam suddenly broke out into violent rebellion, not against his illness but against his treatment with me. He claimed it was very unfair that he should be selected to have psychotherapy and begged instead for more treatment at the hospital where he was indeed treated with special privileges. His resistance to coming to see me was so fierce that his parents were astounded by the strength of his feelings and were scarcely able to cope. They had to bribe him with sweets and bring him forcibly to the clinic. Adam never let me see this rebellion but remained co-operative and polite. I knew from the monster material that he felt cruelly trapped and persecuted by me, and he now developed another means of showing me how he felt picked on. With the sweets needed to bribe him to come to treatment, Adam developed games in which each sweet was chased, trapped and "sacrificed" (i.e. eaten by him) in turn. The games had to appear as though the evasion of sacrifice could be achieved by skill, but in fact the choice of victim was arbitrary and depended upon an imaginary dice. I thought these games showed how Adam felt picked on by fate and how he feared that his number would come up, however cleverly he tried to avoid it. Here we were near the possibility that Adam might die, but at this stage only the fantasies of sacrifice were mentioned. Meanwhile his sense of injustice increased. His mother reported that at home he was no longer charming but constantly complaining about being nagged, bullied and generally "got at" by his parents, teachers and boys at school. He began to retaliate and to get into fights. It was not until the second year of treatment that Adam acknowledged resentment that fate had picked on him to suffer a congenital illness, and with this bitter acknowledgement there came a reduction in his sense of being discriminated against by others.

Edith Jacobson (1959) adds one more observation to the psychopathology of the exceptions in her paper on this theme. She found that a "dangerous masochistic need for punishment" seemed to be present in all the varieties of "exceptions" which she had the opportunity to observe. The masochistic need for punishment may well account for Adam's submission to being sacrificed on the altar of medical treatment, which he was able to claim that he loved. It may also account for the docile way that he accompanied me to treatment, as a lamb to the slaughter. But I think there was another reason for this too. In his fourth session Adam had let me know of his desire to be an exception of quite another kind. He modelled a strange animal with a large open mouth and a tail shaped like a spoon. He named it "a friendly spoon pig" and claimed that because it was "unique and priceless it must have a special farmer to care for it full-time". I think that Adam's rebellion against treatment was mitigated by the reassuring arrival of his very part-time "farmer" therapist, who, like him, had survived a week's separation and was available to care for him again. His treatment gave him more than masochistic gratification; it also sometimes provided the comfort and relief associated with being fed.

Living vicariously

A very different theme had been developing from the beginning of treatment. It concerned Adam's unusual relationship with his sister Susie.

When Adam started treatment Susie was his best and only friend and they played endlessly together. From his first session onwards Adam talked a lot about Susie and I realised that he used references to her to express feelings of which he was unaware. For example, while neatly tidying up his toys he told me what pleasure Susie takes in chucking flour and water about; and when he saw me in the clinic with another child he remarked how jealous Susie is when Mummy plays with him, though he is never jealous of Susie. Once when he drew a secret treasure chest I said, "I suppose that at home Mummy is your treasure." "Oh no!" said Adam, "Susie is." He went on to describe fantasies of rescuing her from all kinds of disaster. Twice he told me that the worst thing he could imagine would be Susie in hospital, and from the context in which he said it I realised that Susie's hospitalisation would mean to him endangering a treasured part of himself.

The form of projection in which we renounce our own instinctual impulses in favour of other people has been described by Anna Freud (1936) as "altruistic surrender". She discusses its effectiveness in relation to the fear of death, "Anyone who has very largely projected his instinctual impulses onto other people knows nothing of this fear. In the moment of danger his ego is not really concerned for his own life. He experiences instead excessive concern and anxiety for the lives of his love objects . . . When his impulses have been surrendered in favour of other people, their lives become precious rather than his own. The death of the vicarious figure means . . . the destruction of all hope of fulfilment."

It seemed to me that Adam was using Susie not just to carry the projections of his unwanted hostile impulses, but also, through altruistic surrender, to preserve the treasure of his life.

Two sessions

I would now like to describe two sessions from the eighth month of treatment. The first session introduces the theme of Adam's contrasting feelings of vitality and limpness and his fear that his body will wear out. The second session illustrates the projective mechanism by which he felt he could displace his vitality into Susie. The role of his early experience of blood transfusions becomes apparent.

Session 22

Adam came to treatment with a purple ice-lolly, instead of his normal supply of sweets, and a limp balloon. From his pocket he produced a packet of seeds and ten old coins which he said had been a present from his remedial teacher, a reward for reading ten books. He briefly described some of them for my interest, and while feeding me with information he finished his lolly.

Then Adam took the balloon and blew it up before he released it to fly across the room and flop on the floor. He was amused by the noises it made and agreed that they sounded like farting.

Next he put the coins under a piece of paper and scribbled over them to make rubbings. He divided the rubbings carefully into "heads" and "tails". I thought he was being careful to discriminate between the head which needs the breath of life and the tail that lets out the fart.

Adam returned to the balloon and blew it up repeatedly in order to fly it again and again, until he was panting for breath. He said "You keep on having to fill it up. It's not like ordinary balloons." I said that his balloon was different and special like he felt. In treatment he liked me to fill him up with interpretations, to blow life into him, but the emotions which made him feel alive were so painful that he let them go and farted them out and that left him feeling limp and weak. Adam said, "There were lots of balloons in hospital when I had Christmas there, but I was the only one having a transfusion." I said that Adam was the special one who needed filling up and the other children were like ordinary balloons which didn't need to be filled repeatedly. It seemed he felt that treatment was like transfusions, something that filled him up and gave him life, but was too painful to keep inside, so he had to let it out and come back for more again and again.

Adam continued to blow the balloon up and then examined it carefully. "If I keep on blowing it up it weakens it and it wears out faster than an ordinary balloon. It won't last long." He sighed. I said he must be afraid that I was wearing him out by blowing so many interpretations into him; this made him feel so exhausted he felt he couldn't live long, just as when he was so weak in hospital he must have felt he might die. "Yes" said Adam flatly. "I always think I might die." I said there had been times in his infancy when he really might have died, but that now his body was healthier than it had ever been. I thought he still feared he would die because he felt so lifeless, he was like the limp balloon which couldn't contain its vitality. Adam smiled and lay back on the couch where he appeared to sleep for the remaining ten minutes of the session.

The second session to be described occurred three weeks later. Adam unexpectedly missed the session immediately before it because of a family excursion.

Session 25

Adam left the waiting room reluctantly. Instead of the usual sweets he brought with him a biro which he had found in the school playground. He said it was blocked up so it couldn't ever take a refill, but it still had some life in it. I reminded him that he had missed his refill from me last week; perhaps some angry feelings about that were making him reluctant to come to get another refill from me today. Adam smiled.

As Adam played with the biro I noticed that he kept pressing it against his arm as though he were pushing in a needle. I remarked that transfusions were another kind of refill. Adam said "You can keep on putting refills into a biro till it wears out." I began to say that this reminded me of the balloon, and while I was speaking Adam abruptly broke the biro in half and took out the refill. "I'll take it home and put it safely into Susie's biro," he said. I suggested that when it felt too dangerous to live in his own body because it might wear out, he felt as though he could remove his life from his body and put it into Susie's. "That's why Susie is so bouncy," said Adam, as though my idea, which he had not heard from me before, was nothing new to him.

He now turned to his locker and took out the packet of grass seeds which had lain there for three weeks. "Will they grow with just water?" he asked. He put them in a dish and watered them and asked me to care for them till next week. "You will keep on having to top it up," he told me. This was his first and almost only request. I think he was entrusting me instead of Susie with some of his precious life and asking for more therapy refills to help him grow and live.

I recorded these sessions in detail because they brought together various themes in treatment and seemed meaningful to Adam who was more closely in touch with me than usual. In a paper on Reconstruction in Child Analysis, Kennedy (1972) mentions the feeling of satisfaction which psychotherapists have when they make a good reconstruction, and I felt reassured that the events enacted in the therapy room seemed to parallel the experiences of the repeated transfusions which Adam had endured in infancy. One differentiation which I made in my interpretations seemed important to me: I mean the differentiation between the life of Adam's body as the container (balloon, biro) and the vitality of his emotions (breath, refill) contained within his body but felt by him to be separable from it. It was easy for me to spell out this difference to Adam because his body was in fact relatively healthy and not in any immediate danger of "wearing out". In the twenty months we were together the probability that he would die young was never mentioned. In retrospect I think that the theme was there, but I only interpreted it as his fear without any acknowledgement between us that this could be a reality. Rodrigue (1968) writes of the difficulty the physician in us has in facing what is "incurable", and Lussier (1960), in a paper on the analysis of a boy with a congenital handicap, implies that there may be room for a little denial which will help to foster development. My denial was unconscious. At this stage I focused my work on the irrational anxieties which were preventing Adam from living within his body, a body which was not wearing out or in imminent danger of death.

Perhaps it was this approach that brought results or perhaps it was simply that in the transference I was now experienced by Adam as the giver of life-giving transfusions instead of as the monster-doctor about to trap and devour him. We can only guess at the factors which facilitate change. Within about two weeks of session 25, Adam had changed dramatically. He held himself erect, walked with a firm stride and hurried ahead of me into my room. His mother reported that he was full of energy; he now ran spontaneously like other children and even ran upstairs.

It was at this point that I would have expected his whole relationship to Susie to change, but perplexingly this had happened six months earlier, in the third month of treatment. Adam had been very sensitive during his first term in treatment to the fact that I had other child patients whose lockers stood in my room. My interpretations of his jealous wishes to be my only patient were accompanied by the expression at home of intense jealousy of Susie. She became his worst enemy and they fought constantly, shattering family peace. About the time that Adam recovered his physical energy his relationship to Susie improved and settled down to become an apparently normal blend of sibling rivalry and affection. I was left wondering "where" Adam had been living during the six months that he was on such bad terms with Susie, before he had vitalised his own body. Perhaps I had misconstrued the problem or had been unaware of some important aspect of the transference.

Adam maintained his gains during the long summer holiday which followed six weeks after session 25. He was reported to have run and romped and kept up in every way with Susie. He also stopped eating as though he were starving and enjoyed venturing on a wide range of new foods. His nightmares had disappeared and he became able to confide his worries in his mother.

In the autumn term which followed his holiday Adam usually seemed to be living in his own body, though his muscle tone varied and he would resume the feeble manner and posture of an invalid when he had a cold or felt particularly tired. His fears of living in his body continued to be expressed in play, and included unconscious fears that his body was itself a trap, and that if he became full of life there would be none left for anyone else.

Twice in treatment I saw Adam change suddenly from normal body tone to the flaccid slump of an invalid. In each instance this happened in response to my interpretations of the fears of annihilation by me which I thought his play expressed. On each occasion he retreated, not metaphorically into Susie, but into deeply absorbed play with an object which seemed to have a life of its own. In one instance this was a high-bounce ball, and in the second, a springy rubber band. Here was a possible answer to my perplexity. Perhaps Adam had another place in which to live, and from which to borrow life: in his absorption in the apparent life of inanimate objects.

A world of his own creation

These observations lead me to another aspect of Adam's material: his retreat into deeply absorbed play. This form of play began in the very first session, when Adam became engrossed in drawing "an invention" in response to the news that there was only five minutes left. He continued to exclude me by withdrawing into his own activities when I disappointed him, and I noticed that he sometimes also withdrew in this way when he felt physically threatened by me. Gradually his retreat into absorbed play became less a defensive means of excluding me and more a means of communication. It became less dominated by his need to produce his own invention and more open to changes suggested by the material, and it was increasingly accompanied by a feeling of delight.

Let me describe the nature of this absorbed play as it appeared in treatment after Adam had gained his physical energy and after the play had lost its manifest intent to exclude me.

Before Adam allowed himself to become engrossed he usually supplied me with a number of colourful anecdotes which he had collected during the week, interesting and sometimes perturbing items designed to give me food for thought while leaving him free to do his own thing. When I had been well supplied, Adam became absorbed in his own pursuits, and this quality of absorption characterised and seemed to lend importance to all the play which I now describe. He called many of his activities "inventions" or "discoveries". Sometimes he relied entirely on the toys which I had provided, usually the paints and plasticine. "Let's see what it becomes," he would say as he splodged paint and water on the paper and watched them run. Or else he might explore the plasticine, cutting it in slices to reveal marks reminiscent of fossils, the entrances of caves or traces of his own earlier excavations. In all these activities there was a two-way interaction, a kind of dialogue, between himself and his material. He thought of something, put it in action and then allowed the effects of his action to give him another idea. The splodge of paint suggested a flower; he added a curve, and it became a seashell, and so on. He was sensitive to colour, preferring pale shades, but sometimes complaining that they were too dull and needed more life, which he always added with red. Often he supplemented my toys with his own collection gleaned from the school dustbins and carefully treasured in his pockets or socks. Pebbles, coins, batteries, springs, broken glass, badges, balls, cigarette cards: these trivial items were fascinating objects of beauty or scientific curiosity for Adam. His visual imagination was so fluid that he once spent half an hour exploring the shapes he could make with a fine gold chain. "A face . . . a cliff . . . a map . . . a rose" and so on, he murmured, more to himself than to me. Sometimes he talked to his treasures as though they were small children, saying "Come here little ball-y" or "Don't be naughty, you silly pebble." The high-bounce ball was one of his favourite treasures and he would often sit and gaze at its action with a rapt expression on his face.

While Adam was happily preoccupied with these pursuits he maintained a friendly relationship to me as long as I did not intrude. He was pleased when I was interested in his experiences and sometimes he actively drew me into them. For example, one day he brought a packet of white sherbet powder and emptied it into a blue beaker. Then he held it up to the light, turning the beaker and shifting the sherbet while he lyrically described a glittering avalanche descending the Alps on a sunny ice-cold day. For a moment the vision he described carried me away, and I returned with a jolt to mundane reality.

Understanding Adam's world

When I struggled to understand this material it seemed primarily concerned with the creation and discovery of a personal world, a world of "me" which excluded the "not-me"; a world in which boundaries could merge to allow the blissful illusion of union; a world of mother-with-baby in which there was no intrusion of masculine symbolism; a world of marvellous creations of body-stuff in which aggression and destruction had no place.

Frances Tustin (1972) has beautifully described the enclosed world of the autistic child. Adam's world was open to limited interchange with reality. In Winnicott's terms I think it would be true to say that Adam was immersed in "transitional phenomena", playing in "the intermediate area between primary creativity and objective perception based on reality testing" which "throughout life is retained in the intense experiencing that belongs to the arts and to religion and to imaginative living and to creative scientific work" (1953).

Where was my place in this world? When Adam supplied me with anecdotes before embarking on his absorbed play he reminded me of a mother fobbing off her child in order to pursue her own important interests. Even when I was no longer actively excluded I sometimes found myself with no place in Adam's world at all, an isolated outsider envying his capacity to find beauty and interest in everyday things; it seemed to me then that I had been allotted the role of the unhappy baby Adam had once been, fobbed off and left to bear his anxieties alone while mother pursued her own creative life. But there was no doubt that at other times Adam required my mutual participation in his activities and even needed to feel merged with me through them. Perhaps he also felt in some way merged with the creative life of his artistic parents. I supposed that his merging was a relief from the threats which he had come to associate with human relationships.

When Adam was absorbed in his own world I was certainly no longer needed to supply life-giving transfusions in the transference, for Adam's world was itself transfused with life. Sometimes he seemed to borrow life from the vitality of his treasures, like the high-bounce ball, and sometimes to impart it to his creations, like the pallid picture which he suffused with red life-blood. In all these activities I think he felt no definite boundary to exist between himself and his materials. Life flowed from the high-bounce ball into Adam and from Adam into his pictures; it ebbed and flowed through his use of his medium.

It was pointed out to me while writing this paper that Adam may well have felt that when he was merged with me he could resuscitate me as well as himself. Even at a superficial level Adam's absorbed play gave me reassurance of his vitality and made me think of what he might grow up to be, rather than that he might not grow up. I could imagine Adam as a small child with his mother at his bedside, quietly playing and making no demands on her, while they escaped together into the realm of play. Through this shared use of illusion he must have felt he could revive her and protect her as well as himself from the cruel threat of death. There is good evidence from Adam's parents that neither of them had openly faced this threat, and in his treatment with me I avoided facing it directly too. In retrospect I recognise that in this area I colluded with his need to reassure me and so missed a possible opportunity to help him further.

The barrier

In the analysis of Adam's own world I encountered a technical problem which rendered my understanding useless. If I interpreted the defensive nature of Adam's escape into illusion, or if I translated his themes into symbols of my own, I was confronted by the barrier of Adam's total withdrawal. He stared mutely into space for as long as I attempted to get through to him. If I fell silent then after five or ten minutes he would resume some form of play, but only in a very desultory and disheartened manner. I think it did not matter whether my interpretations of his own world were right or not; they were simply experienced as intolerable intrusions, impingements of the not-me. And this was in striking contrast to the way he was prepared to accept my interpretations of other material.

Consideration of Adam's barrier revealed the negative counterpart of the blissful, life-enhancing qualities of his transitional play. Adam's barrier told me, through my counter-transference (Heimann 1950), that the alternative to the blissful illusion of merging was to feel annihilated and not to exist at all. Now I could understand another factor in his intense resistance to coming to treatment and the suffering he must have endured in the unbearable gap between sessions. The infant in him was not ready for such an abrupt disillusionment, such a disruption of his sense of "going-on-being". In Winnicott's view (1956) such a disruption produces "a very real primitive anxiety", a "threat of annihilation" which long antedates any anxiety about death. It is tempting to compare the quality of anxiety expressed in Winnicott's "threat of annihilation" with Bion's "nameless dread", the severe contentless anxiety which a baby feels when some failure of mother/baby interaction interferes with the baby's use of the mother as a "container" for his anxieties (Bion 1962). However, Bion's concept is significantly different, for it is based on a complex theoretical relationship to the fear of dying which Bion believes to exist in early psychic life. Bion follows Klein in her assumption of the major role played by the death instinct from the start of life. To do justice to the development of these views would involve a long and controversial exposition which I shall avoid. I would simply say that Adam's use of the barrier to communicate the threat of annihilation was the nearest he came to conveying a primitive idea of death, not death conceptualised in adult terms, but dreaded as the disruption of the personal sense of continuing existence, a sense of going-on-being which at that stage was best sustained when he was merged with me in his own world.

In all Adam's other material death could be successfully eluded. Even if his body were to wear out or be assaulted he could live vicariously through Susie or resuscitate himself in the life-giving exchanges of transitional play. Even when devoured by monsters or sacrificed when his number came up, he developed fantasies of continuing to exist inside his attacker. Adam's material would seem to support Freud's claim that "No one believes in his own death . . . in the unconscious everyone is convinced of his immortality" (1915a).

Technical problem

Let us return to the technical problem posed by Adam's barrier. I could of course have persisted with interpretative work, and tried to use awareness of my counter-transference, to understand and to resolve the barrier. Instead I let Adam know what I thought the barrier was about and I allowed him to continue to use his sessions as he wanted. This did not bring all interpretative work to a halt, for only a portion, usually about half, of each session was spent in transitional play, and even when Adam was immersed in his own world I could slip simple messages across within the terms of his fantasies. For example I could say "You described that avalanche so vividly that I think we both forgot our bodies and were living in the Alps", or I could talk about his loving care of his "dustbin treasures", but to have translated the sherbet avalanche into oral terms or to have called the treasures "anal babies" would have been experienced by Adam as an impingement requiring withdrawal behind his barrier.

Many of the ideas which I have found helpful in understanding Adam's own world have been drawn from Marion Milner's outstanding paper on "Aspects of Symbolism in Comprehension of the Not-Self" (1952). In it she describes her work with a boy who could not experience the relief of disillusion until he had had time to experience and become conscious of the previous stage of illusion. She writes "It is the capacity of the environment to foster growth [towards recognising a world outside oneself] by providing conditions in which a recurrent partial return to the feeling of being one is possible; and I suggest that the environment does this by the recurrent providing of a framed space and time and a pliable medium, so that, from time to time, it will not be necessary for self-preservation's sake to distinguish clearly between inner and outer, self and not-self." In Milner's terms, the setting of psychotherapy provided the framework, while the play materials and I myself, in my adaptability to Adam's needs, provided the pliable medium. Adam had indeed been forced too early for self-preservation's sake to distinguish between inner and outer, self and not-self. He had developed a split between a compliant false self which conformed with the demands of medical necessity and a hidden self which scarcely dared to exist. This split in his personality mirrored the split in his body-image between a hard outer container (Bick's "second skin" 1968) and an inner vulnerable core. In his use of illusion he could temporarily evade this split and had probably long been able to do so. Treatment provided a setting in which the need for illusion could be accepted and made conscious, even though, in this short treatment, Adam could not permit the content of illusion to be analysed. I cannot assess what part, if any, this use of illusion played in Adam's gradual recognition of the world outside himself, but his parents brought evidence that he was becoming increasingly able to respond to the demands of the external world.

This leads me to describe some of the changes which took place in the second half of treatment.

Developments in treatment

Adam brought fewer sweets to his sessions. He now involved them mainly in lively football matches between teams like Toffo Town and Peppermint City instead of in his former sagas of random sacrifice; however the winners still ate the losers.

Play with the toys involved increasingly aggressive themes of fights, robberies and cruelty to animals. Adam was actively involved in the assaults and no longer passively attributed all atrocities to monsters. Much of his time passed doing nothing in particular, somehow waiting for the right moment at which the absorbed play could start.

In early treatment Adam had left deceptions to bridge the gap between sessions, later he regularly left some of his treasures in his locker, beginning with the seeds in session 25; he also left small items hidden in the room in the hope that they would remain undisturbed until next week. And he allowed himself to leave a mess for me to clear up.

In his play I began to see myself symbolised as a container – a letter-box for his messages, a pen for a wild bull, a garage for a car needing repair, a hanger to protect an aeroplane that risked being bombed. This development implied a growing sense of trust in my capacity to protect, repair and understand. Certainly Adam felt more favourably towards me and no longer protested against coming to see me. After about fourteen months of treatment his mother reported that he could remember that he liked me until the eve of his next appointment, but when the day came for it he never wanted to come. His parents were delighted to report that he had become warmly affectionate to them and was able to enjoy physical contact, cuddles and kisses, for the first time since early infancy. They felt that his affection was genuine and spontaneous but they described as partly play-acting his first attempts to express his rage. They also reported that he had become interested in the external world of school and learning, and with his father's help he worked hard at reading and made steady, though slow, progress.

These changes reflected a growing capacity to integrate aspects of internal and external reality; I suggest that this move towards disillusionment could be tolerated partly because of the provision of a reliable setting for illusion and partly because Adam was now sustained by the sense of possessing an internal good object, which was felt to provide his own source of life.

Termination of treatment

Unhappily Adam's treatment ended prematurely. After only fifteen months of therapy I told him that it had been decided to finish his treatment at the end of the following term. This decision was made because I was going abroad for two terms and because Adam's parents would not consider resuming treatment on my return. They were happy with the changes that he had made and hoped that his one remaining failure, to make any friends, would be overcome when his school-work caught up with his peers'. Adam still spent school break-time searching for treasures in dustbins and it seemed unlikely to me that academic improvement would bridge the gap between him and other children.

Adam was devastated by the news that treatment would end in five months' time. Although he characteristically showed no emotional reaction when I told him of the decision, he devoted his entire session to demolishing his valued aeroplane hangar, which had seemed to represent me; he said he would pulverize it to sugar and he broke it up with violent karate chops which left his hand bleeding. At home he became an invalid again and took to bed for a week, although he and his mother both recognised that there was nothing wrong with him but depression. Adam spent his next session building bridges in order to demolish them, and two subsequent sessions painting splodge pictures which grew more and more muddy until they proved impossible to revitalise with red. I was sorry that although his message was transparent, he was still unable to express any feelings to me directly. I think he had come to rely on me to do it for him vicariously, and if treatment had continued perhaps I could have helped him with this.

After a month Adam emerged from his despair and his physical energy returned. For the remainder of treatment he was more defensively isolated and spent less time in transitional play and more in aggressive activities. The anxieties expressed by the original monster material returned as a fear of being trapped and eaten by me, hiding the obverse wish to consume me, like the pulverised sugar, and keep me inside. He also fantasised becoming a baby inside me and being born with perfect health when treatment ended. In his last session he gave me a small rubber lobster to keep. "You can't really eat it," he said humorously, " 'cos it's firmish all the way through." "So are you, now," I said, "and when I look at the lobster it will help to keep alive my memories of you."

This paper is based on these memories, reconstructed from my notes. Working with Adam had had two unexpected effects. It had led me to modify my technique by allowing him to be an exception who enjoyed the special privilege of evading the reality principle by withdrawal into the realms of illusion. And it had supplied me with the motivation to write this paper. I could not fulfill Adam's wish to be reborn with health; instead I have tried to convert my experience of working with a child threatened by an early death into the delivery of a viable paper.

Note

1 *Journal of Child Psychotherapy* 1977 4(3): 5–21. Presented at the ACP Study Weekend 1976.

3 The role of trauma in the development of a borderline state and a foot-and-shoe fetish in a 6-year-old girl[1]

Fetishism in females is extremely rare. It is therefore of particular interest to attempt to understand its origins in a girl who was only 6 years old when she started psychotherapy. At that time she was psychotic and believed herself to be a boy. The traumatic nature of much of her early experience was revealed through her psychotherapy; information from her mother confirmed and amplified some important aspects of her history. The paper follows the difficult and dramatic course of treatment and offers an understanding of the girl's presenting symptoms, including her fetishism.

Referral and assessment

Sylvia Z was referred to our clinic at her mother's request when she was just over 6 years old. Mrs Z complained that Sylvia was hyperactive, unmanageable, had many tantrums and wet the bed; she attended a special school for children with emotional and behavioural difficulties. Sylvia had a younger brother, Enrico, aged 4½ years. Her father, Mr Z, had died in a car crash just before her fourth birthday.

When the psychiatrist and the social worker met Sylvia they were both convinced from her appearance that she was a boy. Mrs Z explained that Sylvia had insisted on being a boy since her father died. She also mentioned that Sylvia had a very acute sense of smell and that she had a habit of wanting 'to love and kiss' shoes; she would even throw herself on the shoes of strangers to kiss them, salivate on them and bite them. Her interest in shoes had been first evident at 7 months old when she appeared fascinated by her father's shiny shoes. She would draw herself up to them, salivate on them and then suck her thumb. Later, as a toddler, she adopted the habit of taking a pair of her mother's old shoes to bed with her, a habit which still persisted.

Mrs Z was a very defensive young woman who seemed eager for her daughter to have help but reluctant to involve herself. She explained that she could talk to no one about her husband or his death, but in fact did give a brief account of the accident. This occurred just after the family had moved house in order to provide a separate bedroom for the children who until then had slept with their parents. Mr Z had been disqualified from driving so his brother drove him to collect a carpet for the new house. Mr Z's brother lost control of the car which crashed and Mr Z died instantly, but his brother was uninjured. Mrs Z said she felt only blank at the time and had never cried.

Mrs Z described herself as the only child of Jewish parents. Her father died suddenly of a stroke when she was 5 years old and her mother never wept for him. She herself was sent away at once to boarding school. She could remember very little of her mother during her childhood and now seldom saw her. Her mother had remarried while she was away at school and she never got on with her step-father. After leaving school she worked as a secretary until Sylvia was born.

Mr Z's family were Italian Catholics who came to England when he was 12 years old. He took many jobs after leaving school, and following his marriage to Mrs Z he studied in the evenings to become an accountant.

Mr and Mrs Z met at a concert, and when she became pregnant they decided to get married, despite bitter opposition from both families.

Sylvia was born early and weighed less than five pounds. She was placed in an intensive care unit for sixteen days and returned home 'feeding three hourly, taking an hour and a half to feed, and screaming when not feeding'. Mrs Z attempted to breastfeed her for a week but stopped when she herself became ill. She recalled Sylvia's early months as an absolute nightmare. Nothing would pacify Sylvia and Mr Z 'was driven round the bend' by her screaming, which he said prevented his studies.

Mr and Mrs Z had always felt that there was something wrong with Sylvia and this was confirmed for them when a psychologist assessed her at the age of 3 years and announced that she was eighteen months retarded. She did not speak fluently or become toilet trained until she was 5 years old.

Enrico was a much easier baby than Sylvia had been and Mr Z became very attached to him in a way which he had never done to Sylvia. Mrs Z was clearly proud of Enrico's development, though two years later, at the age of 6 years, he too was to be deemed emotionally and behaviourally disturbed.

Sylvia's initial assessment at our clinic was inconclusive. The psychiatrist was not sure whether to describe her as 'psychotic' or 'borderline'. The psychologist found her completely untestable, but deduced from her speech that she was likely to be potentially of at least low average intelligence. Arrangements were made for Sylvia to have twice-weekly psychotherapy with me and for Mrs Z to meet with Mrs R, an experienced social worker, for twice-weekly casework. More intensive treatment was not feasible.

Impressions of Sylvia during the initial phase of treatment

Sylvia started treatment with me when she was 6 years and 4 months old. There were ten sessions before the first holiday break and during this period I gained the following initial impressions.

My first meeting with Sylvia was dominated by my conviction that she must be a boy. Sylvia succeeded in appearing unmistakably male, although in fact her hair length and clothes were equally suitable for either sex and her features were not masculine. It must have been her slightly swaggering gait, aggressive manner and assertive body postures which conveyed her masculinity. When she smiled her whole face lit up and had a radiant quality, which was extremely attractive, but she more often looked angry and menacing.

Sylvia was indeed hyperactive. She rarely pursued the same activity for more than a minute and her conversation was as disconnected as her behaviour. Her dark eyes were intensely bright and she was constantly in the grip of extreme and fluctuating emotions. Love, hate, excitement, terror and rage gripped her in rapid succession. The intensity and passion of her ordinary experience is difficult to convey. She seemed helplessly at the mercy of extremely violent feelings which fluctuated arbitrarily, entirely outside her understanding or control.

Sylvia's first two sessions with me differed from subsequent ones in that she was less disorganized and far less violent than she quickly became. She was excitedly concerned with immersing herself in all the paint and glue provided, and made a number of very messy, sticky pictures called arbitrarily, 'Ghost', 'Dragon', 'Worm', 'Machine in the rain' and 'Peanut butter spreading on bread'. She hit the dragon picture claiming it had hit her, and she called the dirty paint water 'wee wee', laughing hysterically as she tipped it over my chair. She expressed the fear that I would hit her like her mother did, and at the end she tried to destroy the light in my ceiling by repeatedly hurling a ball at it.

The first two sessions were only two days apart, but five days elapsed before the third session. When I went to collect her she looked at me in terror and bolted. There followed a long chase through the clinic until I cornered her under a secretary's desk. When at last she emerged she blurted out angrily 'Where *were you?* Have you been away on holiday?' In my room she seized her ball and sank her teeth into it. This action ushered in the first of a long series of extremely violent sessions in which Sylvia threatened to kill me and eat me up. She swore profusely, hurled toys and water at me, kicked and spat and flung the furniture about. At other moments she embraced me, spoke affectionately and begged me to visit her home. At all times she was highly involved in relating to me and never withdrew into activities on her own.

In addition to constantly attacking me, usually for no apparent reason, Sylvia was very preoccupied with fantasies of herself being attacked by monsters. Sometimes she begged me to be her friend and to protect her while she imagined the room to be full of attacking monsters. She called the furniture 'Daleks' and seemed convinced that chairs moved across the room to strike her. Her terror was intense and when she kept cowering and ducking as though about to receive a blow from a Dalek or some other monster, I thought she was hallucinating. At other times, instead of enlisting my help against the monsters, she asked me to play the part of a monster and to frighten her, but she could never tolerate this for more than a minute or two.

I first saw Sylvia's fascination with shoes when I found her embracing and slobbering over another patient's boots in the waiting room. This behaviour often occurred before Sylvia's sessions and Mrs Z did nothing to restrain it although onlookers found it shocking. It happened that I had been wearing a pair of suede boots when I first saw Sylvia, and she was very disappointed about this because she only loved shiny leather.

Mrs Z had not mentioned Sylvia's passionate interest in feet, but this was apparent from the second session when Sylvia excitedly paddled barefoot in water she had spilled, exclaiming 'Now you can see my foot!' Later she begged me to paddle in the sink with her so she could see our bare feet together. She also wanted me to tickle her toes. Sylvia spent much time paddling in the sink in all the following sessions before the Christmas holiday. It made her deliriously happy to sit with the water up to her knees, often playing with wet pieces of paper which she called meat balls, fish and lettuces. Most frequently she said she was washing and polishing lettuces, throwing out 'the dirty lettuces' and 'the nasty kidney' on to the floor. She sometimes remarked that her feet were cheesy and said that she loved cheesy feet.

Sylvia's feet were important to her as instruments of aggression as well as sources of excited pleasure. When wearing her shoes she liked to stamp items underfoot to destroy them and she kicked me and the furniture often and violently.

Sylvia had told me she was a boy soon after we met, when she also remarked that girls were stupid. She did not mind my calling her Sylvia as long as I did not refer to her as 'she' or 'her'.

Sylvia's excitement about paddling at the sink increased from session to session. She wanted to flood the whole room so it would be a swimming pool which she could wee into. At the height of her excitement she stood on top of the sink, pulled down her jeans and pants, and with her hands indicated the invisible arc of urine she supposed to be spurting forth to soak me. I said she really believed she was weeing from a big willy and Sylvia agreed as though she were convinced of it. Next session she announced she was a man diver who would dive into my pool and she managed to take off her clothes and stand naked on the window-sill 'so everyone can see me do it'. All these activities were carried out with tremendous excitement and laughter.

In a later session Sylvia showed some doubts about being a boy. Revealing her pink underpants, she remarked 'Boys *do* wear these, don't they?' And in the same session she also referred to herself as 'her'. When I commented on her doubts about being a boy she confirmed them by squatting and urinating on the floor behind a chair 'to serve you right', in totally different style from the earlier manic deluded moment when she had indicated that she was urinating from a penis.

Sylvia had inadvertently referred to herself as 'her' when we were talking about how she had attacked me in the waiting room. Sylvia explained 'That was the other Sylvia who hit you, not me. I socked *her* in the eye.' She had previously insisted that there were two Mrs Hopkins – a horrid one in the waiting room and a nice one in my room. On many occasions she looked at me quizzically as though bewildered about who I was, and asked 'Where's the other Mrs Hopkins gone?' I thought she was the victim of an extreme form of defensive splitting which she used principally to deal with anxieties about my return after separation. Mrs Z reported that Sylvia had become intensely attached to me, spoke of me continuously at home and could not wait for her sessions. However, by the time I saw her, Sylvia could only greet me with terror and rage, attacking me by hurling toys or running away to hide. I had become the horrible Mrs Hopkins of the waiting room.

The end of each session was also unbearable for her. She clung to me or tried to carry on playing until I had to steer her through the door. Then she began at once to scream for her mother and kept this up until they were reunited.

Sylvia's speech was fluent and ranged from the poetic to the obscene. She spoke of inanimate objects as though they were alive, for example 'The door won't let me open it' or 'I must wake up my sleepy socks – they're falling down'. Her end-less fantasies about monsters and space were sometimes delightfully expressed. 'Be a moon, and we'll have star teas' or 'Inside this space is the darkness of the dream monsters.' Her use of 'I' and 'you' was clear and accurate. When she was angry she swore with a range of obscenities which she was unlikely to have picked up from other children.

Therapeutic approach

During this early period of Sylvia's treatment I struggled to impose some order on her chaos and on my own confusion by simply trying to describe what was happening and by naming the emotions which she was experiencing with me. When I had identified her feelings I tried to link them with the few sequences I understood, for example her anger because she had to wait for me and her terror that I would retaliate whenever she was angry. I emphasized that I was *one* person whom she sometimes loved and sometimes hated and feared, and that there were not two Mrs Hopkins or two Sylvias either. I spoke of her evident bewilderment about whether I and other grownups were friends or enemies, whether we would protect her or kill her, and I indicated how she tried to allay her fears that I would attack her unpredictably by actively trying to provoke an attack under her control. In her quieter moments Sylvia clearly welcomed understanding and found some of my comments meaningful.

Sylvia's enormous erotic excitement about feet, shoes and willies made me very cautious about giving interpretations in sexual terms because of the risk of provoking uncontrollable excitement and exhibitionism. Behind her manifest excitement about sexual matters I sensed an extreme anxiety and this reinforced my caution about interpreting sexual themes, both at this phase and throughout the treatment.

As far as Sylvia's actual sex was concerned, in early treatment I acknowledged that she often needed to believe she was a boy or a man with a willy so she could excite me and feel as close to me as being married. However, I told her that I could see that she really knew she was a girl. I made no comments about Sylvia's excited interest in feet, but I linked her voracious attacks on shiny shoes in the waiting room with her feeling about my absence, the pain of waiting to embrace me and the fear both of my failure to return and of my return to attack her. In order not to excite her interest in my shoes I decided always to wear the same pair of suede boots when I saw her, and I did this throughout the first year of her treatment.

During this first phase of work with Sylvia I did not try to interpret any of her material in relation to her past and present experiences outside the clinic. It seemed essential to reduce her most intense anxieties about seeing me before we could think about the origins of her preoccupations.

Possible diagnosis: traumatic psychosis

After this initial phase of therapy I found myself wondering whether Sylvia had been traumatized by violent treatment. On reflection this impression seemed to be based on the following lines of evidence which I report in some detail, as the importance of trauma in psychotic and borderline conditions may sometimes be overlooked.

Firstly my countertransference. After each session Sylvia left me feeling emotionally bruised, betrayed and bewildered by the constantly reiterated shocks of her sudden switches from affectionate overtures to violent assaults. I thought my experience with her might well reflect experiences which she herself had suffered.

Secondly, my work with three neurotic child patients who had had similarly intense, though more intellectual, preoccupations with monsters, had led me to recognize that such preoccupations commonly represent not just the child's own monstrous feelings, but also the adults who were responsible for arousing these feelings. Analysis of the monsters in the three cases mentioned revealed that they disguised, respectively, a history of physical abuse by the mother, a homosexual assault, and early hospitalization experiences (Hopkins 1977). In each case the monsters represented a compromise between the child's fear of *real* aggressive attacks and fears related to his own aggressive impulses.

Sylvia had not yet mentioned her father but the nature of her monsters and her response to my absences made me suppose she had experienced him as a terrifying person who would return to avenge his death. She appeared to have dealt with his loss by identifying with him, and it seemed probable that this identification, an identification with the aggressor, had begun before he died, in response to her fear of him.

Another suggestive aspect of Sylvia's material was her use of her craziness to camouflage reality. At moments when she was relatively sane she would suddenly escape into distracting psychotic fantasies if I mentioned an aspect of reality she didn't like, such as the coming holiday. It seemed she might be unconsciously exploiting her madness as a camouflage to hide some unacceptable truths. At this stage her capacity for camouflage effectively confused me and prevented me from realizing that her terror was a terror for her life, and not a psychotic fear of personal annihilation or disintegration (Rosenfeld 1975).

Several factors corroborate my impression that Sylvia had been the victim of physical violence.

The literature on abused children offers some external support (Delozier 1982). Sylvia was hyper-alert. Her need to be constantly involved with me had a monitoring quality and she never turned her back. Later in treatment when she no longer defensively split me into two Mrs Hopkins she came to manifest an acute approach-avoidance conflict on first meeting me which is characteristic of abused children.

Stroh's (1974) data on seven children diagnosed as suffering from traumatic psychosis provide an essentially similar diagnostic picture. All of these children suffered from panic rages and extreme contradictory behaviour in which they violently attacked the people they loved, eliciting counter-aggression which repeatedly recreated their early experiences.

Finally, Sylvia's excited, erotic behaviour towards feet and shoes merits description as fetishism, a condition which implicates a variety of physical and sexual trauma in its development (Greenacre 1979; Stoller 1975), but which has not previously been reported in a child with a traumatic psychosis.

When giving her account of Sylvia's early history, Mrs Z had made no mention of family violence. In fact she had told more in this first interview than she was to reveal for a very long time to come. Although she met twice-weekly with Mrs R she quickly became extremely withdrawn and often spent whole sessions in angry or remote silence. She was too threatened by questions to answer any, so many details of Sylvia's history had to remain unknown. However, in her own time she gradually amplified the initial outline she had given with important material to be reported later. But, meanwhile it was to be Sylvia herself who conveyed information about some of her early experiences through her play and behaviour in her sessions with me.

Trauma, reconstruction and exorcism. Sessions 11–31

After Christmas Sylvia enabled me to reconstruct some of her experiences before her father died, two and a half years previously.

She increasingly demanded that I should act the part of terrifying monsters who pursued her with roars and threatened to eat her up. 'Be a Dalek,' 'Be a carpet monster' (draped in a carpet), or 'Be a light-switch monster,' she said. By this means I thought she was trying to localize and control her terrors of being attacked, but it was never wholly successful for she often screamed out in terror that a chair, a light or an unseen monster was attacking her.

I first interpreted one of her dramas as an attempt to communicate the past in a session when she told me 'Be a cross dream!' She made herself a bed and hid under the blanket. 'Roar!' she shouted. When I did, she asked, 'Are you a real Mummy? Are you a Daddy too?' 'Yes,' I said. 'Speak Italian then!' said Sylvia. 'I'm Never Mind Boy in bed. I'm not Sylvia. Sylvia was too frightened.' I said she was trying to remember what it was like when she was little and her mummy and daddy had had terrible roaring rows in Italian and she had been too frightened to bear it. 'Go tap, tap with your feet', said Sylvia urgently. I had to stamp with a regular rhythm. I asked, 'Did mummy and daddy go tap, tap with their feet?' Sylvia replied, '*Not* with their bottoms, silly. With their *feet*.'

This was the first occasion on which Sylvia revealed her confusion between feet and genitals, and also indicated how she had dealt with night terrors about parental violence and sexuality by imagining herself to be a boy. She was moved by my reconstruction and wanted me to tell her more about what had happened in the past. During part of each session she would enact a drama in a particularly urgent manner which I understood as a request for me to reconstruct past events, which were at first more rows between her fighting parents. Sylvia now claimed to remember their fights. 'Dad beat my mummy up', she said with conviction.

Soon Sylvia voiced more memories of her own. One session when she asked me to 'Be a fierce daddy monster and frighten me very much', I said I thought she was trying to remember how she had been frightened of her own fierce daddy. Sylvia suddenly looked at me with great amazement and said, 'My Dad broke up our house! It was another house. He threw all the furniture.' She was perplexed about where this event had happened and I told her I knew she had lived with her dad in a different house which her family left just before he died. Sylvia replied in a disconnected and cheerful way, 'You haven't seen my feet for a long time,' and she proceeded to paddle in the sink. She interrupted this activity to say, 'Be my friendly dad in my house. Come and listen to my record. Get in my bed.' When I came close to her she suddenly changed from friendliness to panic. 'My dad was in my bed. A terrible dream! A giant crane was rising up! And now a screwdriver is coming!' Sylvia held out her arms to protect her abdomen. 'The crane killed me with a sharp knife,' she concluded with a shudder. I said she might be trying to remember being terrified of dad's giant willy. Sylvia didn't appear to listen. She asked brightly, 'What is paper made of?' and returned to washing her paper lettuces.

Sylvia's vivid recollection of her father throwing furniture helped me to understand her terrors of flying Dalek furniture and her own need to overturn and fling the furniture herself. She quickly responded to interpretation about her wish to throw furniture in order to terrify me so I would know how she had felt when her father did it. She lost her terror of being attacked by furniture and also stopped throwing it.

In her role of Never Mind Boy, Sylvia began to think increasingly about the past. Just as her recollection of her father throwing furniture had laid the Dalek monsters to rest, so her recollection that her father had died in a car accident collecting a carpet, led to the disappearance of her need to make me attack her dressed as 'carpet monster' (always pronounced by her car-pit). Sylvia's attacks on the lights in my room and her terror of the 'light-switch monster' seemed related to her intense fear of the dark and her almost equal fear of turning on the light to reveal her monster parents fighting or banging their feet together. Discussion of these fears stopped Sylvia's attacks on the lights, and the light-switch monster also disappeared.

Soon after this Mrs Z told Mrs R that Sylvia had asked her about the old house and Mrs Z had taken her to see it. Whether or not at this time Mrs Z and Sylvia were also able to share memories of Mr Z's violence we do not know, since a whole year was to elapse before Mrs Z at last confirmed Sylvia's memories by confessing to Mrs R that her husband had thrown furniture in his rages and had broken the arms off the chairs. She said he had also beaten Sylvia frequently and had thrown her across the room. When Sylvia was a screaming baby he had 'kicked' both mother and daughter out of the house 'or else he would have killed Sylvia.' His violence outside the home had led him into trouble with the police.

As for Sylvia's possible indication of some sexual advance from her father, no external confirmation was ever forthcoming. I return to this subject later.

After reconstructing some of the events which seemed to have contributed to Sylvia's intense terrors of monsters, she began to bring happier memories about her father. She liked to sit on top of my cupboard because it was just like 'riding on my daddy's back'. She told me with delight how she could now remember going to the park with her daddy and paddling with him in the pool. She began to ask me to 'Be a friendly daddy' while she was Never Mind Boy and we went to the park together. Sylvia was now in touch with her love for her friendly father as well as her hatred and fear of her fierce and angry father. At this stage I seemed to represent in turn both aspects of her father and Sylvia had not yet accepted the reality of his loss.

Sylvia continued to express a persistent desire to see and to smell 'your lovely white feet'. When I told her of the coming Easter holiday she told me how she dreamed of going away with me, taking off my shoes and socks and paddling with me at the seaside. She was very aware of being rejected by me and was acutely jealous of my husband whom she was sure would paddle with me. This holiday was to confront her with the reality of losing me and after it she was able to acknowledge the loss of her father.

By the time that Easter came Mrs Z reported great improvements. Sylvia had stopped having violent tantrums and now talked about what angered her. She had become much more manageable and no longer made advances to strangers' shoes. She had also stopped bedwetting and did not insist she was a boy, though she was still reluctant to admit to being a girl. At school her teacher reported that she had at last begun to learn.

At the clinic Sylvia no longer supposed that there were two Mrs Hopkins and her behaviour in the waiting room and corridor had become much more controlled. She was still preoccupied with monsters but no longer possessed by them. After Easter Mrs R and I both independently observed how Sylvia had lost that radiant quality of beauty which she possessed when she started treatment. A beautiful boy was changing into a plain little girl. The terror and the masculinity had gone and with them the radiance too. I felt as though something comparable to exorcism had happened and I wondered what had been instrumental in achieving this change.

It was my impression that it was Sylvia's recall of past traumatic events, facilitated by my reconstruction, which had alleviated her most florid psychotic symptoms. She became dispossessed of a primitive identification with her father, which had been split into an idealized omnipotent aspect which she embodied and a terrifying persecutory one which she attributed to monsters. Instead of being possessed by images of her father she became able to know about him.

The ready availability of Sylvia's memories had surprised me. Evidently the traumatic events which she recalled must have been registered cognitively by her at the time of their occurrence. My reconstruction effectively gave her permission, in a safe setting, to recall and to share what she already knew. The analytic litera-ture (Bowlby 1979; Khan 1972; Rosen 1955; Tonnesmann 1980) suggests that the therapist's ability to construct external events is of particular importance when the patient has taken psychotic flight from reality or when important adults in the patient's life have put a taboo on knowing. In both these conditions, which applied to Sylvia, the therapist risks colluding with the patient's defences if he treats the traumatic events only as fantasies. He may also risk repeating the behaviour of the original traumatogenic adult for, as Balint (1969) points out, it is common for an adult who has traumatized a child to behave afterwards as though nothing had happened and as though the child had simply imagined it.

In Sylvia's case the shared acknowledgement of terrifying events in her past provided a key to her plight for both of us. Although we could never know the exact nature of her past experience we had both gained a cognitive framework in which to organize evidence. Sylvia now became sufficiently in touch with reality to learn in school. In treatment she had increasing periods of quiet and thoughtful behaviour when she drew pictures and talked about them. After Easter she moved on to acknowledge further aspects of reality: her lack of a penis and the loss of her father. She grew openly depressed and cried recurrently as she genuinely mourned the dad she had loved as well as feared and hated.

However, despite all these positive developments Sylvia could still suddenly become crazy and chaotic. Her progress at this stage must not be exaggerated. Her moods continued to change arbitrarily and although she no longer fought me as though fighting for her life she remained extremely aggressive.

Fetishism, incest and revenge

In the second year of treatment Sylvia continued to make educational progress and behaved well at school. She also gave up her fetishism and began to become aware of some of her emotional problems. She felt herself to be seriously damaged and she feared going mad. This development was associated with less desirable changes. Sylvia felt both suicidal and vengeful and she revelled in punishing and humiliating both me and her mother.

I will now describe and comment on these developments and their relationship to the possibility that Sylvia had been the victim of incest.

Firstly, it should be mentioned that in addition to using shoes and feet as fetish objects, Sylvia had another fetish which she used exclusively for sexual purposes. This was a tobacco tin which she always used when she masturbated. It had been given to her by 'Sir', her class teacher, and it contained 'magic words', Sylvia's name for flash-cards used for reading practice. Sylvia called masturbation 'swimming on my tin'. She lay happily on her stomach under my desk with her head on two cushions and her genitals pressed against the tin, rhythmically moving her hips. Ideally she liked me to 'tap-tap' with my feet while she did this.

Cases of female fetishism are extremely rare in the psychoanalytic literature, but Sylvia's form of masturbation was reminiscent of that used by an adult female patient (Zavitzianos 1971) who could only masturbate to orgasm if she employed a fetish symbolizing her father's penis. However, Sylvia's fetish comprising Sir's magic words in a tin seemed to symbolise the penis in the vagina, while Sylvia 'swimming' under my desk could be interpreted to represent father in intercourse with her mother. By adding the rhythmic noise of my feet she reproduced her version of their sexual act, with herself as a participant and not as an excluded observer.

Sylvia gradually gave up masturbating in sessions and I thought this was related to her growing awareness of being a girl. This new awareness greatly increased her envy and jealousy of Enrico, and Mrs Z reported that she had become most intolerant of him at home. She expressed the wish to bite his willy to bits and she tried to steal his masculinity by borrowing his underpants, his cowboy costume and his tie, which she often wore during sessions. His clothes restored her self-esteem and made her confident of winning my affection. Without them, at times when she accepted being a girl, she was liable to complain that I didn't love her at all.

It had been known from the start of treatment that Mr Z had loved Enrico much more than Sylvia. Mrs Z now confessed that she had convinced herself when pregnant that Sylvia would be a boy and had bought only boy's clothes for her. When she gave birth to a girl she was glad that the baby was taken into special care and that she could leave the hospital without her.

Sylvia's fascination with footwear slowly diminished for reasons which I did not understand and I began to be able to wear a restricted variety of shoes without exciting her. However, the desire to see and smell my feet and to paddle with me remained at high pitch. It only abated after more work was done on its meaning. This work was facilitated by information given by Mrs Z.

I had often wondered what part Sylvia's parents might have played in her choice of fetishes. I had become convinced that she had been over-excited by someone tickling her feet and pretending to eat her toes when she was little. I also thought it likely that she had slept at the foot of her parents' bed so that she had seen their feet move in intercourse.

Mrs Z now told Mrs R that her husband had often encouraged Sylvia to play with his bare feet. In particular she remembered Sylvia as a toddler putting marbles between his toes. Mrs Z also mentioned that he always slept naked and walked about the house naked too. When Sylvia was about 2 years old she had screamed at the prospect of having a bath and would only take a bath sitting on her father's lap, which she regularly used to do.

On the next occasion when Sylvia played at paddling with daddy I asked her if she remembered paddling with him in the bath. 'Oh yes!' said Sylvia ecstatically, 'With his nice friendly willy'. Then immediately she enacted a terrified girl in a park, attacked by a nasty man with a crocodile who broke into the park through a hole. He was shot by a bow and arrow. I said she seemed to have two sorts of memories about daddy's willy in the bath. Sometimes it had seemed nice and friendly, but sometimes she had felt it was fierce like a crocodile and would break into her hole and hurt her. It was safer to be a boy with a bow-and-arrow willy, like Never Mind Boy, than a girl with a hole who could be hurt.

If Sylvia had been so frightened of her father's penis, why had she found it reassuring to bath on his lap when she was about 2 years old? Did she feel safe from assault by seeing his penis between her legs and imagining that this frightening organ was her own? Or did the sight of her own and her father's feet in the water help to reassure her that genital differences did not exist? Such relevant material as Sylvia brought before the next holiday confirmed her focus on feet as a displacement from genital differences. It also suggested that Sylvia had enjoyed sexual stimulation in the bath for she asked me to tickle her genitals while pretending I was her daddy bathing her.

The episode of the break into the park through a hole led to my first mention of Sylvia's vagina. She soon brought much more material which could be understood in terms of her having a vulnerable hole which could be violated by her father's penis. For example, she brought three rubber crocodile monsters to visit her in her bed where she greeted them with an orgy of kissing and sucking before she screamed that they were attacking her. Then she pulled down her pants to show me her genitals and anus, in a manner intended to be very offensive. 'See! That's my blood!' she said. I spoke of her need to convey to me the horrifying shock that she felt when she imagined that her body holes were wounds made by an attacking willy. At this point Sylvia's dominating identification with her father had given way to a more primitive identification with her wounded mother.

Episodes like this were a reminder of the possibility that Sylvia had herself experienced genital assaults or acts like fellatio. Since her early dramatization of attack by crane and screwdriver, which was repeated on three occasions, other suggestive evidence of abuse had come mainly from Sylvia's provocative habit of copious spitting.

When Sylvia spat at me she aimed mainly for my mouth and was triumphant when she hit it. She called her spitting 'being sick' and spoke of spitting out poison and of spitting at me to kill me. At first I thought Sylvia's confusion of 'spit' and 'sick' might arise from observations of her baby brother 'spitting' up milk or simply from her fantasy. However Sylvia told me, 'Willies are sick' and 'I'm sicking out white like a willy'. Perhaps Sylvia had experienced ejaculation in her mouth which had made her feel sick, but I never felt sure enough to suggest it. Certainly Sylvia spat most at times when she was dominated by identification with her father, and as this identification diminished, so did the spitting.

Did Sylvia experience sexual advances from her father or could such mechanisms as identification with her mother and erotization account for her interpretation of violent sexual assaults being directed against herself? Greenacre (1953b, 1968) has described how in the pre-fetishist there is a prolongation of the early state of primary identification with the mother, on account of an insecure, unstable body image which impedes separation of the 'I' from the 'other'. In addition to such an identification, Sylvia may have erotized the many beatings she is known to have received from her father, for it is believed that pain and distress in infancy always arouse both sexual and aggressive drives (Freud 1924; Greenacre 1968).

Although identification and erotization may help to explain Sylvia's feelings of having been sexually assaulted, it should also be added that Mrs Z with great reluctance admitted to Mrs R that as a child she herself had been sexually abused by her step-father; she would not give details. It is known that some mothers who were sexually abused in childhood condone the sexual abuse of their own daughters. Certainly Mrs Z had not protected Sylvia from viewing full details of sexual intercourse which is likely to have been very violent on occasion.

With hindsight, now that I am familiar with recent evidence on child sex abuse (e.g. Renvoize 1982), I think it is very likely that Sylvia had not only witnessed violent intercourse, but had played with her father's penis in the bath and had experienced fellatio and possibly even attempts at penetration. She had apparently enjoyed the sex play and in association to this she played games in treatment in which she was a princess who proudly controlled the erections of a crane (a chair-leg under a blanket). However, fellatio seemed to have been associated not only with excitement but with extreme anxiety, humiliation and disgust, while the risk of penetration was clearly terrifying.

During Sylvia's treatment I lacked confidence to reconstruct her sexual activities with her father explicitly, but I described the themes of sex play, fellatio and penetration in terms of her wishes and fears, and also related them to her difficulty in distinguishing what she had seen happening to her mother from what she had supposed was happening to herself.

Following this work Sylvia lost interest in my feet and her mother reported a similar improvement at home.

It seemed to me that Sylvia's foot fetishism, like her masturbatory fetishism, had represented a recreation of sexual acts. Sylvia's first aim was to see, smell, suck and salivate over a pair of feet (or shoes), thus reproducing the act of fellatio, displaced from penis to feet. Her second, and more important aim, was to paddle with the feet so that there were two pairs of feet together. When Sylvia had bathed with her father at the age of 2 she may have felt that their feet together reproduced the sexual union of the parental couple. The similarity of their feet allowed Sylvia to disavow their sexual differences, while simultaneously Sylvia seems to have been in some ways aware of her father's 'friendly willy', either as a possession or a source of stimulation. Freud (1938b) describes how the split in the ego of fetishists enables them to maintain two such contradictory attitudes at once. Splitting allows them to disavow their perception of a woman's lack of a penis while simultaneously recognizing its absence and experiencing castration anxiety. Freud's fetishistic patients were all men. In Sylvia's case it seemed that she had disavowed sexual differences and armed herself with the fantasy of possessing a penis in order to protect herself from an underlying fear of violation. However, in so far as she still actually believed that she possessed a penis she may have been liable to castration anxiety. Greenacre (1979) claims that symptoms of fetishism only develop in females in whom the illusionary phallus has gained such strength as to approach the delusional. Sylvia certainly had a major delusion of this kind when treatment started, and although by this stage she had already recognized her lack of a penis and had wept about it, it is possible that the delusion may still have persisted in the enclave of her fetishism. However, it could also be possible that in females fetishism might arise in response to the terror of violation, and that the illusionary phallus and castration anxiety are secondary to this fear.

At the same time as Sylvia lost her excited interest in feet she became conscious of a pervasive sense of bodily damage. For example, she identified closely with 'a squashed rabbit bleeding from its bottom' and a hedgehog alleged to be torn apart and eaten by a Turkish family. She dramatized herself as the victim of terrifying forces which had destroyed her bodily integrity. She also became aware of being psychologically damaged and expressed the fear that she would grow up crazy.

Sylvia had been reasonably well-behaved at the clinic for some time, but now when she had an audience she delighted in displaying her disturbance. She aimed deliberately to shock people and show them she was damaged. She spat on other patients and shouted obscenities, 'So they think I'm mad' and 'So they'll know it's all your fault'. '*You* broke me.' 'You tore me apart.' She repeatedly threatened to throw herself down the stairwell, 'So everyone will know how horrid you've been,' and at home she talked of strangling herself. She drew obscene pictures of me and attacked me with her faeces. She revelled in humiliating me and was revengeful and triumphant. In these moods, which mercifully never dominated treatment, her intense hatred had a new and vengeful quality and I found her loathsome.

Although Sylvia now felt seriously damaged she made no intellectual connection between this and her traumatic history. Perhaps it was too distressing to think that her loved parents were responsible. The earliest and most serious trauma she had suffered was probably her mother's failure to protect and comfort her. Now that I had helped to remove the protection of her fetishism Sylvia took revenge on me.

These detrimental changes baffled me until I understood them in Stoller's terms (1975). He describes fetishization as an act of cruelty whose unconscious aim is to seek revenge on the original loved traumatizing object, to desecrate it and humiliate it. The accompanying excitement is not due to voluptuous sensations so much as to 'a rapid vibration between the fear of trauma and the hope of triumph'. The trauma feared is the repetition of a childhood event, sensed as life-threatening, and the triumph is the fantasy of revenge on the original loved traumatizing object.

When Sylvia ceased to express these complex feelings through her fetishism it seems that they became expressed instead in object relationships. The triumph of the fetishistic re-enactment of traumatic sexual scenes gave way to acknowledgement of a sense of trauma and a desire for revenge.

Casework with Mrs Z

Mrs Z now insisted on stopping treatment in order to take a job, while the psychologist attached to Sylvia's school thought Sylvia was ready to transfer to a school for normal children. Plans had to be made to end treatment after two years of work.

Mrs R had had a very difficult time working with Mrs Z who had remained extremely resistant throughout. However, it had been possible, to a limited extent, to help her to mourn her husband and to become able to speak about him with her children. Work had also been done on her over-identification with Sylvia, expressed by Mrs Z as being like one person going into another and dissolving them. Mrs Z's parents had intended that she herself should have been a boy, so her identification with her own unwanted girl baby dated from Sylvia's birth.

Mrs R's work with Mrs Z was crucial to the success of Sylvia's treatment for she managed to maintain her co-operation in spite of her recurrent threats to break off treatment, and also enabled her to make changes which benefited Sylvia. Sylvia must have been further helped by having the same man teacher throughout her treatment, for 'Sir' was a kindly father-figure whom Sylvia loved.

Treatment was nearly over before Mrs Z admitted how 'utterly brutal' her own relationship to Sylvia had always been and continued to be. Sylvia was certainly extraordinarily provocative but Mrs Z's collusion with this was most unfortunate. It seemed that Mrs Z needed to continue a violent relationship with Sylvia, although she also loved her and wanted to help her.

It had taken two years of patient work with this defensive mother to reveal the extent of Sylvia's rejection from birth and of both parents' murderous feelings towards her. Sylvia's inability to acknowledge that it was her parents who had threatened her life and her misattribution (Bowlby 1973) of this threat to monsters may have been partly due to the overwhelming terror associated with the realization that both her parents had often wished her dead.

At the end of treatment Mrs Z also revealed that her step-father, who had sexually abused her, had been a shoe-fetishist. This perversion can scarcely have been a complete coincidence, and it may explain the great importance which Mrs Z had attached to Sylvia's first display of interest in her father's shiny shoes. Dickes (1978) has described how parental reactions influence the development of their children's fetishism. As a rejected baby on the floor Sylvia may have been first attracted to shiny shoes as a substitute for faces with their shiny eyes, but her later passion for shoes seemed to stem from their relationship to feet and from the fact that shoes could be possessed, taken to bed, bitten and sucked without retaliation.

Termination

During the last term of her treatment Sylvia always wore skirts, which she now preferred to jeans. She maintained a rigid split between her loving self which appreciated and depended on me, and her damaged and revengeful self which continued to delight in fierce attacks. She still switched from one self to the other without apparent reason or awareness. The main work that was done was on the conflict she experienced between 'wrapping herself inside her mother' and separating from her, and the relationship of this theme to her sexual identity which was still very confused. She began to think more about me as a separate person with a home and family of my own from which she felt painfully excluded.

Sylvia had been very upset by the decision to end her treatment. In spite of her distress she kept the final date constantly in mind and told me with feeling how much she would miss me. At the end she embraced me in tears and said, 'I cannot bear to say goodbye'.

Follow-up

Sixteen months after treatment ended, when she was nearly 10 years old, Sylvia came to see me again at her own request. She asked me to arrange treatment for herself and for Enrico and was angry when I explained that Mrs Z could not manage to bring them at present. She drew obscene pictures of me to express her rage, but followed them with 'a lovely picture' of me to make amends. This was the first reparative gesture I had ever seen her make.

Mrs Z reported that Sylvia had maintained her gains and there had been no recurrence of her fetishism. She was coping adequately in her normal school where her behaviour was good, but she took it out on her mother after school and was often very difficult to manage. She was growing in independence and successfully performed errands on her own.

Despite her great improvements Sylvia remains a borderline child who is likely to encounter very serious problems at adolescence, such as psychosis, promiscuity or attempted suicide.

Summary

The interest of this paper lies in the unusual nature of the patient's symptoms and in their apparent relationship to early trauma. The patient was a 6-year-old girl with a foot and shoe fetish who was at first psychotic and convincingly appeared to be a boy. In the course of her psychotherapy it emerged, and was later confirmed, that she had been the victim of terrifying, life-threatening assaults by her father who had died before she was 4 years old. It also seemed probable that she had had an incestuous relationship with him. The paper explores the defensive nature of the girl's psychotic illness and masculine identity, and considers the possibility that her fetishism represented a re-enactment of sexual trauma.

Treatment freed the girl from her presenting symptoms and enabled her to attend a school for normal children.

Acknowledgement

I would like to thank Dr John Bowlby for his helpful comments on the manuscript.

Note

1 *International Review of Psycho-Analysis (1984)* 11: 79. Also published in Lubbe, T (ed.) (2000) *The Borderline Psychotic Child: a selective integration* London & Philadelphia: Routledge.

Attachment and child psychotherapy

Introduction

In an unpublished paper given at a conference in Leeds, Juliet Hopkins enlarged on her relationship to Bowlby's work on attachment:

> . . . from the start I embraced my uncle's attempt to recast psychoanalytic theory in terms of contemporary science with the aim of making it open to research. He liked to quote Freud's definition of psychoanalysis as " a science of unconscious mental processes" (Bowlby 1988: 39) and I have always seen attachment research as an example of that science, the scientifically-based face of psychoanalysis that has gradually developed to become a two-person theory of conflict and defence.
>
> (Hopkins 2010)

This 'scientifically-based face of psychoanalysis' was not always acceptable to the mainstream psychoanalytic community – indeed, for many years it was viewed as heretical and non-analytic, seen by some as turning away from the purely internal conflicts of the rather solitary Freudian child and more importantly being viewed erroneously by many as an attack on Freud. Nevertheless . . .

Juliet Hopkins has over many years encouraged her colleagues in psychotherapy and allied professions to engage with the attachment theorists and has been important in making this field directly accessible through her writing and talks. The four papers that follow (all reviewed and updated by her) were designed to give the reader a good introduction to attachment theory and its relationship to psychoanalysis. In addition, they show these ideas in action: psychoanalytic and attachment thinking come together in both the knowledge base and the clinical approach. It was this desire 'to make attachment findings relevant to clinicians' (Hopkins 1998) that led to chapter 5 – the earliest of this group of papers – which was given in 1987 at an ACP (Association of Child Psychotherapists) conference to celebrate John Bowlby's 80th birthday and published in the same year.

The first three papers were written between 1987–1990, a period in which professionals working with children were learning to recognise the existence of child sexual abuse and to perceive sexualised behaviour in childhood as related to abusive relationships and not simply to the internal process of the ego's struggle against id drives.

While child and adolescent psychotherapists were wrestling with this challenge to prevailing views of Freud's theoretical position and, perhaps as a consequence of engagement with children as their patient group, beginning to adopt the findings of attachment researchers into their clinical practice, adult psychoanalysis was perhaps slower in its adaptation. The first paper here, 'The observed infant of attachment theory', was to be published in a journal that would extend its audience to those who also worked with adults. That there was an assimilation of attachment thinking, and a widening of its perceived relevance and uses, can be seen in the fourth paper, chapter 7, presented in 2000 at a Tavistock Clinic conference on 'Attachment in new relationships'.

Finally, 'Facilitating the development of intimacy between nurses and infants in day nurseries' stemmed from a specific incident and the reaction to it. In 1983 a cot death had occurred in a nursery not far from the Tavistock clinic. The public inquiry that followed noted impersonal care by multiple carers. This provided an opportunity for intervention, helping the nurses reflect on the nature of their attachments to the children and of the children to their parents, carers and nurses:

A colleague and I together planned a course for nurses from seven state-run day nurseries. We aimed to improve the quality of care offered to the infants by developing the nurses' capacity to observe and to reflect upon the children in their care and upon their own experience of caring for them. Our work was facilitated by knowledge of Menzies' contribution on institutional defences. The project was successful in increasing the nurses' involvement in their work and the resulting paper has been adopted by the National Children's Bureau as a basic text for teaching significant factors affecting the quality of day care, including the need for on-going staff support and consultation.

(Hopkins 1998: 5–6)

In her desire to make a wider and more scientific knowledge base – one that calls on relevant research from a range of sources outside as well as within psychoanalysis – available to her colleagues, Juliet Hopkins has been particularly diligent in her explication of attachment theory. This introduction would best end with her own words, reminding her audience of the role of the child in internalising his attachment experiences:

Bowlby was aware that, influential as parents might be, children also shaped their own psychological development. He created the concept of "internal working models" to avoid the difficulties inherent in the psychoanalytic concept of "internal objects" and to explain the tendency for children's attachment patterns gradually to become a property of themselves. Although the family context continues to influence the child, the perpetuation of his attachment patterns becomes increasingly a matter of self-regulation. Once this is so the child is recognized to play a major role in the creation both of his own environment and of his internal world.

Importantly, Bowlby believed that because working models of relationships develop in transaction, the child internalises both sides of the relationship and the working models of the parents and of the self are complementary. For example, if a child has experienced reliably responsive care-giving he will construct a working model of the self as competent and lovable, but if he has experienced much rebuff he will construct a model of the self as unworthy of help and comfort. This view that in childhood we see ourselves as we perceive our parents to see us is a view that Winnicott (1970c) also reached but otherwise does not seem to have been a significant aspect of psychoanalytic theory.

(Hopkins 2010)

AH

4 The observed infant of attachment theory[1]

Introduction

The infant of attachment theory has been created to explain the behaviour of infants rather than to explain the free associations of adults on the couch. Consequently few psychoanalysts have become attached to it. This would not surprise its originator, John Bowlby, who has recognized the need of our insecure profession to cling to established theories and to their parental figures rather than to risk exploring new territories. Our clinical work is fraught with anxiety and uncertainty, and we need to rely on familiar theories to sustain us as we work. As clinicians we value the security provided by the familiar, but in our role as scientists we must risk exploring the new. Attachment theory is centrally concerned with this in-built polarity between the need for security and the desire for exploration and mastery of the environment, a polarity that is most obvious in toddlers but is with us throughout life. It has added a new dimension to psychoanalysis, a dimension from safety and security to danger and fear.

Why should psychotherapists explore this new territory and familiarize themselves with the attachment infant? One good reason might be a wish not to be left behind. Attachment theory is the chosen language of an increasing number of developmental psychologists and of professional workers in child mental health, in both America and Europe. It is, for example, the development within psychoanalysis which is now widely adopted within the World Association for Infant Mental Health. It has stimulated a significant advance in child development research and its contribution has been widely welcomed by child psychologists. A further good reason to explore it is the increasing relevance of attachment research for developmental psychopathology and for preventive mental health. The psychoanalysis of adults is unlikely by itself to give us further insights into the infantile origins of pathology. It is likely that more can be learned by relating these insights to observations of parent-child interactions. As Winnicott (1957: 114) wrote, "By constantly co-operating, analysts and direct observers may be able to correlate what is deep in analysis with what is early in infant development".

In the course of Bowlby's work on attachment and its corollary, loss, he reformulated psychoanalytic theory in terms compatible with contemporary scientific thinking. His trilogy "Attachment and Loss" (1969, 1973, 1980) combines ideas derived from ethology, systems theory and cognitive psychology. The theoretical essentials of this new approach have been ably summarized by child psychotherapist Victoria Hamilton (1985).

In this chapter my emphasis is on empirical findings of attachment research on infancy, with reference to their clinical relevance.

Evolution and the need for attachment

Bowlby approached the early mother-child relationship from the standpoint of a biologist. He appreciated the need to formulate psychoanalytic thinking within the central biological theory of our time: evolution. Our ancestors spent more than two million years as hunter gatherers before history began. They inhabited an environment in which only the fittest survived to reproduce. Our instinctive behaviour evolved to increase our chances of survival in these conditions. Freud was never satisfied with his own instinct theories and Bowlby decided to avoid Freud's use of the term 'instinct' with its outmoded concept of some internal driving force, and substituted the term 'instinctive behaviour'. This is conceived as a pattern which is activated or terminated by particular internal or environmental conditions and which can be observed in action, an idea borrowed from the science of ethology.

Attachment behaviour is an excellent example of such instinctive behaviour. Bowlby conceives of it as being separate from the instinctive systems serving feeding and sexual behaviour. It is activated in infancy by the internal conditions of fatigue, hunger, pain, illness and cold, and by external conditions indicating increased risk: darkness, loud noises, sudden movements, looming shapes and solitude. When it is activated the child seeks contact with one of his particular attachment figures whom he has learned to discriminate.

Babies are clearly pre-programmed at birth to learn the specific details of a few caretaking adults. For example, they have been shown to recognize their mother's voice at birth; they have learned her smell by five days and they can discriminate her visually from a stranger from two or three days old. They show their capacity to discriminate by their preference for their mother's familiar qualities. Although clear preferences develop from birth, the full intensity of the baby's attachment behaviour is only manifest from the latter half of the first year.

When attachment behaviour is activated at low levels it is possible for a mother to calm her infant by voice and proximity alone; but when the infant is very upset, only close physical contact can terminate distress. The aim of all attachment behaviour is proximity or contact, while its subjective goal is felt security. Anxiety is experienced throughout life when we are threatened either by a hostile environment or by the withdrawal or loss of our attachment figures. As adults, we still need attachment figures and we still seek physical contact at times of acute anxiety, trauma or loss. Our attachment system remains active throughout life.

In summary, Bowlby sees infants as being pre-programmed, given an ordinary expectable environment, to develop attachment behaviour which decreases the risk of danger and increases safety. A toddler's clinging to his mother in a strange situation is therefore conceived as an adaptive action and not as a manifestation of cupboard love, greed, sexual possessiveness or omnipotent control, which some psychoanalytic theories have supposed it to be. Bowlby's view shocked psycho-analysts when first presented to them in 1959: among other objections they felt it was a disloyal attack on Freud. Bowlby (1988), however, liked to quote Freud's 1925 definition of psychoanalysis as both a particular therapeutic method and as a science, the science of unconscious mental processes, the science which Bowlby had started to pursue.

The evolutionary approach provides a simple explanation for the vast increase in infantile sleeping disorders in recent years: more infants are now expected to sleep alone. Anthropological studies reveal that, in all pre-agricultural societies investigated, babies invariably sleep beside their mother, often between the par-ents (McKenna 1986); this practice is also the norm in industrialized Asia. It is interesting that parents in these societies, when told of Western sleeping practices, regard them as a form of child abuse. Babies are highly adaptable, but in evolu-tionary terms, being alone in the dark is a situation of high risk, and when babies become aware of their isolation they are liable to insist on parental presence. There are of course ways of overcoming babies' fears without sleeping beside them (see Daws 1989), but pursuing the aims of Western civilization can prove exhausting.

Bowlby's initial research focused on the effects of physical separation of young children from their parents, usually in hospital or residential institutions. When sel-dom visited, they were observed to pass through three stages of adaptation that Bowlby called protest, despair and detachment. Later attachment research has focused on the nature of the mother's availability when she is present – her sen-sitivity and responsiveness. Bowlby's colleague, Mary Ainsworth (1985), found evidence that the toddler who knows his mother is reliably available when he needs her can use her as a secure base from which to venture to explore his environment. He can concentrate well and play independently because he feels safe. Research has repeatedly shown a strong positive correlation between the security of children's attachments and their capacity to co-operate with adults, to concentrate on play, to persist at problem-solving and to be popular with peers (Prior and Glaser 2006).

The concept of security is not entirely new to psychoanalysis. In 1959 Sandler suggested the notion of safety as a feeling state quite distinct from sensual pleasure. He went on to describe how patients might thwart analytic work by regressing to childhood relationships associated with punishment or pain, because the security associated with these relationships made them more rewarding than the insecurity and isolation associated with new ventures. Thus, some instances of the negative therapeutic reaction could be understood in attachment terms.

Similarly, the heightened attachment which abused children develop to abusing parents can be understood as clinging to the little security that they know rather than risking the unknown. Safety for all of us is felt to reside in the familiar.

Security of attachment: The observed infant

Attachment research has focused on the parent-infant relationship. Since biologists have found each organism to be highly adapted to its environment, Bowlby has always supposed the infant to be more influenced by real aspects of parenting than by internal fantasy. This assumption has been supported by Ainsworth's research (e.g. 1985) which reveals that certain characteristics of a mother's parenting are more important for determining the infant's security of attachment at a year, than any innate quality of the infant that has yet been assessed.

The concept of security was introduced by Ainsworth (1971) in her attempt to understand the results of her "Strange Situation Test", a test which she intended to reveal individual differences in infant development. In this standardized test the infant is frightened by being left briefly alone in a strange room and then reunited with his mother; his reactions on reunion are considered indicative of the nature of his security, since they reveal the expectations he has developed about her physical and emotional availability.

Early research was done exclusively with mothers; research with fathers will be mentioned later.

i) Secure attachment

In general, patterns of behaviour on reunion with mother fall into two broad categories. The exact proportions of babies falling into each category vary with the sample (many nationalities have been assessed), but roughly speaking some two thirds or less of babies are described as securely attached to mother. On reunion these babies immediately seek contact with their mother; on being picked up they are quickly comforted by her and they soon ask to be put down so that they can pursue their exploration of the toys provided. They may express some anger with mother, especially if she tries to interest them in the toys too soon, but their crossness is easily assuaged. These babies show no approach/avoidance conflict and express their feelings directly. They can be said to have developed basic trust.

ii) Insecure attachment

The remaining third of babies are classified as anxiously attached. Ainsworth thought that this category comprised two groups: those with avoidant and those with ambivalent (resistant) attachments. These two groups appear to correspond with the two groups of adult patients whom M. Balint (1959) had designated as philobats and ocnophils respectively. Although Balint's terminology is not widely known, all psychotherapists must be clinically familiar with the distinction between these two solutions to insecurity. Philobats can be briefly designated as self-sufficient explorers who evade close contact, while ocnophils are dissatisfied, clinging dependents who rely on physical proximity to feel safe. The revelation of Ainsworth's research is that these patterns of response to stress are clearly established by the first birthday. Further research (Beebe & Lachman 2002) has shown that these patterns may be evident as young as four months.

a) The infant with an avoidant attachment

The characteristic response of these babies on reunion in the Strange Situation is not to greet their mother, and, in some instances, not even to look at her. Any approaches tend to be abortive. If picked up they may lean away or squirm to get down. Frequently they divert their mother's attention to a toy or distant object. However, it is clearly perplexing that stressful events which normally heighten attachment behaviour apparently diminish it. Bowlby (1988: 132) interprets the avoidant response to indicate that "already by the age of twelve months there are children who no longer express to mother one of their deepest emotions, nor their equally deep-seated desire for comfort and assurance that accompanies it." Fearfulness, dependency and hostility are not expressed. This behavioural strategy of apparent detachment allows the baby the safety of physical proximity without risking the rejection of intimacy.

b) The infant with an ambivalent attachment

These babies are intensely upset by the separation and are highly ambivalent to the mother on her return. They want to be close to her but are angry with her and so are very difficult to soothe. They cling, resist being put down and are slow to return to play. Analytic understanding of this strategy indicates that the baby cannot accept the mental separateness of the mother and so lives in a confused identity with her.

As Ainsworth has pointed out, the psychological significance of the three patterns of attachment behaviour which she described rests upon their close association both with mother-infant interaction in the home, and with their persistence over time.

iii) Observations in the home

reveal that the reaction of babies in the Strange Situation is closely related to the nature of the mothering which they have received during their first year.

a) Briefly, babies with a secure response have mothers who have proved responsive and accessible. These mothers are able to read their babies' signals and to respond to them sensitively and reliably, especially to their bids for attachment and close physical contact. At home their babies are observed to be happier and more co-operative than babies who manifest an insecure attachment.

b) Babies with an avoidant response have mothers who are restricted in their range of emotional expression and who usually exhibit an aversion to close physical contact; these are babies whose bids for comforting have been consistently rebuffed. Their mothers hold and carry them less comfortably than other mothers do, tending to avoid close ventro-ventral contact. Their babies have been found to be no less cuddly at birth than other babies are, but by a year they neither cuddle nor cling but are carried like a sack of potatoes. Their mothers tend to express affection by kissing rather than by cuddling.

Bick (1969) has described how some of these infants develop a "second skin" as a means of holding themselves. Balint recognized that adult philobats depend upon an illusion of self-sufficiency to sustain their adaptation.

An avoidant attachment does not necessarily result in manifest pathology. Avoidant adaptation ranges from the self-contained and emotionally distant personality (said, for example, to be characteristic of the English upper classes) to the severely withdrawn, obsessional or schizoid.

c) Babies with an ambivalent attachment have mothers who enjoy physical contact, but who provide it erratically, often in response to their own needs rather than in response to their babies' needs. They are in general inconsistently responsive and tend to be interfering and intrusive. Their babies' anger towards them can be understood as an attempt both to express frustration at their inconsistent handling, and to force their mothers to provide the care and comfort of which they know they are capable. Balint (1959) recognized that, as ocnophils their "real aim is not to cling but to be held without even needing to express the wish for it". He found that they had the illusion that as long as they were in touch with a safe object they themselves were safe. In view of the fact we now know that their mothers' moods have been inconsistent and unpredictable, it is not surprising that ocnophils feel that physical contact is necessary in order to keep "in touch".

The difference between an ambivalent and an avoidant view of life may be reflected in some of the differences between the theoretical infants of Melanie Klein and Anna Freud. Melanie Klein struggled to explain the intense involvement and the destructiveness associated with an ambivalent attachment, while Anna Freud endeavoured to keep the more detached, objective stance associated with an avoidant adaptation.

The infant with an insecure disorganized-disoriented attachment

Further research revealed that not all babies fell neatly into Ainsworth's three groups. In 1986 the insecure disorganized-disoriented attachment was described by Main and Solomon. This infrequent attachment is usually found in conjunction with infant behaviour characteristic of one of the other major attachment categories, but whereas the avoidant and ambivalent infants can maintain their consistent strategies for dealing with stress, the disorganized infants cannot. In the Strange Situation, they reveal their inability to cope in a variety of individual ways. For example, the infant may freeze motionless, fall prone, exhibit tic-like stereotopies or a simultaneous display of contradictory behaviour-patterns, such as approaching with head averted. It seems that impulses to flee, fight or freeze are interfering with their approach to the parent. Main saw these infants as being locked in an approach-avoidance conflict. The infants could not approach because of their fear of the parent and could not flee because of their attachment, an irresolvable paradox.

The first suggestion to explain the origins of their behaviour was that they had had experiences with frightening or frightened parents. However, psychoanalysts have long known that parents do not have to threaten or maltreat their children in order to become objects of hatred and fear. It is particularly striking, for example, to observe how the internal representation of a loved and trusted parent can become a monster or a witch after a young child experiences a traumatic separation or a loss. Bowlby predicted that all experiences in infancy which activate strong attachment-seeking without terminating it would result in disorganization of the attachment system. These frightening experiences can include separation, loss, illness and neglect as well as experiences with alarming or alarmed parents. All these experiences are felt to threaten infants' survival. All evoke extreme longing, pain, terror and rage. Main (1995) named this constellation "fright without solution." These are the infants who are most likely to manifest later pathology, including borderline personality disorder.

Fathers

Fathers have so far had to take second place in attachment research because they so rarely are the baby's main caretaker and so are less available for study. However, two most important findings have emerged from the research.

Firstly, fathers are found to have a capacity equal to mothers to offer babies a secure attachment. Both sexes have the same proportions of securely and insecurely attached infants.

Secondly, contrary to psychoanalytic expectation, the infant's relationship to his father cannot be predicted from the nature of his relationship to his mother. It is independent of it and reflects the qualities which the father himself has brought to the relationship. This means, moreover, that the nature of the infant's security is not a function of his general temperament but depends on the history of interaction which he has had with each caregiver.

In 1938 Freud described the child's relationship to his mother as "unique, without parallel, laid down unalterably for a whole lifetime, as the first and strongest love-object and as the prototype of all later love relationships, for both sexes" Freud 1938a). Although attachment research has clarified that the early attachment to the mother is *not* the prototype for the attachment to the father, it has not yet been established whether Freud was right about its significance in determining later love relationships. One study is in line with Freud's view.

Main and Goldwyn (1986) found that six-year-olds' representation of attachment, revealed in projective tests, was based on the relationship to the mother not the father. For these children mother had been the primary caretaker and it would be interesting to know what consequences follow when father plays an equal or major caretaking role. Without question, both the relationship to the mother and the father, together with those to other significant early figures, are brought forward into the psychoanalytic transference. But the relative significance of these relationships in sexual object choice is not yet understood.

Whatever the case, it seems possible that the prototypes of the earliest relationships which determine all later love relationships are based on those parental characteristics which determined the nature of the child's attachment; that is, on physical and emotional availability, sensitivity and responsiveness.

Changes in attachment pattern

Attempts to predict the course of child development from individual characteristics assessed during the first year had always failed until the nature of the child's attachments to both mother and to father at the first birthday emerged as factors with significant predictive power. This must be because the attachment pattern is an aspect of a relationship, not just of the child himself, so as long as the child continues within the same relationship, the stability of the attachment pattern is high.

However, changes in attachment patterns do occur, especially in unstable populations, such as a deprived inner city sample. They are found to be a function of the availability of the parent concerned. For example, with regard to mothers, attachments are likely to become more secure if mother gets more support, whether from her husband, her mother, a friend or a professional worker. Attachment to mother may become less secure when mother goes out to work, gives birth to a sibling, is depressed or bereaved. However, as the child grows older his attachment pattern becomes increasingly a property of himself, and is less responsive to changes in parenting.

Several studies have shown that the provision of additional support for mothers during the baby's first year increased the likelihood of the development of secure attachment. Social policies to support new parents are needed. Infant-parent psychotherapy (Chapter 8) can also contribute. In this psycho-analytic approach infant and parent are seen together and their relationship can usually be improved more rapidly than when the parent is given individual help. Results can be rapid because the baby's representation of the relationship is not yet self-regulating and is still able to change responsively to changes made by the parent. The implications for early intervention are evident.

Classification

For many clinicians the most obvious contribution of attachment research has been the new ways of classifying children's relationships with regard to security. As clinicians we usually do not need special assessments to reveal children's attachment strategies. They reveal themselves in response to everyday separations and reunions and especially in the particular ways that children seek comfort and care when distressed.

Psychoanalysts have recognised attachment categories to be simplistic. Bowlby agreed that the insecure categories were certainly complex and contained characteristics of each other. I have found this to be evidently true when unconscious aspects of children's communications are considered. For example, six year old Clare (Chapter 13) was strongly avoidant in her relationships but conveyed that when she was dancing she felt herself to be merged with both her parents. It is helpful to know that observable attachment behaviour may not coincide with unconscious fantasy and that insecure categories are not mutually exclusive.

Lyons-Ruth (2003: 888) attempts an interesting link with psychoanalysis by suggesting that infantile attachment strategies could be one way of conceptualizing

Bollas' concept of the "unthought known", those early implicit but unsymbol-ised representations of ways-of-being-with which have yet to be translated into thought.

Internalization

Early mental representation has always been a central aspect of psychoanalytic theorizing and Bowlby felt this was necessary too. He developed the idea of 'internal working models' to resolve some of the difficulties inherent in the psy-choanalytic concept of internal objects and to explain the tendency for a child's attachment patterns gradually to become a property of himself. Although the family context continues to influence the child, the perpetuation of his attach-ment patterns becomes increasingly a matter of self-regulation. As Bowlby (1973: 368) describes, "present cognitive and behavioural structures determine what is perceived and what ignored, how a new situation is construed, and what plan of action is likely to be constructed to deal with it. Current structures, more-over, determine what sorts of person and situation are sought after and what sorts are shunned. In this way an individual comes to influence the selection of his own environment."

It is proposed that the infant constructs models of the world which enable him to interpret events, predict the future and plan action. Because working models of relationships develop in transaction, the child internalizes both sides of the rela-tionship, and the working models of the parent and of the self are complementary. For example, if a child has experienced reliably responsive caregiving he will construct a working model of the self as competent and lovable, but if he has experienced much rebuff he will construct a model of the self as unworthy of help and comfort.

It is possible to conceive of internal working models as composed of the RIGs (representation of interactions which are generalized) proposed by Stern (1985). Indeed, attachment theory is entirely compatible with Stern's work, and comple-mentary to it, since it provides what Stern lacks: a psychology of comfort and distress and an explanation of the specificity of infant attachments.

For a relationship to proceed optimally each partner must have reliable working models of each other, which can be revised and updated in accord with commu-nication between them. Here there is a striking difference between the directness of communication between the secure and insecure infants and their mothers. Secure couples show more eye contact, verbalization, emotional expression and shared interaction with toys than do insecure pairs. This disparity is even more marked when the infants are distressed. The secure infants remain in direct com-munication with mothers and express their anger, fear and desire for her, while, for example, avoidant infants only engage in direct communication when they are content.

These differences persist. Main's longitudinal study (Main & Goldwyn 1986) found that at six years of age children with mothers who had shown a secure pattern of attachment five years earlier, engaged in free-flowing conversation, including a wide range of topics, personal issues and expression of feelings. Six-year-old children who had had an avoidant pattern with mother at a year had limited conversations which avoided both personal issues and feelings.

Such obstruction in communication indicates the operation of defensive strategies. Defensive exclusion is believed to occur in response to intolerable mental pain or conflict. As Bretherton (1987: 1093) describes, "Clinical case material suggests that such conflict arises when an attachment figure habitually ridicules a child's security-seeking behaviours, reinterprets rejection of the child as motivated by parental love or otherwise disavows or denies the child's anxious, angry or loving feelings towards attachment figures. Under such circumstances, it is common for a child to exclude defensively from awareness the working model of the "bad" unloving parent, and retain conscious access only to the loving model."

In addition to the defensive strategies adopted by the child in response to the frustration of his bids for security, the child's self-model is profoundly influenced by how his mother perceives him. Whatever she fails to recognize in him he is likely to fail to recognize in himself. In this way, major parts of his personality can be split off and unintegrated. The situation is further complicated if the mother falsely attributes to the child intentions and feelings which he does not have. This view that in childhood we tend to see ourselves as we perceive our parents to see us is a view that Winnicott (1967b) also reached but has not become a widely accepted contribution to psychoanalytic theory.

Bowlby (1980) points out that there is often a discrepancy between what a parent says and what a parent does. Severe psychic conflict results when parental generalizations clash with the child's actual experience, and defensive exclusion of personal feelings and/or memories may be used as a means of continuing to see the attachment figure in a good light, and so to maintain security. Infantile phobias can be understood as a means of preserving a secure relationship to an attachment figure while attributing fears belonging to the parental relationship to some external object. For example, a two-year-old boy developed a phobia of all books containing monsters after his mother had read him a story about a dragon which blew smoke and flames. In therapy it emerged that she had often controlled him with threats of cigarette burns and had actually burned him on one occasion. Bowlby (1973) reinterprets Little Hans' phobia of horses in terms of his anxious attachment and terror of losing his mother.

Intergenerational transmission

Psychotherapists will not be surprised to learn that there is a significant correlation between parents' representation of their own childhood attachments and the nature of their child's attachment to them. This finding stemmed from the work of Ainsworth's former student, Mary Main (Main, Kaplan & Cassidy 1985) who developed the Adult Attachment Interview (AAI).

When interviewed with the AAI about their childhood experiences with their own parents, parents reveal as much by the defensive or direct nature of their communication as they do by the content of their replies. Parents whose infants are resistant or avoidant with them are alike in giving accounts which typically are characterized by unrecognized inconsistencies and contradictions, but their accounts also differ from each others' in predictable ways. Parents with resistant infants generally give a lengthy account of unhappy, entangled relationships, with ample evidence that they have remained entangled with their own parents or with memories of them. Parents of avoidant infants give much briefer accounts, partly because they minimize the importance of relationships and partly because they tend to have forgotten childhood experiences. They are likely to make generalized statements about having had happy childhoods, but to be unable to support this with evidence, which is either lacking or contradictory. Parents of disorganized infants frequently express bizarre or irrational thinking about the topics of abuse and loss which indicates that these traumas remain unresolved.

In contrast to the parents of insecure infants, parents of secure infants give a fluent, consistent and coherent account of their childhoods in which they treat relationships with significance and recall events with appropriate affect. The vast majority of these parents have had secure childhoods themselves, but among them are a number who recall childhoods of extreme unhappiness and rejection. They have thought and felt deeply about their experiences and have tried to understand them. Some of them have remained very angry with their own parents while others have achieved forgiveness.

The outcome of this research clearly supports the clinical finding of Fraiberg et al. (1975) that the repetition of adverse childhood relationships can be avoided when adults come to terms with their unhappy past. It seems that this can happen when they recognize what happened to them, acknowledge how they felt about it and are aware that their parents contributed significantly to their unhappiness, which was not entirely of their own making. What they have achieved is a capacity for reflective functioning, that is, an ability to mentalise and reflect on their experience. It is this capacity, rather than any other significant variable, such as parental sensitivity, that has been found more recently to best predict the likelihood of creating a secure attachment to their child (Fonagy 2001). The reflective dialogue between parent and child provides an internal feeling of containment for the child, a secure base of inner strength and confidence. Attachment theory and psychoanalysis are now united in recognising that parents provide the interpersonal context in which children discover and learn to use their minds and that this capacity is related to issues of both security and containment.

Developments within attachment and psychoanalysis have brought these two approaches closer today than they have ever been. Their mutual collaboration should provide psychotherapists with sufficient security to recognise attachment as a fruitful endeavour to continue the science that Freud began.

Note

1 *British Journal of Psychotherapy* 1990: 460–470.

5   Failure of the holding relationship

Some effects of physical rejection on the child's attachment and on his inner experience[1]

Introduction

Bowlby's immense contribution to our awareness of the importance of holding in the early mother-child relationship was acknowledged by Winnicott in his last public lecture (1970a: 225). "John Bowlby has done more than one man's share of drawing the world's attention to the sacredness of the early holding situation and the extreme difficulties that belong to the work of those that try to mend it."

In this chapter I participate in Bowlby's work of drawing attention to the early holding situation, in order to consider some implications for the child psychotherapist in trying both to understand and to mend it.

Winnicott's term, "the holding situation", was used by him to cover many aspects of the early mother-child relationship besides the actual physical holding of the baby. But here I restrict myself to that aspect alone: that is, to the mother's provision of physical holding and body contact for her young child. I illustrate its significance by reference to the response of children whose mothers, though present, are physically rejecting of their infants. I bring together contributions from attachment research and clinical work, and finally consider some implications for psychotherapy.

The role of holding in the early mother-child relationship was never developed as a theme by Freud. Winnicott (1954: 284) pointed out that Freud himself had enjoyed good enough mothering to be able to take many aspects of its reliability for granted and to provide them for his patients in the secure and comfortable setting of his consulting room. Winnicott set out to remedy Freud's omission of the theme of holding; he developed original ideas about the role of holding in the mother-infant relationship and its parallels in the analytic situation. In 1952 he wrote that "the earliest anxiety is related to being insecurely held", and followed this with the statement that the physical holding of the infant is a form of loving (1960: 49). "It is perhaps the only way in which a mother can show the infant her love." In 1963 he described how the analyst symbolically holds the patient and how "this often takes the form of conveying in words at the appropriate moment something that shows that the analyst knows and understands the deepest anxiety that is being experienced or that is waiting to be experienced" (1963a: 240). Clearly this implies that the function of holding, in addition to conveying love, is to relieve anxiety. It follows that a child who is not adequately held must feel both unloved and anxious.

Meanwhile Bowlby had approached the early holding relationship from a different angle. In his seminal paper, "The Nature of the Child's Tie to his Mother" (1958), he observed that the baby manifested at least five instinctive responses: sucking, clinging, following, crying and smiling. These responses served the function of attaching the child to the mother and eliciting her responsive care and protection. When this paper was published, children's disturbances were generally ascribed by psychoanalysts to problems in feeding, weaning and toilet training, but Bowlby (1958: 371) boldly suggested that the mother's responsiveness to her child's need to cling and to follow was potentially of more pathogenic importance. "The association which constantly impresses itself upon me is that between form and degree of disturbance and the extent to which the mother has permitted clinging and following, and all the behaviour associated with them, or has refused them."

Attachment research

Attachment theory has from the beginning been built on empirical research as well as on clinical insight; it has also generated further research. Two of Bowlby's followers, Mary Ainsworth and Mary Main, have provided substantial evidence of the effect on a baby of a mother who does not readily permit clinging or following, but is physically rejecting of her child. I will summarize some of their major findings (Ainsworth 1982, Main 1977, Main & Stadtman 1981, Main & Weston 1982, Main & Solomon 1986).

Most strikingly, research has shown that home-reared babies whose mothers have been physically rejecting have, by the age of twelve months, developed a characteristic form of attachment, classified by Ainsworth as "anxious avoidant". Whereas babies with a secure attachment to their mothers actively seek physical comfort from them after a very brief, but stressful, separation, avoidant babies do not. Their characteristic response to reunion after such a separation is not to greet their mothers, and, in some instances, not even to look at them. Any approaches tend to be abortive. If picked up they lean away or squirm to get down. Frequently they divert their mother's attention to a toy or distant object. Avoidant behaviour is commonly thought by these mothers to indicate mature independence. However, it is clearly perplexing that stressful events which normally heighten attachment behaviour apparently diminish it. Bowlby (1988: 132) interprets the avoidant response to indicate that "already by the age of twelve months there are children who no longer express to mother one of their deepest emotions, nor their equally deep-seated desire for comfort and assurance that accompanies it".

When Ainsworth initiated her research on infant attachment she expected to find that different mothers would prefer different modes of communication with their infants, some stressing physical contact, for example, others relying more on vocalisation or eye-to-eye contact. However, she discovered that desirable forms of maternal behaviour tended to occur together. Mothers who were sensitive to their infants' signals tended to respond with all the modes available to them, and when distal modes of contact failed to soothe their infants, they picked them up and cuddled them. However, mothers whose babies developed an avoidant attachment all manifested what Ainsworth called "the rejection syndrome", characterized primarily by deep aversion to bodily contact which led them to rebuff their infants' attempts to initiate physical contact. In addition these mothers were liable to be rough or threatening with their infants and to perceive their infants' demands as conflicting with their own activities. They were noticeably restricted in their range of emotional expression, conveying detachment or stiffness, which could be interpreted as an effort to control expression of their resentment. These findings mean that babies whose mothers are physically aversive have mothers who are also liable to be emotionally out of touch. The effect of physical rejection cannot be considered in isolation from the effect of lack of emotional rapport.

It might be supposed that infants who have developed an avoidant attachment by a year were more difficult or less cuddly than other babies in their earliest months, but research (Main 1990) has shown that this is not so. However, by the age of nine months these babies do not respond positively to their mothers' initiation of contact; they neither cuddle nor cling but are carried like a sack of potatoes. At this age they still initiate as many contacts to their mothers as other babies, though often mainly to mother's distal parts, like her feet.

In the second year, babies with an avoidant attachment show no anger with mother after a short stressful separation, although secure babies do. However, they show a high incidence of angry behaviour towards the mother in stress-free settings. This anger is often out of context and seems entirely inexplicable, for example, suddenly hitting the mother's legs while smiling. Bowlby (1988) has described how the avoidant child's attempts to be self-sufficient in order to avoid rebuff may lead to personality organization which is later diagnosed as narcissistic or as a false self, of the type described by Winnicott.

Main and Weston (1982: 54) postulated that the avoidant infant was the victim of an irresolvable and self-perpetuating conflict, caused by his mother's aversion to physical contact, "The situation is *irresolvable* because rejection by an established attachment figure activates simultaneous and contradictory impulses both to withdraw and to approach. The infant cannot approach because of the parent's rejection, and cannot withdraw because of its own attachment. The situation is *self-perpetuating* because rebuff heightens alarm and hence heightens attachment, leading to increased rebuff, increased alarm and increased heightening of attachment . . . In other words, by repelling the infant the mother simultaneously attracts him."

Four years later Main and Solomon (1986) published their discovery of the disorganised/disoriented attachment pattern. Main realised that the "irresolvable" and "self-perpetuating" conflict which she had attributed to infants with an avoidant attachment was actually at its most intense in infants who also showed disorganisation. In retrospect, it seems that the three children described in this chapter would have been classified as manifesting a disorganised-avoidant pattern of insecure attachment.

A psychological constellation associated with physical rejection

Reading Main's work made me wonder how often this irresolvable and self-perpetuating conflict of infancy is at the root of later psychopathology. I turned to the records of children I have seen in psychotherapy in search of evidence of the effects of physical rejection on their inner experience.

In the clinical material that follows I present material from three children whose mothers provided convincing evidence that they had avoided physical contact with them as far as possible in their infancy. All three children came from intact families with well-intentioned parents; there were no hints of physical abuse. I have omitted further mention of the fathers who in each case played a minimal part in their children's care and were often absent for long periods.

Material from these patients enabled me to distinguish a psychological constellation which I believe to be associated with the experience of repeated physical rejection in infancy. This constellation consists of the conflict which Main has described, associated with a terror of physical rejection and an almost equal dread of physical acceptance lest physical contact results in mutual aggression. In addition there are feelings of intense pain and a self-representation of being in some way untouchable and repellent.

Clinical material

Clare was referred for psychotherapy at the age of six years on account of failure to settle on starting school: she could not learn or make friends. During the course of weekly casework her mother gradually revealed the extent of her rejection of Clare. She had resented her arrival and found her physically repellent as a baby, though she had gradually come to enjoy talking and playing with her. She had always propped Clare's bottle and kept her in a playpen all day until she started nursery school. She thought that Clare had always resisted being cuddled. As soon as Clare could walk she walked away from her mother and was liable to get lost. She had always been stoically independent, never asking for help except when she had hurt herself. Her mother described her as "accident prone" and felt that she had accidents to gain the attention which she had no other means of seeking. Even when she had hurt herself she did not cry.

The psychiatrist who assessed Clare described her as having a false personality (Winnicott 1960a). She was strongly identified with her mother whose phrases and gestures she accurately reproduced. It seemed that she did not need her mother because she had become her. Similarly, in therapy, Clare took over my capacity to make interpretations and gave them to herself so that she would not need to depend on me. Once, when I spoke to her of her hidden wish to cry, Clare explained, "I never cry because if I started I would never stop." I understood this to mean that she feared there would never be anyone to comfort her.

In the second year of her therapy Clare spoke of her worry about lepers which gave her bad dreams. She explained that lepers were contagious which meant that "if they touch someone they die". She thought they could be cured by the laying on of hands. As therapy proceeded Clare became aware that she felt herself to be a leper whom no-one wanted to touch because she would kill them, and she also became aware of her longing to cry and to be comforted. In her sessions she was tortured by the longing to touch and be touched by me which conflicted with her terror of it, and by her longing to cry which she fiercely resisted because it was "so silly and only babies do it".

Clare first allowed herself to seek comfort from me when she melted into tears while pretending to cry in the role of a small baby. She held out her arms to me and I responded by picking her up and holding her. Later in therapy she sought physical comfort from me a second time when she allowed herself to fall heavily from my desk onto the floor. It was after this event that Clare's mother reported that Clare came to her to be comforted when distressed for the first time. Mother, who had been greatly helped by her own case-worker, was ready to respond to Clare and thereafter Clare continued to turn to her mother when upset and began for the first time to confide her worries to her. She became cuddly and, before long, very clinging and demanding, and no longer accident prone.

Laura, 16 years, suffered from depression and compulsive eating. In therapy she recounted a recurrent nightmare of finding herself alone in a desert, covered with a revolting skin disease. In association to this dream she mentioned that she had a collecting box for Hindu "untouchables". No-one in Laura's family had ever suffered from a skin disease, but Laura's mother, like Clare's, could not tolerate physical contact with her throughout her infancy. However she had been able to enjoy cuddling Laura's younger sister when she was a baby. In therapy Laura represented herself as a tortoise and her sister as a cuddly rabbit.

I have found it common for physically rejected children to dramatize or draw themselves as physically repellent or unstrokeable creatures, like tortoises, toads, crocodiles and hedgehogs. They feel themselves at depth to be unattractive though this is sometimes over-compensated for with pretty clothes.

In a session in the second year of her therapy in which she suffered great distress, Laura became obsessed with the image of the moth's fatal fascination for the candle flame. She wept as she expressed her horror at the moth's repeated return to the flame that burned it, and said that she experienced the pain of the burning acutely in her own skin.

This image of the moth and the candle flame is a dramatic reminder of Main's finding that, by repelling the infant the mother simultaneously attracts him. I thought that for Laura it expressed the conflict between her burning desire to be loved by her alluring mother and the burning pain and rage associated with the continued rejections which she had experienced.

Before Laura's preoccupation with the image of the moth and the candle flame she had been concerned with being frozen rather than being burned. Her images had been of icebergs, snow and refrigerators.

Children's images of being frozen are familiar to psychotherapists. The burnt child dreads the fire and the frozen withdrawal of the avoidant child prevents any further risk of being burned. Laura's shift from freezing to burning imagery was accompanied by intense awareness of her longing for physical love and of her hatred of her mother for her rejection of her.

After getting in touch with the feelings represented by the moth and the candle flame, Laura lost her urge to eat compulsively. This would not surprise Bowlby who has expressed the view (1982) that oral symptoms can develop in response to the frustration of a child's attachment to his mother. However, I think that Laura's compulsive eating was not an arbitrary displacement activity. The way in which she had felt compulsively drawn to the desired but hated food mirrored the moth's addiction to the candle flame. This parallel has made me wonder whether the compelling lure of the physically rejecting mother may contribute to other compulsive or even addictive practices.

Both Laura and Clare suffered acute pain, verbalized as "burning" and "torture" as they faced the issues inherent in their experience of physical rejection and their desire for and dread of physical contact. Winnicott (1963b: 88) has described how the toddler's need for his mother becomes "fierce and truly terrible". When this need is frustrated by a physically aversive mother then I believe that the pain which is aroused is also fierce and truly terrible, like burning or torture, stabbing or biting. It seems to me that the infant experiences the pain as a physical assault, not as a psychological rejection.

In their book on psychotherapy with severely deprived children Boston and Szur write of the long struggle through which deprived children must come to terms with pain and loss: "Central to this struggle seems to be the transformation of pain from something which has the character of an overwhelming physical attack into something which can be considered in the mind as an experience" (Boston and Szur 1983: 75).

Claire and Laura were both intelligent and articulate; they had been able to translate the pain of their physical rejection into symbols which could be understood. My third clinical example concerns the therapy of a three-year-old, Paddy, who was incapable of symbolic expression when his therapy began. I present his material in some detail in order to illustrate how the conflict which Main described could first be deduced from his behaviour, before it emerged in symbolic form in the context of the constellation which I have come to associate with a history of physical rejection. Paddy's therapy, like Clare's, also touches on the issue of the role of physical contact between therapist and child patient, a topic to which I return.

Paddy was the only child of Irish parents. He was referred for psychiatric assessment at the age of three and a half years by a paediatrician who wondered whether he was mentally defective or psychotic; today he might be considered to be on the autistic spectrum. He had no speech and was not toilet-trained. His parents reported that he had never shown signs of preferring them to anyone else; he had never greeted them on arrival or protested at their departure. He showed no awareness of danger and would wander off and get lost unless kept locked indoors. When he injured himself, even severely, he appeared to feel no pain. He regularly ate dirt and rubbish, and even occasionally his own faeces. He rejected being cuddled and was a constant thumb-sucker. He did not play but wandered about "getting into things". Although he never cried, he was upset if other children did, and was also upset by the sight of mess spilled on the floor. In spite of the many worrying features of his development, Paddy presented at the clinic as a jolly little boy who usually made good eye contact, though there were times when his eyes glazed over and he became inaccessible.

What sort of history lies behind such extreme disturbance? Paddy's mother was a chronically depressed and very anxious woman who had made several attempts at suicide in her teens. She suffered from severe eczema and explained that although she loved Paddy she had always avoided touching and cuddling him for fear that his germs would infect her skin. She reported that Paddy's birth had been normal and he was a healthy baby, but she lost all her confidence as a mother when he was a month old and a paediatrician suggested that he might have Down's Syndrome. At this time breast-feeding failed and mother employed a series of au-pairs to help with Paddy's care; however, none of them stayed longer than a month because conditions in the home were so chaotic. The marriage was unstable and father did not help.

Paddy showed no sign of anxiety at meeting me, a complete stranger in a strange room. I was surprised to find that he was immediately interested and pleased by the way that I verbalized his activities and reflected his feelings. Although he usually seemed vastly cheerful his anxiety suddenly became very acute at any moment that there was a loud noise or a threatened loss of control, like spilling water. At such times he attempted to bolt from the room, and when I held the door shut he turned his back to me and indulged in a variety of tense nervous manner-isms such as pulling his ears and rocking. At times when he was especially pleased and happy he also avoided eye contact, by closing his eyes while grasping his nose and mouth and seeming acutely abashed.

Attachment theory (e.g. Main & Weston 1982) explains how, by turning his back, closing his eyes or attending to an inanimate object, the avoidant child reduces the rejecting mother's power to elicit flight or aggression, and is thus enabled to stay safely in her proximity. By deduction, Paddy avoided eye contact at moments when he most wanted physical contact and so feared both my rejection and the expression of his own hostility. At times when he had no particular desire to be held he easily made eye contact while being perfectly comfortable for me to touch him, for example, by helping him undo his coat.

One of the clues to Paddy's fear of bodily contact was manifest in what became the central activity of his therapy sessions. With enormous effort he erected piles of wobbly furniture. He aimed to put a cushion on the top, climb up and sit on it. However, the furniture was always stacked too insecurely to make this possible, and I had to intervene to prevent him from falling. I thought Paddy's building represented both his wish for a mother with an available lap, and his fear, based on experience, that she would never prove strong enough to hold him.

Paddy took great pleasure in having or doing the same as me. He would be thrilled, for example, to discover that we both had hankies and that we could draw circles together. This need for sameness has been described as mutuality (Winnicott 1970b) or imitative fusion (Tustin 1986). It can be used as a means of enjoying togetherness or of denying a separate identity and therefore denying the possibility of separation. Paddy not only sought refuge from his approach-avoidance conflict in this way, but also by hiding inside safe places. He would lie for long periods under the couch or sit wrapped in a blanket with his head inside a cushion cover. Such behaviour has traditionally been understood as an expression of the wish to be safe inside mother. More poignantly, it might also be considered as an attempt to create a secure base when there is no mother available, a nest or a den instead of a lap.

As the first term of therapy progressed Paddy sometimes risked coming close enough to touch me when distressed. On the first occasion he bumped into me backwards and then sat down and held my shoe. This new ability to touch my extremities was accompanied by occasionally thumping me hard for no apparent reason. As he grew bolder and began to approach me from in front, he clutched his mouth very tightly. From observation of his movements I interpreted his apparent longing to use his mouth to cry, to kiss and to bite, and his fears of doing so.

During the first term of therapy Paddy blossomed into speech and also toilet-trained himself. These developments were of immense reassurance to his parents who no longer feared that he was mentally defective. They attended the clinic for regular weekly casework themselves; their marriage stabilized, they showed increasing interest in Paddy, and mother's eczema healed.

In his second term of therapy Paddy risked more direct physical contact with me by jumping off the window-sill into my arms. He did this with clenched teeth and fisted hands, not snuggling into me but wildly thrashing the air as though fending off an assault. Soon after he had trusted me to catch him he began to greet me in the waiting room and to resist leaving me at the end of sessions. This was an extremely painful period for his parents who had to observe their son manifesting an affectionate attachment to his therapist which he had never shown to them. I wondered whether I had been too explicit about Paddy's wish to be close to me and too accepting of his advances. I tried making myself less physically available and I emphasized his wish for physical contact with his parents. Paddy felt crushed. He withdrew from me, and various of his mannerisms, which had almost disappeared, returned. In the third term of treatment I again made myself more available and spoke directly of his longing to be held and comforted by me when distressed, while also acknowledging his negative feelings.

At the time of his referral Paddy had seemed oblivious to pain. His reckless climbing led to many bruises which he completely ignored. I verbalized his need not to know that he was hurt because he feared that there would be no-one to comfort him. Bowlby (1988: 156) has emphasized the link between emotion and action. "Failure to express emotion is due very largely to unconscious fears lest the action of which the emotion is a part will lead to a dreaded outcome." This close link between emotion and action has also been demonstrated in the work of Fraiberg (1982). She found that toddlers who had seemed oblivious to pain became able to respond to their injuries with cries or screams once they had established a relationship with their mother in which they could expect consolation. The same proved true of Paddy with me. In his third term of therapy he began to whimper when he hurt himself, and eventually one day when he had injured his thumb, he climbed into my lap, crying loudly. After this he not only sought my lap when he hurt himself, he took better care to avoid injury. However, when Paddy climbed on my lap for consolation, traces of his anxiety about physical contact remained. Like Clare, he kept his head averted from me.

When the first year of therapy ended I was worried that I had seduced Paddy away from his parents whom he still ignored and rejected, in spite of many positive changes in their attitude to him. However, during the long summer holiday Paddy caught measles, and it was while his mother nursed him through this illness that he first sought refuge and comfort in her arms. After his illness he became affectionate and sometimes clinging to both his parents.

Paddy's acute approach-avoidance conflict had been apparent in his behaviour from the start of therapy. It was only in the second year of his treatment that he achieved the capacity to express it symbolically and to convey accompanying fears of being both physically repellent and contaminating.

When Paddy first began to speak one of his most repeated phrases was "dirty boy". He gradually brought increasing associations to his sense of being disgustingly dirty and identified with "smelly poos", only fit to be flushed down the toilet. It seemed that behind his habit of eating rubbish and faeces were fears that his mother had rejected him on account of his dirtiness, and that this dirtiness was also the cause of her eczema. Like Clare with her fears of leprosy and Laura with her skin disease, Paddy felt repellent and dangerous to others. Like them he feared the physical acceptance which he also longed for, because he might cause harm. This fear of hurting was exacerbated by powerful wishes to hurt which Paddy began to express in endless fantasy fights between crocodiles. In these fights, which were enacted with great urgency, Paddy and I were both crocodiles who intended to eat each other up while protecting ourselves by biting and scratching each other. Paddy often described our sore and bleeding wounds and he found it meaningful when I likened these wounds to his mother's sore and scaly skin. The crocodile fights seemed to represent the acute approach-avoidance conflict of Paddy's infancy and the agony he suffered when longing to be close enough to eat his mother up while dreading rejection and mutual assaults.

Paddy ended therapy at the age of five and a half years when he entered his local primary school. He settled well and made progress. His parents' only remaining worry about him was that he was indiscriminately friendly to strangers.

Implications for psychotherapy

Physical contact between therapist and child patient

Paddy's and Clare's use of my lap for comfort may be considered a controversial technique. When Freud advocated abstinence throughout the course of treatment (1915c), he intended that language and interpretation should suffice. However, Winnicott (1963a) wrote that in the course of therapy, "Occasionally holding must take a physical form, but I think that is only because there is a delay in the analyst's understanding which he can use for verbalizing what is afoot". With regard to children, it could be added that there may also be a delay in the child's understanding which needs to be bridged by physical holding. I doubt whether for Paddy or Clare there could have been a satisfactory alternative to the availability of my lap at a critical time in their therapy.

Main (1986) concluded that what has most meaning to an infant is not the *amount* of physical contact which he receives from his mother; it is her physical *accessibility* in response to his initiative that matters. Where the treatment of young avoidant children is concerned it is probably essential to respond with more than words to their first initiatives for physical consolation when distressed. Not to do so would be to repeat the history of rejection which they have endured from their parents, and so could nip a new beginning in the bud.

Once a new beginning has been made with the therapist, the question remains of how it can be transferred to the parents. This happened immediately and spontaneously for Clare whose mother was eagerly awaiting the opportunity to comfort her. Clare only needed my physical comfort twice before she turned to her mother to meet this need in future. From then on in her therapy, in the manner of older children like Laura, she was able to use the cushions for comfort while feeling herself symbolically held by my capacity to be verbally "in touch" with her feelings. Paddy is the only child I have worked with who for a while preferred intimacy with me to closeness with his own parents. I am left not knowing how I could have managed this better.

Another area of technique about which I am uncertain is the degree of intimacy which it is helpful to develop in therapy with very young children. Even after accepting comfort on my lap both Clare and Paddy continued to show their fears of a more intimate relationship by averting their faces. I did not comment on this behaviour for fear of seeming to want to draw them into a more intimate contact which I felt belonged in their relationship with their parents. However, although their parents described both children as becoming "cuddly", I never learned how intimate they became, and it seems possible that further exploration of these issues in therapy could have been valuable.

Untouchability

A final implication for our work concerns the understanding of the avoidant child's feelings of being untouchable, repellent or contaminated. These feelings need ideally to be traced to their origin in the parents' treatment of their child, and not ascribed only to the hatred and guilt which the child inevitably feels. Failure to do this may increase the child's tendency towards self-blame, depression and low self-esteem.

Freud discovered that what has been remembered and understood need not be repeated. Further research by Main (Main & Goldwyn 1986) provides some evidence that when early rejection is understood and recognized as a function of the parent, not of the self, then the risk of repetition is reduced. Children who know that their parents rejected them on account of their parents' own failings are less likely to reject their own children.

Conclusion

This paper has brought together research and clinical evidence to demonstrate the central significance for healthy development of the mother's physical availability at times of her infant's need. In doing so it has described some adverse effects on development when she fails to provide this secure base. Bowlby and his co-workers have enabled us to recognize that the reliable availability of a responsive and sensitive mother is more fundamental to satisfactory personality development than conventional issues concerning feeding, weaning and toilet training. We can now explore in detail the psychopathology associated with the various deviations in maternal care which attachment workers have shown to be significant.

In a recent contribution to the Association of Child Psychotherapists, Bowlby expressed the hope that the time had come when a wider understanding of attachment theory would be used to improve clinical understanding and therapeutic skills. I hope that this paper will encourage other psychotherapists to explore the exciting new territory which Bowlby has so brilliantly opened up for us. Our patients will reap the benefit.

Note

1 Originally given at the Association of Child Psychotherapists celebration of John Bowlby's 80th birthday in February 1987 and published in the *Journal of Child Psychotherapy* 1987 13: 1.

6   Facilitating the development of intimacy between nurses and infants in a day nursery[1]

The gap between ideals and practice in child care is often inexplicably wide. This paper examines why the care of infants in day nurseries often becomes impersonal rather than intimate, and suggests means of counteracting this.

Background

Two recent research studies (Bain and Barnett 1980, Marshall 1982) were made in state run day nurseries which provided care for infants from disadvantaged families in London. Although the two nurseries studied were of good repute and employed trained nursing staff, the care of the children was found to be very inadequate. In particular it was impersonal and fragmented. Nurses were observed to focus on the physical care of the children and on the domestic tasks of the nursery and to avoid personal and playful interaction with the children.

For example, in Marshall's detailed study of the care of a group of nine infants under two years of age, it was observed that the attention of adults flitted from one child to another and rarely lasted for as much as thirty seconds on any one child. A child with a dirty nappy received the longest bout of sustained attention (up to 4 minutes), but this was directed only to his buttocks. It was usual for a nurse not to make eye contact with the infant she was attending to, but to direct her attention to another infant at a distance. Not only was the infants' care fragmented in its brief and episodic style, but also in the discontinuity of personal attention which it provided. There was no assignment of infants to individual nurses and it was, for example, common for a toddler to be sat on a pot by one nurse, to be wiped by another and to have his pants pulled up by a third. Physical contact between adults and children was kept to the minimum and staff did not attempt to comfort distressed babies by holding them, but by moving them, for example, from cot to floor or back again. Very little speech occurred between adults and infants. Throughout most days the infants remained silent, without any babbling or jargoning of their own. Contact between the nurses and the infants' parents was restricted to a few pleasantries at the times when the infants were left at the nursery and when they were collected.

These findings may seem unbelievable. How can staff who have chosen to make a career with children and have been trained to do so, treat them so distantly, impersonally and interchangeably?

One of the obvious reasons for the poverty of care was the inadequate staff/ child ratio. Although the recommended ratio for the care of children under two years of age in these state day nurseries was one to three, staff coffee and lunch breaks and the shift system often meant that only two staff were in charge of nine infants. Moreover staff shortage was exacerbated by the high rate of staff sickness. In the nursery studied by Bain and Barnett, staff absenteeism averaged 53 days per nurse per annum. Such a high level was both a reflection of the stress of the job and a cause of it, as nurses at work struggled to cope in the absence of others. Staff turnover was also found to be extremely high.

However, the inadequate staff/child ratio seemed insufficient to explain the extent of the staff's detachment from the children and of their evident unaware- ness that they were giving the infants less than optimal care.

Approach

In 1983 in a similar state-run day nursery, close to the author's clinic, a cot death occurred. The official inquiry revealed that the baby who died had been handled by four different nurses that morning, and that she had been put outside in her pram and forgotten because she was no one individual's responsibility. The publicity surrounding this event led the author to approach the local department of Social Services in order to offer an intervention aimed to understand why impersonal and fragmented care so often becomes the mode of practice in day nurseries and whether this practice could be reversed to provide the more intimate care recom- mended for young children. In undertaking this project the author was encouraged by the work of Bain and Barnett in achieving beneficial changes in the day nursery which they studied.

The Social Service Department responded by arranging for twelve nurses, responsible for the care of infants under two years of age, to be released for one afternoon a week to attend group discussions at our clinic for a period of six months. Two nurses, one senior and one junior, came from each of five nurser- ies, and two juniors from two other nurseries; they represented a wide range of experience. The group discussions took place in two periods. One period, led by a colleague, focussed on the care and development of individual infants, while the other period, led by the author, focussed on topics selected by the nursery staff. Topics covered included such subjects as admission procedures, settling babies in, relationships with children's parents, handling aggression and the assignment of children to individual staff members.

Neither the author, nor her colleague, ever visited the seven day nurseries where the nurses were employed, and therefore did not know how closely conditions of care in them corresponded with those reported in the two research studies cited. However, since the staff/child ratios and the staff training were the same and the infants were selected from similarly disadvantaged backgrounds, it would be surprising if there had been major discrepancies. The main difference was prob- ably a recent change in Social Services' policy which now requires that each infant should be assigned to the care of an individual nurse, or "key worker".

This recommendation turned out to have been variously interpreted in five of the nurseries and to have been ignored in two. In each of the nurseries the majority of the infants stayed for the whole of a working day, some of them for as long as nine hours. They had been allocated places on account of parental need, associated with such problems as child abuse or neglect, depression or ill health. Some indication of the problems presented by children from such disadvantaged families is given by a recent London survey which found that children, aged two to four years, in day nurseries had four times as many behavioural problems as those in nursery schools, and ten times as many behavioural problems as those in play groups (McGuire and Richman 1986).

Many papers have dealt with the adjustment of young children to the provision of alternative care. This paper is entirely concerned with the experience of nurses in providing this care, as reported by them in the group discussions. It describes how the discussions changed and enriched the nurses' experience.

Understanding the conflict between ideals and practice

All the nurses already claimed to accept the ideal of babies developing intimate, individual relationships with their nurses. This ideal has spread among London nurseries in recent years, in accord with the views on attachment of Bowlby (1982) and Ainsworth (1974). It replaced an earlier ideal that close relationships between nurses and children should not be allowed to develop because such relationships were potentially damaging for children and created difficulties for staff (e.g. Tizard & Tizard 1971). Proponents of the old ideal argued that if a child became closely attached to a nurse he would suffer a great deal when she left or went off duty, and that it would both weaken his relationship with his mother and make him more difficult to manage by his nurse. Although all the nurses in our group had apparently accepted the new ideal, all the original arguments against it were reproduced by them unchanged. They were perplexed about the clash between the new ideal of intimate attachments and the apparently adverse effects of practising it. Many of the nurses had had experiences early in their career of developing an intense attachment to a child and they still vividly recalled the pain caused to them and to the child when they parted. They had also had experiences of children who became attached to them demanding excessive attention and being jealous and possessive; they wondered if they had spoiled them. And although they were uncertain whether an intimate relationship with a nurse weakened a child's relationship to his mother, they were very much aware that some mothers became jealous of their children's affectionate relationship to their nurses. So, although the nurses expressed themselves in favour of closer relationships, they feared the consequences.

The group discussions revealed two other major sources of conflict with the new ideal: notably the ideals of equality and of independence.

Nurses believed that children should be treated equally and given equal attention, or else some would miss out. In practice this seemed to mean avoiding any lengthy involvements with individual children, for fear that others were being ignored or getting jealous; they also feared that favoured children might become spoiled. The nurses' struggle not to favour some children more than others emerged in the discussions as a reaction against the strong wish to do so. Their feelings towards the children were not at all equal; they found some of them appealing and lovable, others uninteresting, some annoying and a few unbearable. The nurses deprecated their biases and felt especially guilty about their dislike of some of the children. It was a relief to them to discover that the group leaders regarded this as a problem to be understood rather than as a failure to be condemned.

The counterpart of the belief that all children should be treated equally was the apparent belief that all nurses should be equal, and therefore equally interchangeable within the groups of children who knew them. Bain and Barnett believed this to be one of the factors associated with high absenteeism: nurses felt that any other nurse could do their job just as well.

The ideal of children attaining physical and emotional independence was one which had been fostered at the nurses' training school. Nurses were proud when infants moved from bottle to cup, when they learned to feed themselves and when they achieved toilet training. Nurses had also been led to admire infants who were undemanding, quiet and self-contained. And they were aware that once infants formed individual attachments these qualities were often lost and gave way to much more emotional behaviour.

An additional conflict with the ideal of individual, intimate relationships was the threat it appeared to pose to both infants' and staffs' relationships to the infants' parents. Staff were afraid of offering the infants happier relationships in the nursery than they enjoyed at home in case this undermined their relationship to their parents; and they did not want to make inadequate parents jealous or envious of their own relationships to the children. Consequently staff avoided displaying signs of affection to the infants in front of their parents, and some said they even felt guilty if they gave the infants a cuddle when their parents had gone.

Development of awareness of the importance of feelings

As group discussions proceeded, nurses' perceptions changed in two main directions. They became more aware of the children's individuality and of their needs for attachment, dependency and emotional expression; this change was reflected in the more detailed and sensitive observations of the children which they reported. They also became increasingly aware of the impossibility of fully meeting the infants' needs, because of the inadequate staff/child ratio and the special needs of disturbed and disadvantaged infants. Greater awareness of the children's needs was accompanied by a greater response to them and more pleasure in doing so; in this way the job became more rewarding. But greater awareness of the impossibility of providing sufficient care made the job more painful and frustrating. It increased the staff's anger with their employers, the Social Service department, which seemed to be demanding 'the impossible' while paying 'a pittance' for it. Three staff said that they would give up nursery nursing unless the pay and the staff/child ratio improved.

The development of the expression of the nurses' feelings in the group discussions went hand in hand with their growing awareness of the children's feelings. The group leaders challenged some of the nurses' assumptions about the value of independence in such a young age group. They drew attention to the difference between genuine self-reliance and detachment, and between distress and disturbance. They indicated that it was natural for infants to be distressed several times in the course of a nursery day and to need physical comfort from a known nurse. Some nurses stopped using distraction as the main technique to deal with children on the brink of tears, and began to find that there were benefits in picking them up and allowing them to have "a good cry". For example, Peter, aged 18 months, had appeared to pass each day during the month he had spent at the nursery tremulously on the brink of tears. When his nurse stopped diverting him with toys on his arrival, but picked him up for a cuddle when his mother left him, he sobbed on her shoulder and then for the first time settled down to play. Nurses were surprised to recognise that tears and fuss could be a sign of a child's security in his relationship with his nurse, and not simply a sign of her failure. They became more accepting of displays of emotion and less unquestioning of the virtues of detached independence.

As Anna Freud wrote in her book on the institutional care of infants (1974), "It is not the absence of irrational emotional attachments which helps a child to grow up normally, but the painful and often disturbing process of learning how to deal with such emotions."

Although nurses were relieved to find that there could be blessings in tears, opening up the whole subject of the children's emotions was a very painful one for them. They became increasingly aware of the extent of many children's unhappiness, both at the nursery and at home, and of the high incidence of emotional disturbance among them, manifest in such problems as tantrums, screaming, head banging, provocation and teasing, aggressive assaults and compulsive masturbation. Looking at the feelings of these disadvantaged children was a bit like opening Pandora's box, and sometimes created a feeling in the nurses' group that everyone there could do with a good cry.

The development of intimate attachments

During the six month period of the group discussions, several staff risked forming more intimate relationships with the infants than they had done before. Their reports of how this affected both them and the infants were of special interest.

Firstly, the change gave the nurses a new sense of self-importance. It now mattered to them to be reliably at work to ensure the happiness of the children who depended on them. Illness or absence was a serious matter. They took an especial pride and interest in the babies who became attached to them, and surprised themselves by referring to them as "my Harry" or "my Jane". Two nurses were also surprised to find themselves spontaneously using "baby-talk" to babies who had become attached to them. This drew the whole group's attention to the fact that "baby-talk" had not previously been used by staff in any of the nurseries; they said it would have seemed silly.

A further spontaneous development in response to the formation of individual attachments was concern on the nurses' part about the transfer of infants from one nursery group to another, as the infants grew up. Plans were made to postpone some of the transfers and to make other transfers very gradually, to ease the loss for both nurse and child. Increased concern for the infants also led staff to attempt more communication with the infants' parents in order to co-ordinate their care at home and in the nursery.

However, the nurses' increased affection for the infants also made them more distressed about the inadequacy of the parenting which some of the infants received. Two young nursery staff spoke of spending sleepless weekends worrying about the happiness and safety of "their" babies. Commitment to these disadvantaged infants was achieved at a considerable emotional cost.

Changes reported among the infants who had developed special attachments to individual nurses were diverse, depending, it seemed, on the nature of the attachments which they had formed. All attached infants were reported to show an increase in communicativeness, especially in the use of language. For example, two toddlers whose speech had been markedly delayed suddenly blossomed into sentences as soon as each had a nurse whom he could call "mine". Some attached infants showed other positive developments. They were reported to settle more easily on arrival, concentrate better on play and be less attention-seeking than before. Presumably these were infants who had formed secure attachments, and were able, as Bowlby has described, to use their new attachment figures as a secure base from which to explore. However, other attached infants developed the characteristics predicted by adherents of the old ideal of detachment. They became intensely demanding, especially of physical contact, and were jealous and aggressive towards other children.

Nurses observed that infants who had developed secure attachments to them greeted their mothers more enthusiastically than before. They showed less ambivalence towards their mothers, and this seemed to indicate that they had found the long day's separation less painful now that they were assigned to an individual nurse.

However, two infants, who had developed secure attachments to their nurses, provided apparent evidence that their relationship to their mothers had been undermined. When their mothers came to collect them, they howled, clung to their nurses and resisted going home. This was very upsetting to both nurse and mother. One of these children, Jane, aged 19 months, seemed to be showing an angry, retaliatory reaction to having been left by her mother; this made staff more aware of the way Jane's mother was frequently rejecting towards her. The other child, Tom, aged 21 months, seemed more frightened of his mother than angry with her, and this confirmed staff's suspicions that he was being maltreated at home. These two children's new attachments to their nurses had enabled them to express feelings towards their mothers which had previously been hidden and were valuable for staff to know about.

No evidence was brought that any child's relationship to his mother was actually weakened by his attachment to his nurse. Discussion of these issues drew attention to how little is actually known about the effect of an infant's various current attachments on each other. Such anecdotal evidence as there is, for example, on children in hospital and in foster care, seems to suggest that a secure attachment with one figure builds up a capacity for trust and an increased capacity to form secure attachments to other figures (see Chapter 7).

Evidently, nurses had been correct in supposing that offering individual attachments to the infants in their care would lead to trouble. The reasons which had sustained the old ideal of detachment became clear. The available evidence indicated that it was infants who enjoyed a secure relationship to their mothers who were able to develop secure attachments in the nursery, and who presented no problems in their management. But infants who had insecure, anxious attachments to their mothers developed relationships to their nurses which were fraught with difficulty. This finding is in line with Sroufe's research (1983) which showed that children who had insecure, anxious attachments to their mothers in their second year subsequently developed very dependent and demanding relationships to their pre-school teachers; in particular they sought attention in very negative ways.

The period spanned by these discussion groups was too short to discover whether, with time, infants who had made insecure, anxious attachments to their nurses might become more secure. The nurses' own view was that this could only be achieved by offering these infants one-to-one individual care. With the existing staff/child ratio they felt that they could not provide sufficient attention to make the development of secure attachments for disturbed infants possible.

Impersonal care as a defence

In conclusion, work with this group of nursery staff clearly supported the finding, reached by Bain and Barnett, that impersonal care develops as a defence against the anxieties, pain and frustration associated with intimacy. Once the nurses could be helped to tolerate and understand the distress which was inevitable in their work they were able to offer more intimate relationships to the children in their care, and this greatly increased their pleasure in their work. Infant care was experienced as more rewarding and interesting, as well as more painful, and the staff were convinced that both they and the infants benefitted, in spite of all the difficulties. When the group discussions ended, the nursery staff no longer paid lip-service to the ideal of infants developing intimate, individual attachments to their nurses, they were fully committed to it.

The group discussions

The changes achieved through the group discussions were reached through combining the nurses' knowledge and experience with the group leaders' psychoanalytic understanding of group processes and of child development. The group leaders made it clear that they were there to help the group to learn from each other and to find their own solutions to problems, rather than to tell them what to do. Inevitably the nurses knew far more about daily life with disadvantaged infants than the group leaders did, and this in itself contributed to the nurses' self-esteem. Their self-esteem was enhanced further by the group leaders' respect for their work and recognition that they were playing important therapeutic roles, while coping with major stress, rather than "simply playing all day with babies", as one of them had put it.

Weekly attendance at the clinic provided the nurses with a secure base from which to explore their thoughts and feelings about their work. They valued the respite from the pressures of the nurseries and the opportunity to have some time for themselves. What mattered to them most seemed to be the opportunity to meet with each other; their attachment was primarily to their peer group, and they seized opportunities to chat informally to each other outside the group discussions. They pointed out that nurses at work also need time available to chat to each other, as well as regular opportunities for serious discussions. As one nurse explained: during the era of impersonal care she had worked in a nursery where the nurses chatted all day to each other, but now she had become involved with 'her' babies she felt deprived of other nurses' companionship.

Although the nurses' main allegiance appeared to be to their peer group, they were evidently influenced by the group leaders' approach. In particular, the leaders' individual interest in them and their work probably contributed to their own growing interest in the individuality of the children in their care, while the leaders' toleration of their feelings helped them to feel more tolerant of the infants, and, to some extent, of the infants' parents. Perhaps it is worth mentioning that the question of the nurses' relationships to the infants' parents was often discussed but never resolved. Pressures towards greater involvement with parents came from the nurseries' policy makers, from the nurses' own wishes to help, and from some of the parents themselves. Pressures against involvement with parents came from the acute shortage of staff, their lack of training for work with adults and their animosity towards some of the parents, who were often described in very pejorative terms.

Not all nurses gained equally from the group experience. Three nurses quickly dropped out, apparently because their nurseries could not spare them. Two nurses spoke very little and it was difficult to know what they had assimilated. The more experienced nurses probably gained most from the climate of thinking and understanding, and from the capacity to conceptualize their work and hence to explain it to nurses whom they supervised. More junior nurses chiefly gained an increased interest in and understanding of infants and of the stresses inherent in their job. All nurses seemed to gain a new sense of the importance and value of their work, and of the necessity for continuing discussion and support. One outcome of the intervention was requests for regular consultation to each nursery.

Recommendations

It is obviously very difficult to overcome the pressures towards the impersonal care which is so repeatedly observed in institutions, such as nurseries and hospitals (e.g. Coser 1963, Menzies 1960). However, this brief intervention, like the much more thorough study of Bain and Barnett which preceded it, does illustrate that retraining and support of staff can facilitate the development of intimacy.

The basic training of nursery nurses must develop beyond the physical care of children to include understanding of their needs for attachment, dependency and emotional expression. It also needs to include understanding of the psychological stresses of the job of the nurse. Once nurses are trained, they need on-going support and opportunities for discussion of their difficulties, and those of the infants and their parents. However, good training and on-going support can only be effective if individual case assignment and adequate staff/child ratios make rewarding attachments between nurses and infants possible. If all these conditions are provided, nurses should not need to retreat behind impersonal institutional defences in order to cope with their sense of frustration and failure (Menzies Lyth 1982); they should be able to provide the opportunities for intimate attachments which infants need. Yet, the question remains whether such optimal conditions can ever be reliably and consistently provided, and therefore, whether the institutional care of infants under the age of two can ever be satisfactory. Alternative methods of supporting disadvantaged parents with their infants must also be developed.

Note

1 *Early Child Development and Care* 1988 33: 99–111. Adopted by the National Children's Bureau as a teaching paper on the quality of day care.

7 Overcoming a child's resistance to late adoption

How one new attachment can facilitate another[1]

Summary

The paper describes the difficulty which late-adopted children may have in forming attachments to their new parents. It considers the nature of the disorganised/controlling attachment response which many of these deprived, abused children display and the origin of this response in experiences of 'fright without solution.'

The psychotherapy of a 9 year old, late-adopted boy is used to illustrate long-standing resistance to new attachments to adoptive parents on account of defences on which security is felt to depend, and the persistence of loyalty to prior internal attachment representations. Change becomes possible through psychotherapy in which earlier negative attachment models are externalised together with their associated feelings of fear, hate and humiliation. For this boy, a long period of punitive rejection of his therapist gave way to a friendly capacity to play together; this was associated with the development of affectionate attachments to the boy's adoptive parents.

Introduction

One of the risks of adopting children in care is that they may perpetuate their deprivation by rejecting the loving care offered them. Clinical experience shows that, when this happens, it can sometimes be possible to facilitate children's attachment to their new parents by involving them in individual therapy.

This paper aims to describe the difficulties inherent for these deprived and rejected children in making new attachments and to consider how a new relationship to a psychotherapist may help these children to take the risk. Looking at this familiar process through an attachment lens may enable familiar patterns to be seen afresh.

In order to explore these issues, I describe some aspects of the developing attachment made to me in therapy by 9 year old Max. Max had been adopted five years previously by a couple who already had three children of their own – two teenagers and a son a year older than Max.

Max was born to a mother with a history of mental illness. He lived with his birth parents until his mother was hospitalised when he was two years old. His parents' relationship had been violent. After short stays in two foster homes, Max lived with an unsatisfactory foster family for about two years until his adoption. He was reported to be very disruptive and aggressive in day nursery care and was assessed as very disturbed prior to his adoption at the age of four years.

His adoptive parents were caring, concerned and thoughtful people who hoped to overcome the adverse effects of his early history within a year or two of his adoption. However, Max refused to accept the permanence of his adoption and did not become affectionately attached to his adoptive parents or his new siblings. As five years passed by, he continued to reject the care he so badly needed and drove his parents to desperation by being outrageously defiant and manipulative. He was in trouble for stealing, lying and destructive behaviour. He did not like to be touched, held or cuddled. At school he was supported by a special needs teacher but his disruptive behaviour was barely contained. He was a bully in the playground, was scarcely learning, had no sense of number and no sense of time (Canham 1999). Intelligence testing resulted in a WISC performance IQ which was average, but a verbal IQ which was only 85. A child psychiatrist noted Max's inability to make any warm attachment or show any strong emotions. He was diagnosed as having Attention Deficit Hyperactivity Disorder (ADHD). In short, he showed a pattern of development which is familiar in children, especially boys, with similar early histories.

The disorganised /controlling attachment pattern

Children like Max, who appear to care for no one and to turn to no one when hurt or distressed, are often said to be suffering from an "attachment disorder". Although there are varying opinions about exactly what constitutes an attachment disorder, what is not debatable is that such children commonly manifest a "disorganized/controlling attachment pattern" (Lyons-Ruth and Jacobovitz 1999) with all its characteristic, perplexing, contradictory features.

Children who enter the care system have experienced abuse and neglect at the hands of their care-givers, the very adults on whom they depend for their safety and well-being. Main (1995) describes how maltreatment by the attachment figure places the infant in an irresolvable paradox in which it can neither approach the frightening parent, nor shift its attention, nor flee. She summarized the subjective experience of this irresolvable conflict as "fright without solution" (Hesse and Main 1999: 484). The effects of repeated exposure to this experience are already apparent in infants one year old. In the Strange Situation test, impulses to fight, to flee or to freeze conflict with the urge to approach their attachment figure. The result is manifest in the disorganised and contradictory behaviour which characterises the disorganised/disoriented (D) attachment (Main and Solomon 1986).

Fright cannot be borne for long without solution. As D infants grow up, if abuse and neglect continue, they master their helplessness to achieve safety by developing powerful defensive strategies which characterise the disorganized/controlling attachment pattern. They become extremely controlling of adults, most often in a punitive way. The punitive need to control adults can become the basis of opposition and defiance, as it did with Max. The aim is self-sufficiency. Bowlby (1980) explained how the defensive processes associated with this attachment pattern lead to segregated systems – extreme forms of dissociation that separate attachment information from consciousness. Attachment behaviour, feelings and thoughts become disconnected both from consciousness and from each other but continue to break through in fragmented, irrational and unpredictable ways. In order to maintain their defensive strategies, these children become hypervigilant: any sudden or unpredictable change may trigger behaviour that seems totally disproportionate and irrational. If they become adopted they will evidently erect two barriers to making new attachments in adoptive homes: a deep distrust of relationships and a defensive armoury which protects them from intimacy and which makes them behave in ways which are at least perplexing and at worst as impossible to tolerate as Max's behaviour had become.

Therapy

Although children like Max are often regarded as too emotionally damaged to be suitable for psychotherapy, there has been a long tradition of treating them at the Tavistock Clinic. In 1983 Mary Boston and Rolene Szur published their groundbreaking book on *Psychotherapy with Severely Deprived Children*, which drew on the experience of some 80 children in care who had received psychotherapy at the Clinic. Many of these children had experienced both abuse and neglect. The book described the steady progress which most of these children could make provided the therapist could stick it out in the difficult phases.

There was nothing remarkable about the course of Max's therapy, except perhaps the persistence and intensity of his challenging behaviour. It epitomised many of the themes which emerged in the therapy of the severely deprived children described by Boston and Szur (1983). It is probably typical of how much and how little can be achieved in two years and a term of twice weekly work with such a disturbed child.

While I was working with Max, a colleague was working, on a much less frequent basis, with his parents who were determined to overcome five years of impasse between Max and themselves. Although adoptive parents may not appear to be contributing to the problems that their children present, understanding these problems and their own painful and sometimes violent feelings can make a vital difference to their children's capacity to change.

Issues of control: testing the limits

Attachment theory is concerned with survival, with the dimension from protection and security to danger and fear. The therapist aims to provide safety and to be experienced eventually as a secure base, but this poses a colossal threat to children like Max whose only sense of security resides in the stability of their defensive system (Hamilton 1987). A therapist who offers sensitive attention directed towards recognising and empathising with the child's feelings and intentions threatens to arouse the longing for care which segregated systems keep actively at bay. The therapist needs to play it cool, but nevertheless the impact of the initial sessions may lead to a major explosion of all the defensive operations at the child's disposal, as it did for Max.

Max was a big, athletic boy with a crop of blond hair. His therapy began with a wild display of extremely provocative and disruptive behaviour. He could not stay in the therapy room but escaped all over the building, climbing up and down the banisters of the deep stairwell in a way which courted serious danger. He threw toys and water at me and out of the window. He created havoc in the toilets. He broke into my drawers and threw files and paper everywhere. He repeatedly dialled 999 to summon police and have me arrested, and, when he did stop for a moment to handle toys, his brief enactments with them were classically catastrophic (Main and Cassidy 1988). Baby dolls were selected for particular torture, being burned alive and hung on hooks to be used as bait for sharks. Ambulances deliberately ran people over and teachers enjoyed poisoning their pupils. Themes like this in which supposedly helpful people do horrible things are of course common in the play of abused children.

Max claimed that he was never afraid of anything. He aroused panic in me with his danger-seeking and his mixture of flight and fight behaviour, but he seemed genuinely not to feel fear himself. I had to accept that Max could not allow me to keep therapy safe as long as safety with an adult represented danger, the danger of a dependent attachment. Meanwhile I had to tolerate my dread of his sessions, my hatred of his treatment of me and my helplessness to help.

Underlying Max's wild behaviour was a powerful need to be in control, to maintain his defensive system and to regulate the emotional distance between us. He soon discovered that he could always have the upper hand. When he leapt onto the forbidden window ledge and started to kick the glass, he knew I would rush to stop him so he could leap past me and bolt out of the door. Discovering that he could go when he chose helped him to feel safe enough to stay for longer.

Max continued to test me out with outrageous behaviour for a couple of months before it was clear that he was going to allow therapy to happen. During this time of extreme testing, Max must have discovered my refusal to play the roles assigned to me, either as a rejecting and punitive adult or as a helpless, defeated child. I was not going to imprison him for stealing, send him away, surrender, or let him walk over me. He appeared to have discovered what unconsciously he may have been seeking, that therapy offers a new developmental opportunity (Hurry 1998), a relationship in which to externalise the aftermath of adverse and abusive experiences, a relationship in which he did not have to be either aggressor or victim, either hostile or helpless (Lyons-Ruth, Bronfman and Atwood 2000).

Boston (Boston and Szur 1983: 9) describes how children in care make 'endless evacuation into therapists of chaotic, confused and unwanted feelings.' Naturally, young children cannot talk about their experiences of rejection and abuse, when they may not even recognise that these are what they have had. Their hope of recovering from the impact of these experiences is to externalise them with someone who can safely tolerate being hated, humiliated and helpless without retaliating or collapsing, and, more than that, who can tolerate being experienced as deliberately cruel and abusive. Those who deal intimately with these children have to accept the many negative ways that the children perceive them while also tolerating the powerful negative emotions that the children arouse in them.

I thought that I had passed this test with Max when he briefly settled to make a drawing. It depicted a burglar, armed to the teeth. Max stuck it on the outside of the window, ready to break in. I said the burglar believed the room held something worth having, a space, I imagined, for Max's rage and deprivation.

Developing attachment

Max's possessiveness quickly widened to include the room and all the clinic, '*my* room' and '*my* clinic' as he came to call them. It infuriated him that he could not have access to all the cupboards in my room and all the rooms in the building. He found ways of breaking locks on my cupboards and entering forbidden areas of the clinic. 'There'll be no problem,' he said 'when I grow up and buy the clinic and be the boss.' This development of an initial attachment to the territory, rather than to the therapist, is common in deprived and abused children.

Bowlby (1980) predicted that children like Max, who had retreated into emotional self-sufficiency after suffering loss, would reject new attachments but betray the existence of their segregated attachment systems in isolated thoughts and actions. Max's attachment to my territory while maintaining his ongoing hatred of me appeared to be a classic example of this; it proved to be the beginning of a new and very gradual growth of positive feelings for me. After six months of treating me with extreme contempt and heaping me with playground obscenities, he allowed me to become firstly the woman he loved to hate and then the woman he hated to love. His tone of contempt began to mellow as he became a pop singer who crooned songs in which words of love were replaced by terms of abuse. 'You are a bitch and an arse-hole' was a favourite song. After a couple of terms these songs sometimes conveyed quite an affectionate feeling. He started to open the window and shout 'I love you' at bemused passers-by before turning to spit 'You shit-head!' at me. When I asked if anyone could love a shit-head he sang in return, 'I love you shit-head.' Affection leaked out in other fragmented ways. Instead of physically avoiding me as though I were contaminated, Max now brushed against me and asked me to catch him when he jumped off the furniture. His parents reported their awareness that Max was now ambivalent about therapy instead of wholly against it. At home his fearlessness yielded to anxiety when he refused to go upstairs alone any more.

Max's growing affection was a torture to him. The pain of this was reflected in deliberate attempts to hurt me and pleasure in doing so. He drew a picture of a torture camp where a man arrives thinking it's a restaurant, only to discover the trickery too late. This theme of deception was already familiar to me, since Max repeatedly broke promises or offered to show me something I'd like, only to throw it in my face. These sudden oscillations between contradictory moods, characteristic of the disorganised/controlling pattern, are extremely confusing to adults who complain that they "never know where they are" with the child. Segregated systems deprive children of a sense of continuity: the children are often oblivious that their moods have switched.

Playing together

It was in the context of this tortured love/hate relationship that Max initiated a game which involved my participation. A year had passed before this first move to develop both playing and togetherness.

Without warning, this macho kid suddenly collapsed helplessly at my feet. He said he was a robot that was stuck and needed to be screwed together. He required me to touch him all over to tighten imaginary screws. The game developed. Robots had names like Knuckleduster, Peewee and Scavenger Cat who liked to be stroked. They had imaginary buttons which I had to locate and press – the 'speech button' which said 'I'm me', the 'feeling button' which said 'I feel you' and the 'mad button' which screamed. Sometimes whole sessions passed in which I could never find the elusive buttons. Perhaps this was Max's way of saying how frustrating it can be to attempt meaningful contact with an unavailable adult.

Soon Max moved from collapse on the floor to a more comfortable collapse on the couch where I sat beside him. He called 'our song' the ritual recital of body parts which needed to be screwed up. He said that screwing him up turned him into a boy. It seemed to me that Max was unscrewing his rigid defences by risking friendliness and body contact with me. The pain of this was reflected in the request that I should screw him so tight that it hurt. I said I thought it hurt to have such a gentle touch because he realised how much touching he had missed and that he wanted more. This was a reminder that good experiences with adoptive parents may be too poignant to accept. Max continued to take pleasure in hurting me and now introduced a threat to hurt himself. He questioned me about suicide, threatened to jump out of the high window and wound the window-blind cord repeatedly and tightly around his neck as though to hang himself, suggesting themes of guilt.

Max's attachment also brought concern. When I cancelled on account of illness, Max feared I'd drunk a poison potion he had made and on his return he made a point of being nice to me for a whole session. On another occasion he interrupted his physical attacks on me to explain he was frightened that he'd really kill me and when I'd gone he'd be sorry.

During the robot games Max was very relaxed. He began to play that he was no longer a robot but a baby, a baby who wanted to play baby games. He took off his shoes and asked me to play with his feet. Max was now eleven and I had already had my doubts about the wisdom of body contact needed to screw up the robots, but when I asked if he knew 'this little pig went to market,' he said 'yes' with such delight, that I did not resist playing this game with his toes. Max tried to recall another game from when he was 'very little' and I suggested it might be 'Round and round the garden' or 'Ring o' roses.' These were not the games he had in mind but he enjoyed playing them anyhow, in an entirely childlike manner. Max was now using his growing security with me to link a pleasure, probably derived from his past, coherently with the present through the safe medium of playing. However, I do not want to give too rosy a picture of Max's play. There was mutuality in our pleasure, but I was allowed little spontaneity and I felt myself to be as much Max's slave as his play partner.

Loyalty conflict

Although Max's baby games revealed how pleasures experienced in a past attachment might be revived to enrich the present, there were also ways in which Max's attachments to the past interfered with developing new attachments in the present. Both psychoanalysts and attachment theorists are united in giving significance to loyalty conflicts and to the subjective safety of the link to familiar objects, even when this may involve the repetition of negative experiences. Like most deprived children, Max made very few references to present or past life outside the therapy room. However, he told me several times that he did not want to be adopted and that he hated his new mother when she came 'to choose' him. 'I was all right until they took me. I was free.' Chillingly, his few references to his adoptive family were all in terms of 'they' and 'them,' not 'we' and 'us.' He didn't want 'them,' he told me, he wanted to go back to Wayne, a boy who had shared his foster home. He and Wayne had had a gang and 'went outside and did things everywhere.' Even though Max had not seen Wayne since he was four years old, he searched the clinic in case Wayne had come for therapy too. Max seemed to be seeking an idealised fantasy of a gang life without the need for parents. He told me his foster parents 'were great 'cos they didn't bother me.' The tag he chose for himself, which he managed to engrave in numerous places in my room, was the letter 'B', the initial of the name of his birth mother and of his foster parents. He covered the 'No Smoking' signs in the clinic with 'Yes Smoking' signs and it was not difficult to guess the fact that his birth parents and foster parents had smoked and that his adoptive parents disapproved of it. This clash represented the nub of the problem. If Max accepted his adoptive family's values he would have to give up his identity as a tough, independent, streetwise kid and recognise his failure to be the good, co-operative child that his new parents wanted. Fairbairn (1952) describes the tie to bad objects; he explains how a new mode of relating is felt to involve not only a guilty betrayal of the early relationship but a fear of the loss of the sense of self. A negative therapeutic reaction may sometimes be understood as a return to the residual security inherent in previous attachments, however unsatisfactory, rather than facing the sense of betrayal and loss inherent in developing new relationships.

In Max's last session, he drew a cartoon of a smoker with 4 cigarettes in his mouth. This expressed a more favourable self-image than that of the armed burglar. It also expressed Max's continuing allegiance to his earlier families. The nature of this loyalty was complex: love, guilt and a deep feeling of identification with them because they were bad like him. In order to relinquish his loyalty he might need to become aware both of how badly they had treated him and of how deeply he felt abandoned by them. The nearest Max came to acknowledge the failure of his birth mother was to hurl insults at *my* mother and then express utter amazement that I did not cry.

Changes

Max's relationship to his adoptive parents improved gradually during his two years of therapy. He began to refer to his relationship with them as 'we' and 'us' at about the same time as he achieved togetherness with me in play. Although we know from research (Main and Weston 1981) that the baby's attachment patterns to mother and to father are virtually independent of each other, the success of psychotherapy depends upon positive developments in one relationship becoming generalised to other relationships. As yet there is no systematic study of when this transfer begins and what facilitates it. In Max's case I did not know in which relationship 'togetherness' began or whether it developed in therapy and home simultaneously.

Although Max achieved togetherness with his parents, he never referred to the existence of any of his three adoptive siblings. It seems likely that their long-established presence in the adoptive home had been a major reason for Max's resistance to accepting his adoptive placement. Recognising and talking about his acute jealousy of my other child patients may have helped to make the rivalry at home more bearable.

The development of Max's new attachments was accompanied by a reduction in his defensive behaviour. He stopped stealing, he became less reckless, less uncooperative and more popular with his peers, but still sometimes disruptive, still showing signs of ADHD and still behaving in a disorganised/controlling manner. He gave up his exaggerated working class accent and spoke more like his educated adoptive family. His shift from torturing baby dolls to enjoying being a baby himself was accompanied by a kinder attitude to pets and the successful adoption of a hamster. At times he made great efforts to be good and expressed the wish to be good enough to marry and have children when he grew up. Instead of projecting all his fears, he could now contain and talk about some of his worries, his failure at school, his dread of attack and of being given away. He surprised me by his insight when he said, 'When I'm not stressed and crazy, I just feel empty.' His behaviour as an *enfant terrible* had evidently protected him from feeling empty and unloved while also ensuring that adults kept him actively in mind.

Despite Max's improvements, his sense of safety remained lodged in his defensive system as far as his response to any sudden, unpredictable change was concerned. If a car back-fired outside or a new carpet appeared in the clinic, Max immediately leapt into wild, disruptive behaviour, usually throwing anything to hand. I thought that Max had become so sensitised to the risk of further trauma that any unpredictable happening led him to re-enact an involuntary fight response (Perry et al. 1995). I tried to help him recognise how his terror of sudden changes triggered these alarming reactions. On an occasion when Max seemed to have heard me, he drew a man in the grip of a monster. The picture conveyed how frightening it feels to be in the grip of dissociated impulses, impulses which may once have originated in response to an actual monstrous adult. Max typically dealt with an involuntary upsurge of these violent impulses by exaggerating them, by 'upping' his aggression and by clowning about. To an outsider he appeared to be suddenly inexplicably impossible. To Max himself it seemed he was just beginning to become aware of feeling possessed by impulses which he could scarcely recognise as his own.

Max's therapy had to end when he transferred to a distant specialist secondary school. We had four months to prepare for this separation and Max managed it without a return of his most impossible behaviour. He was able to say that he would miss both me and the clinic.

Max's mother reported that, just before therapy ended, she and Max recalled the last time Max had seen his birth mother. Max's jaw began to tremble and he asked his mother why. He did not realise that he was crying. Mourning for his birth mother had apparently begun in the context of a new closeness to his adoptive mother. His capacity to weep was no longer a segregated component of his attachment system. Max's recent discovery of grief about ending therapy probably helped to make this development possible.

Discussion

Max illustrates how adopted children can use their therapy to risk new attachments to parents whom they have previously rejected. This positive outcome can be obtained because the disorganized/controlling attachment pattern is unstable. Self-sufficiency can never be achieved. Children with this pattern depend on others to receive the projection of the negative emotions that they cannot tolerate in themselves. Others must bear the rejection, hurt, humiliation and despair that they have experienced but have been unable to assimilate. The therapist is open to receiving and working with these negative enactments and projections. The most crucial contribution to the child's willingness to risk further attachments is probably the therapist's capacity to contain all the negative emotions of 'fright without solution' as these are gradually externalised. Previous negative attachment models, such as aggressor/victim, and their associated feelings can then be expressed in a context in which they are tolerated and acknowledged in words, not by enactment. This means that the child becomes able to see beyond his attempt at enactment and to discover that alternative attachment possibilities are less threatening than he had supposed. A new attachment, that is, an attachment responsive to the therapist's actual qualities can begin. And, importantly, this can happen without the need to reconstruct trauma or consciously to revisit the past. Before the past can be confronted, a sufficient sense of self, a capacity to mentalise and an attachment secure enough to hold the pain are all needed. Max was on the verge of looking back at his negative experiences when therapy ended. At home he asked angrily about his history, 'Why did it have to happen to me?'

Late-adopted children are often a very tough assignment for therapists who wonder how adoptive parents can cope at all. With Max I endured repeated dread, alarm, anger, betrayal, humiliation, helplessness and hopelessness. I was supported by my knowledge of theory which enabled me to see the frightened, helpless child behind the controlling tyrant, an insight which facilitated my empathy and affection. Theory also assured me that Max's attacks were not personal, were necessary and could be understood. Even so I needed colleagues for support and encouragement. If therapists need support to cope, then adoptive parents need much more. It may be some small comfort to them to know that when a therapist frees a new capacity for attachment in their child, this is not because the therapist is more significant to the child than they are, but the reverse. Therapists can be tested and risks can be taken because there is much less at stake. They provide a trial ground where new developments can be explored before they are taken safely home.

Note

1 This paper was presented at the conference 'Attachment in New Relationships' at the Tavistock Clinic, London in March 2000 and published in the *Journal of Child Psychotherapy* 26: 335–347 in the same year. An expanded version, 'Individual psychotherapy for late-adopted children: how one new attachment can facilitate another' with additional case material from another child, was printed as chapter 9 in J. Kenrick, C. Lindsay & L. Tollemache *Creating New Families: Therapeutic Approaches to Fostering, Adoption and Kinship Care* London: Karnac 2006. This version is a revision of the 2000 paper.

Infant-parent psychotherapy

Introduction

Infancy is the time when we are least modified by culture, most obviously product of two million years of human evolution, not yet shaped by language and symbolism. It is fascinating to observe how responsive infants are to the communication of emotion expressed in touch, holding, voice and eye contact. My experience as a psychotherapist with infants and their parents has rewardingly confirmed how easily infants respond to changes in their parents' feelings towards them by changing their behaviour.

(Hopkins 1998)

It was, said Juliet Hopkins, at a conference in the mid 1980s that she discovered infant-parent psychotherapy, and its promise excited her interest. This was to lead not only to engaging in clinical practice with infants and their parents together but to joining Dilys Daws – its founder – on the original committee of the Association for Infant Mental Health (UK). It was more than compatible with her developed interest in infancy, family and the making of attachments.

She has commented that

Selma Fraiberg's famous paper on "Ghosts in the Nursery" provided clear examples of the intergenerational transmission of family trauma 5 years before Mary Main's intergenerational work with the Adult Attachment Interview. Fraiberg's paper seems to have provided the first clear statement within the child analytic literature of parental transferences that distorted infant development. Before this of course child psychotherapists knew that parents had their own problems but, following Klein, we always focused on how children distorted their perception of their parents rather than vice versa. This new theoretical slant must have encouraged more therapists to work with parents and young children together and so reap the benefit of observing their relationship rather than relying on parental report.

(Hopkins 2010: 11)

In this section we have included her overview of infant-parent psychotherapy, beginning with Fraiberg's integration of psychoanalytic (particularly object relations) thinking and attachment findings and moving to more recent thought. The second paper, on crying, adds 'an original approach to the psychodynamics of infant crying by considering its possible meaning to the baby' (Hopkins 1998: 5).

AH

8   Infant-parent psychotherapy

Selma Fraiberg's contribution to understanding the past in the present[1]

Infant-parent psychotherapy was first named and developed by an American child psychoanalyst, Selma Fraiberg. She described the work in a ground-breaking book, *Clinical Studies in Infant Mental Health*, published in 1980. Since then many significant clinical and theoretical contributions (e.g. Stern 1995, Lieberman and Zeanah 1999, Barrows 2003, Baradon et al. 2005) have been made to this field. The subject has expanded to include a wealth of complexities of interpretation and technique, but the value of Fraiberg's original psychoanalytic insight remains unchallenged.

Fraiberg relied on the assumption that there is no such thing as individual psychopathology in infancy. This does not mean that babies do not contribute difficulties from their side of the relationship. It does mean that symptoms in the infant can best be treated by treating the infant-parent relationship, rather than by treating either infant or parent separately. Like all short-term therapies, infant-parent psychotherapy is focussed, and the focus is on the development of the infant who is always usually present in the sessions. The infant's presence ensures that parental feelings towards him are readily available in the here-and-now for exploration and interpretation. Interpretation, as practised by Selma Fraiberg, utilized a combination of "object-relations" and "attachment theory" to understand the ways in which the parental past interfered with relating to the baby in the present. The symptomatic infant was found to be the victim of negative transference, haunted by "ghosts in the nursery" (Fraiberg 1980: 165). Infant-parent psychotherapy was the treatment of choice whenever the baby had come to represent an aspect of the parental self which was repudiated or negated, or when the baby had become the representation of figures within the past. The primary focus of the work was on understanding the parents' negative transference to their baby, rather than on understanding their transference to the therapist.

However, interpretative work was only part of Selma Fraiberg's therapeutic approach. She combined it with what she termed "developmental guidance", a rather misleading name, since it very rarely involved giving advice. Developmental guidance comprised a multiplicity of interventions aimed to support the parents emotionally, to demonstrate their own unique importance to their child, and to help them observe and think about the reasons for their child's behaviour. The infant's presence allowed the therapist to witness the infant's own contribution to the problems, to appraise his development, and to share his achievements with his parents. "We move back and forth, between present and past, parent and baby, but we always return to the baby" (Fraiberg 1980: 61).

The clarity with which Fraiberg formulated the essentials of infant-parent psychotherapy offered me security when I made my first tentative move from working exclusively with individual children and parents to working with mother-infant couples and young families. In addition to Fraiberg's ideas, I brought from my British psychoanalytic tradition the benefits of working with the therapist's counter-transference, a development within psychoanalysis which Fraiberg did not explicitly recognize. In the clinical examples that follow I shall supplement my illustration of Fraiberg's method with reflection on the clinical significance of my counter-transference experience as evoked in sessions.

Case illustration 1

Kiran K, aged 24 months, was referred by a paediatrician who had been seeing her regularly as an outpatient for the past six months. She had gained no weight for this period and was persistently unhappy, crying and whining all day and unable to sleep at night unless her mother shared her bed.

The family were Kenyan Asians who had come to London when Kiran was eight months old. There was an older sister, Sandip, aged four years, who was said to be no trouble at all. I invited the whole family, but Mr K did not come because he felt unable to leave his shop. When I collected Mrs K and the two little girls from the waiting room, Mrs K insisted that Kiran should walk unaided down the long corridor in spite of her repeated pleas to be carried. In my room Kiran plaintively demanded her mother's lap, but Mrs K put her briskly on the floor, demanding that she be a "good girl". Mrs K's first communication to me was a placating expression of gratitude for the move to live in England, "your lovely country". I aimed to reassure her that criticism was also acceptable by pointing to the pouring rain and saying that I knew some things, like the weather, were better in Kenya. Sandip at once settled silently to draw, while Kiran made constant overtures to her mother, which were all rejected. Mrs K was eager to talk, but from time to time I turned from her to the children to bring them into our conversation and to encourage their play. Mrs K told me of her anxieties about Kiran's failure to thrive, her insatiable demands and her persistent misery. As a baby Kiran had mainly been cared for by an ayah, until the move to London when she was eight months old. Then Kiran had begun to cry, whine and to refuse food, problems which steadily grew worse. Mrs K had left behind many loved relatives in Kenya and a luxurious life with servants. She was now largely alone, performing the servants' duties herself and seeing little of her husband who worked long hours. She sounded gleeful when she said that Kiran doesn't even allow her to sleep with her husband any more. It was a painful interview in which I found Mrs K's rejection of Kiran hard to bear, while the extent of her depression and of her antagonism towards her husband made me feel despondent. I ended by saying that this was a problem which would take some time to solve and that we would need to include her husband in our next meeting.

Three weeks later, Mrs K returned with her daughters, explaining that her husband had not come because there was no need. She herself had only come to thank me and to ask what I had done. Kiran had been happy by day, was eating heartily and sleeping alone in her bedroom at night. I said I was as amazed as she was. In fact I had noticed from the moment that I met them that Mrs K had felt differently about Kiran for she had swept her into her arms, carried her down the corridor and sat down with her cradled in her lap. Kiran had then felt sufficiently secure to slither down to explore the toys with concentration. Mrs K explained that everything had changed because she had learned from me how to play with her children. She had never played with them before because in Kenya this was a job for servants, but now she knew how to do it and it had made them all happy. This surprised me further, since I had scarcely played with her children at all.

What had enabled this mother to change her attitude towards her own role and towards her children so dramatically? I do not know, but I think that in the course of talking with me she had discovered something new about herself: the extent of her grief about the loss of Kenya and her resentment towards her husband for bringing her here, depriving her of her extended family and turning her into a servant. When she had told me about the move, I had given her permission to feel grief by commenting sympathetically upon what anyone would feel under the circumstances. After she was in touch with her loss, I suggested that Kiran might also have missed Kenya and her ayah and since then had been complaining and grieving for both of them. A further significant moment occurred when I had drawn Mrs K's attention to Kiran's repeated approaches to her and had said that they were not only tiresome demands for attention, but also signs of Kiran's affection for her mother and of her wish to be close to her. Finally, there had been an opportunity to focus on Sandip by talking about her picture of nice and nasty spiders in terms of the way these two little girls had divided the nice and nasty roles between them, instead of each being able to be both nice and nasty.

The speed of Kiran's transformation in so many areas of development remains unique in my experience. Happily, it has made for a conveniently concise, if very atypical, account of brief work with infants. However, dramatic symptomatic changes do occur in this work although they certainly cannot be relied upon and some families need long term intervention. What can seem surprising is that significant changes in behaviour can occur without the parent's or the child's behaviour ever having been a focus of attention. As Daniel Stern (1995) has said, infant-parent psychotherapy is not a behaviour-orientated therapy, but a representation-oriented one. In this case, Mrs K's self-representation as good and grateful was attributed to Sandip, while Kiran represented her own resentment and misery. As long as Mrs K needed to repudiate and negate these feelings in herself, she projected them onto Kiran who enacted them for her. Probably Kiran's initial distress about the move from Kenya, when she was 8 months old, had made her a natural target for her mother's projection. When my intervention had helped Mrs K to accept her resentment and to mourn her loss she became able to empathize with Kiran, to comfort her and to reciprocate her affection. As Selma Fraiberg has described, when someone hears a mother's own cries she becomes able to comfort her baby. In retrospect, I realized that Mrs K had left me feeling so despondent after our first meeting because she had been able to communicate her cries at an emotional level. I have learned that parents who can communicate their distress at this level are more likely to benefit from the therapeutic encounter with me.

These changes were made in the context of a positive relationship to me, which led Mrs K to identify with me as someone other than a servant who could enjoy playing with children, thus giving her permission to enjoy this activity as a mother and not a servant to her children. This could be called a transference cure. Such transference cures are not to be dismissed. They can prove more lasting in infant-parent psychotherapy than they might in individual work. Once the vicious cycle of the child enacting the parent's projections has been broken, the child is freed to develop other strategies and may not collaborate with a pathological enactment if called upon to do so again. In Kiran's case the referring paediatrician found that there had been no recurrence of her problems six months later.

Case illustration 2

My second case illustration is one in which the baby had become the representation of figures from the parental past as well as negative aspects of the parental self.

Sukie S, aged 24 months, and her single mother, Ms S, were referred by their health visitor. Ms S was worried that her little daughter was "a monster" and "exceptionally clinging". The health visitor was more concerned about Ms S's parenting. I learned that when Sukie was nine months old, Ms S had entirely destroyed her own flat, in order, she said, not to destroy Sukie, and to get help with the care of her daughter. Since then Sukie had been on the "at risk" register and had received daily foster care, whilst Ms S had had weekly support from a social worker. Ms S still found Sukie's company very hard to bear and particularly disliked being touched by her.

When Ms S and Sukie came to see me, I encountered a stout Irish woman and a small freckled child in a buggy. Upon entering my room, Ms S left Sukie in the buggy against the door and chose to sit as far away from her as possible. She at once embarked upon a tirade of hatred against her daughter, her extended family, social services and other authorities. She was furious that "they" hadn't let her have an abortion, that "they" hadn't allowed her to give Sukie up for adoption and that no-one had helped her with Sukie's care. Sukie seemed entirely unperturbed by this diatribe. She sat silently in her buggy, looking with great interest at the attractive toys which I had set out in the centre of the room. She made no flicker of protest. Mrs S's irate monologue continued. I found myself unable to listen. It required all my resolution simply to sit still and not to rescue Sukie from her mother's hatred and to free her to play with the appealing toys. I felt frightened of Ms S, battered by her onslaught, furious with her social worker (who clearly should have arranged for Sukie's adoption), and helpless to work with such a hopeless case. Minutes went by. I longed for rescue. I even found myself thinking how hard the counter-transference is to bear in infant-parent psychotherapy in contrast to individual work. If only I had seen this mother on her own I would have been able to listen to every word she had said.

I mention my feelings for two reasons. One is that, in thinking about training for this work, the capacity to contain emotional distress while listening and without taking sides is something that has to be attended to and developed. I will return to this issue later. The other reason is that these feelings, the counter-transference, are valuable as a source of insight. We can use our counter-transference to understand and to interpret the patient's transference, as proved to be necessary to gain Ms S's co-operation. And we can use it to help select the focus for short-term therapy. Daniel Stern (1995) has described how the baby's behaviour provides valuable cues to relevant themes on which to focus the therapy. So does the counter-transference. In this case these two sources of information reinforced each other. Sukie's inability to protest at her confinement suggested themes of intimidation and abuse which were echoed by my feelings. In addition my urge to enact the role of rescuer suggested a further and more hopeful theme.

While struggling with my own emotions I looked at Sukie who had started to rock gently back and forth. I thought at first that she was doing this for comfort, but then I realized that she was now gently inching her buggy towards the toys. Sukie's determination gave me courage to interrupt Ms S and to begin to work.

I began by acknowledging Ms S's anger and her disappointment that having a baby had proved such a terrible burden and that she had had no satisfactory help with it. I said I thought her anger about coming to see me was to do with her fear that yet another authority would fail to help; she might be afraid that I would only criticize her and make things worse, when she really needed rescuing. Ms S calmed down enough to begin to describe her exasperation with Sukie. "She follows me everywhere at home. She wants to suffocate me. She terrorises people. She messes up the flat. She wrecks everything." It was hard to reconcile this picture with the inhibited child who had now moved her buggy to the table and was tentatively touching the tea set. Ms S went on to express her fear that she would flatten Sukie. She said that she had days of terrible depression when she could not get up for fear that she would batter her. She would lie in bed preoccupied with whether to give up Sukie for adoption or not. Sukie had learned to stay in her room when Ms S was "in a mood". She was always put to bed very early and had never called her mother in the night. Ms S said she had come to see me to make me tell social services that Sukie should spend an extended period in residential care to enable Ms S to finally decide whether she wanted her adopted or not.

Ms S was surprised to be asked about her own childhood. She described it with calm detachment as though it had happened to someone else. Her father had been extremely violent and had selected her from among her siblings to be the particular victim of his hatred. She had been hospitalized three times on account of the injuries which he had given her. He was a tyrant and a wrecker. Her mother had never protected her and had lied about the cause of her injuries to protect Ms S's father from the police. Her home was like a prison and she ran away as soon as she was sixteen.

I asked if Ms S had ever wondered if her present difficulties were related to her childhood experiences. She was astonished. I pointed out the similarities in what she had said about Sukie and about her father. At the moment when I mentioned the way she had felt imprisoned in turn by each of them, Ms S got up and un-harnessed Sukie so that she was freed at last to play. At that point Ms S appeared to feel able to empathize with Sukie and did not have to force her to continue her own experience of imprisonment. This was a beautiful illustration of Selma Fraiberg's finding that remembering saves one from blind repetition because it enables identification with the injured child (Fraiberg et al. 1975; in Fraiberg 1980: 197). It gave me hope for change and enabled me to suggest that we should have a few more meetings in order to explore the problems which lay behind Ms S's preoc-cupation with thoughts of giving her unbearable daughter away.

When Ms S and Sukie returned for their next appointment, Ms S told me that it had been "a mind-blowing experience" to think that her problems were related to her past. She had contacted her three siblings and together they had shared memo-ries of their childhood which they had never mentioned before. Ms S felt immense relief that her version of abuse was confirmed. She said she had stopped blaming herself for everything and no longer feared she might be mad.

Ms S was not willing to commit herself and Sukie to regular appointments. I saw them for eight appointments spread over ten months before Ms S dropped out of treatment without explanation or goodbye. In each of our meetings Ms S had recalled appalling events from her childhood with an increasing amount of feeling, and in each meeting she had shown an increasing capacity to relate posi-tively to Sukie. In our fifth meeting she said that she had realized Sukie isn't really a little monster, she had simply imagined her so. She recounted how for the first time she had done something other than routine care for Sukie's sake – she had taken her to the park. She also related, with embarrassment about being "so soft", that she now took Sukie on her lap when they watched TV together. Her own mother had never cuddled her. She said she had suffered no more depression and for the first time she made no mention of adoption.

In what proved to be our last meeting, Ms S spoke warmly of feeling at last that she and Sukie belong together. She had lost the impulse to flatten her and had amazed herself by starting to play with her. These changes were achieved after Ms S visited her father in Ireland and confronted him with his violence towards her in childhood. Instead of denying it, as he had always done before, he acknowl-edged it and begged forgiveness. No doubt this moving encounter was responsible for another change that I saw that day. When Sukie fell and hurt herself, Ms S acknowledged that it hurt and comforted her with a cuddle. In previous sessions she had responded to all Sukie's bumps with laughter and remarks like, "She's faking tears" and "She's so clumsy she brings it on herself." It seemed that she could respond to Sukie's hurt now that her father had responded to hers.

As Ms S changed, so did Sukie. She became self-assertive and talkative. She listened increasingly to our adult talk and was pleased to be included. Ms S was surprised to realize how much Sukie understood and followed my lead by talking to her more. Sukie lost the compulsive compliance which was manifest in our first meetings and started to defy her mother. She also started to attack me when I ended the sessions, but she never risked trying to hurt her mother. Her sleep became disturbed by nightmares of monsters and she took refuge in her mother's bed. It seemed that Ms S was beginning to become a secure base for Sukie, but a really secure attachment remained a distant prospect. Their relationship was still full of conflict, rebuff, teasing, threats and slaps.

There is always the drawback, when trying to write a coherent account of therapy, that all sense of the anxiety and confusion which accompanies the work is lost. I should emphasize that I found this work stressful. I worried at first that I had made a bad situation worse by reducing the likelihood of adoption. I worried when I decided not to report an incident of battering. I worried when appointments were missed and I did not know if Ms S and Sukie would return. I worried when they drifted prematurely out of therapy and missed further opportunities for progress. Fortunately I have colleagues to turn to, since opportunities for discussion are essential in supporting this work.

Understanding the past in the present

When trying to understand the many baffling problems which arise in infant-parent relationships, I have found it helpful to work with Emde's hypothesis (1988) that the experience of becoming a parent evokes representations of the parent's own early infant-parent relationship. These representations, which may have lain dormant for years, become available for re-experiencing, for projection and enactment. They involve both sides of the parent's own early relationships. This means that the new baby may be experienced either as a representation of the parent's own childhood parent or of the parent's own childhood self, or both. This can be, and often is, an enriching experience. But when the early representations are negative their projection can lead to difficulties. Ms S provides a tragic example of a mother who appears to have experienced her daughter both as her father (tyrannical, imprisoning) and as her childhood self (hated, rejected). She also experienced herself both as her violent father and as her desperate childhood self, longing for rescue. The role of her uncaring mother who had failed to protect her seems to have been mainly attributed to the Social Services. Ms S entirely denied the existence of their helpful interventions, perhaps because they had not understood that the primary protection which she had needed was from the ghosts of the past. The social worker who supported Ms S had never mentioned the possible contribution of Ms S's childhood. A vital opportunity had been lost through lack of training.

I do not want to exaggerate the importance of interpreting the intrusion of the past, because, as I shall emphasize, it is only part of what therapists have to offer. But before going further, I would add that exploring the influence of the past does more than offer the possibility of a dynamic disconnection between past representations and present realities, i.e. unhooking the baby from the parents' hang-ups. As Ms S demonstrated, it can ease an exaggerated sense of guilt and self-blame and it can give permission to know and to feel what may previously have been forbidden (see Bowlby 1979).

This case involving severe childhood trauma may illustrate some points well, but happily such a dramatic re-enactment is not typical of the negative influence of the past. This usually shows in more subtle ways, not necessarily available to recall. A brief example will illustrate this.

Case illustration 3

Daniel D was referred by his family doctor at the age of seven months because he was excessively demanding by day and sleepless by night. He was the first child of professional parents, Mr and Mrs D, who were said to be utterly exhausted by him.

In my first meeting with the family I encountered Mrs D's great distress about her baby's impossible demands and her own sense of failure as a mother. "He won't even let me have a cup of coffee. I know I'm doing everything wrong." She was bewildered that after managing a demanding career she could not cope with a small baby.

Daniel was indeed extremely demanding. He insisted on being held in arms and fussed incessantly to get the continuous attention which his parents felt compelled to provide. Mr D felt helpless to support his wife and bound to emulate her practice of responding to Daniel's slightest need. By the end of an hour the room felt full of babies and I had to resist a strong urge to take over and impose tough limits. I summed up humorously by saying that Mr and Mrs D seemed to feel that they had given birth to a half-a-dozen babies. They laughed. Mrs D explained that she actually had been one of a dozen babies in the baby room of an Israeli Kibbutz. She had no memories of the Kibbutz which her family left when she was seven years old, but she had determined to bring up her own baby entirely herself. Unfortunately the experience of motherhood was making her feel that she would have to find a day-nursery for Daniel if I could not help.

It seems that becoming a parent had revived Mrs D's representation of her unmet infantile need for devoted maternal care. She attributed this to Daniel who was then felt to require the uninterrupted care which she had longed for and never had. Mrs D's expectation that Daniel always needed adult attention and could manage nothing himself seemed to have been communicated to Daniel so that he enacted Mrs D's insatiable infantile demands. Looking at it this way directed my attention to the prime importance of looking after Mrs D's needs in the present, in order to free Daniel from enacting her past. Mrs D was surprised to have her needs taken seriously. She thought that I would put the baby first, but she was relieved that I felt she could be entitled to her cup of coffee and to talk to her friends. With her husband's help she thought of various ways of reducing the stress of baby-care and allowing herself some space.

In this case, the past was chiefly useful in making sense of the present. Although Mrs D could not recall her childhood she recognized that her decision to care for Daniel herself expressed negative feelings about it. She could understand that it was difficult for her to know when Daniel had had enough attention because she had never had enough herself. I explained Daniel's need to develop his own resources and to learn to play by himself. In our sessions Mr and Mrs D practised ignoring his fussiness and were surprised to find that he could begin to amuse himself. Within a month he accepted the use of a play-pen while Mrs D did her housework and drank her coffee, but his sleeping problems took much longer to solve (see Daws 1989), requiring appointments spread over several months.

This is an example where a limited understanding of the past was supplemented by developmental guidance about the baby's needs. By resisting the impulse to take over and impose rules as the Kibbutz had once done, I was able to support these parents in finding a middle way between complete indulgence and institutional care. It is also an example of the sudden emergence of representations which have lain dormant for a long time. Mrs D claimed to have had no experience in adult life of feelings of deprivation, of insatiable demands or of incompetence and helplessness. Motherhood had brought rewards buts its revival of the past was extremely distressing. For Mr D, parenthood was less of a shock. His father had been very dominating and he seemed to expect to be dominated by his son, who was named after his father.

Understanding the interference of the past in the present provides both a possible explanation of the origin of infant-parent problems and a means of changing them. However, it is not the only way to intervene successfully in infant-parent relationships. Behavioural methods too have their successes, for changes in behaviour can bring changes in representations, just as changes in representations can bring changes in behaviour. The preliminary results of research conducted by Cramer, Stern et al. (1990) established that infant-parent psychotherapy and a behavioural intervention were both highly effective in selected cases. The first evaluations of outcome, assessed when both these brief therapies had just ended, after an average of six weekly sessions, revealed no difference in the success of the two methods. Further follow-ups have not been published but I can think of reasons why infant-parent psychotherapy might have a more enduring effect. It takes time to assimilate the past. Ms S provides a striking example of a parent who was still initiating changes based on her re-evaluation of her childhood long after she first recognized its relevance. Parents who have partners often support each other in exploring the past, once the therapist's intervention has raised the issue. They can help each other to reassess the influence of their backgrounds and to come to terms with them. This means mourning the parents they would have liked to have had, and deciding how they wish to be different. As Main (1985) has shown, parents who recall and acknowledge their own parents' contribution to their childhood difficulties are less likely to repeat their own parents' mistakes.

Additional therapeutic factors: "Holding" and "containment"

The overall effectiveness of both psychodynamic and behavioural methods points to two things: the extreme flexibility of adaptation within the infant-parent relationship and the amount which the two therapies have in common.

The capacity for rapid change in infant-parent relationships is a reflection of the flexibility both of the infant and of his parents. It seems that within their first two-and-a-half years or so, before internal representations become firmly established, infants retain a remarkable behavioural flexibility. Further, the anxiety and turmoil attendant upon becoming parents make parents particularly accessible to issues regarding their infant. Their identification with their baby, which is part of the re-experiencing of early relationships, can bring with it a capacity to regress in order to attempt a new beginning and hopefulness about change which increases motivation. Some families are so well motivated that they can use the time and space provided by the therapist to tell their story and to work out their own solutions without the help of interpretation or developmental guidance. However, the therapist's contribution remains essential, even if it is simply to provide a "holding environment" in Winnicott's sense, and "containment" as described by Bion. It is this capacity for holding and containment which both psychodynamic and behavioural approaches have in common. Whatever the orientation of the therapist, the family know that their concerns have been heard, that they are not alone with their troubles, that they are not blamed for them and that there is hope of change. If all goes well the therapist is experienced as a benign parental figure who may be felt to replace a curse from a wicked fairy godmother with a blessing. The internal representation of a critical undermining parent may thus be temporarily displaced by the representation of an approving, supporting one, and so allow a new pattern of interaction to be initiated. Stern has called this "the good grandmother transference" (1995: 186).

Holding and containment are easier to describe than to do. I have tried to draw attention to my own difficulty in this respect in order to emphasize this issue. It can be very hard to contain distress and uncertainty and to resist the urge to take sides or to intervene didactically. Experience helps. And so does knowing that these feelings and impulses are both inevitable and valuable. Recognising them and thinking about them make them easier to contain and can also throw light on the work of infant-parent psychotherapy as I have tried to illustrate.

Selma Fraiberg's book has inspired and influenced several generations of clinicians and researchers in infant mental health world-wide, who have elaborated on and expanded her ideas, bringing the practice of parent-infant psychotherapy international recognition.

Note

1 This chapter is a modified version of an article in the *Journal of Child Psychotherapy* 1992 volume 18 (1): 5–18. In its current form it was published in L. Emanuel & E. Bradley (eds.) (2008) *"What Can the Matter Be?" – Therapeutic Interventions with Parents, Infants and Young Children. The work of the Tavistock Clinic Under Fives Service* London: Karnac.

9   Therapeutic interventions in infancy

Crying babies: who is crying about what?[1]

Summary

Infants are liable to many symptoms of emotional disturbance. However, it is now widely agreed that there is no such thing as individual psychopathology in infancy. Infantile disturbances are considered to be a function of current relationships. This paper briefly summarizes available psychodynamic approaches to problems in infant relationships. It argues that more case studies of therapeutic interventions in infancy are needed to increase our understanding of early disturbances and of their treatment. Two contrasting case studies of intervention in persistent crying attempt to understand what may sustain this distressing problem. In each case the possible meaning of the crying both to the babies and to their families is considered.

Introduction

Can babies be maladjusted? Certainly disturbances in the first year of life are legion. Babies can suffer from 'behaviour disorders': sleeping problems, incessant rocking, breath-holding, persistent masturbation, head-banging and other forms of self-harm. They are susceptible to 'disorders of mood': persistent crying and screaming, whining and misery, apathy and withdrawal. They may show autistic features or even merit the diagnosis of autism. A range of feeding disorders can also be added to the list of potential problems: failure to thrive, food refusal, pica (eating non-food substances) and rumination (chewing regurgitated food). Finally there are illnesses which have been traditionally termed 'psychosomatic disorders': vomiting, diarrhoea, constipation, asthma, eczema, some allergies and unusual susceptibility to infectious illness. In the second year of life all the dis-orders associated with toilet training and speech development can be added to this catalogue of woe.

In spite of this impressive array of available symptoms, babies have defied attempts to fit their ills into psychiatric categories. Indeed, recent opinion in the field of infant psychiatry is that "there is no such thing as individual psycho-pathology in infancy" (Sameroff and Emde 1989). This is obvious if we agree with Winnicott that "There is no such thing as a baby", only a mother-baby couple. Infants' symptoms can only be understood as a function of their current relationships. However, this does not mean that babies do not contribute problems from their side of the relationship. It is of course well known that infants differ widely in temperamental endowment. It does mean that the treatment of infant symptoms is often best conducted by treating the infant-parent relationship rather than by treating either infant or parent separately. The exact age at which infantile problems become sufficiently internalized to be susceptible to individual psychoanalysis remains uncertain and may well be variable. However, clinical experience shows that infants under the age of about two to two-and-a-half years are usually quickly responsive to changes in their parents' feelings and behaviour towards them. Early intervention reaps this great advantage.

Psychotherapy with infants and their parents

The work of Selma Fraiberg (1980) in America marks the start of systematic thinking about psychotherapeutic approaches to infancy. Fraiberg introduced two terms to describe her work: 'developmental guidance' and 'infant-parent psychotherapy' (also known as 'parent-infant psychotherapy').

Developmental guidance consists of supportive counselling in which advice is very rarely given. Parents are helped to observe and think about their baby while coming to recognise their own unique importance to their child. This approach is often sufficient to resolve minor difficulties and the restrictions of this method are necessary for parents who are not ready to consider the role that their own relationships may play in their baby's current difficulties.

Infant-parent psychotherapy goes further. The method involves an interpretative approach aimed at understanding the way that the parental past may be interfering with the parent's capacity to relate to the baby in the present. Fraiberg believed that this was the treatment of choice whenever the baby had come to represent an aspect of the self which was repudiated or negated, or had become the representation of figures from the past, "the ghosts in the nursery". (This method has been described in Chapter 8.)

Therapeutic approaches to infants and their parents have increasingly developed in this country. Winnicott (e.g. 1941, 1971) seems to have been the first to report working with the baby in the presence of the mother. Daws (1989) developed a psychodynamic approach within a G.P. practice. Byng-Hall and Stevenson-Hinde (1991) used attachment theory to develop his approach to families with non-verbal infants. Baradon et al. (2005) provide a more recent example of a psychodynamic approach. Another relevant development has been the growth of the practice of infant observation (Bick 1964). Experience of this method of observing babies in their families is an excellent background for training in therapeutic work with infants (Miller 1992).

Therapeutic intervention in infancy can make a significant contribution to understanding the genesis of psychopathology. It helps to disclose the factors sustaining deviant development by changing them. More individual studies are needed, both as a source of hypotheses about infancy and as an addition to the general knowledge available to the clinician. This paper aims to add to this literature by describing intervention in two cases of persistent crying.

Persistent infant crying

Studies suggest that at least 10% of healthy infants suffer from this problem (e.g. St James-Roberts 1991). Severe cases of crying in the early months are often labelled 'colic', although there are no accepted clinical criteria for this term. Persistent crying and colic do not occur in very depriving institutions for infants (e.g. Provence and Lipton 1962); babies simply give up. This is a reminder that crying is always a function of a relationship, as well as of the baby's endowment.

Crying is an intensely powerful communication. It expresses strong feelings and it arouses them. The reaction of parents to persistent crying depends upon the meaning which they ascribe to it. This in turn will depend in part upon the nature of their baby's cry, its intensity, its emotional tone (anger, misery or fear) and its particular aversive qualities. Persistent crying makes most parents desperate. It is not surprising that it is associated with abuse. Clearly someone or something is felt to be to blame and it may seem to be the fault of a monster baby. Scapegoating can start from here. In contrast to, and often along with, their feelings of fury and frustration with their baby, parents experience themselves as helpless and rejected failures. Compassion for the baby is normally mixed with both anger and self-doubt. It can be a great relief to hold 'colic' responsible.

What does crying mean to the baby? This question is usually avoided. Babies are simply described as having 'low thresholds of irritability', 'difficult temperaments' or 'problems with state regulation'. It can be hard to imagine that they are crying about something when all their needs appear to have been met. No doubt some babies are prone to cry much more easily than others. They bring their own genetic endowment and their own histories of pre-natal life, birth and early experience. For example, one group of infants especially prone to persistent crying has been identified by Brazelton (1985). These are babies who are born small for gestational age and have been malnourished in the womb. Whereas 'colicky' babies usually stop crying at around 3–4 months, these babies continue with their aversive cry until 5 months. Parents who are sensitive enough to discover that they require particularly calm, quiet and steady care are able to soothe them.

Since so many babies cry excessively in the early months, they cannot all be offered specialised therapeutic help, nor do they need it. Most families get by with the support of grandparents, friends and health visitors or the help of voluntary organisations, like CRY-SIS. Happily crying is usually outgrown, although the association of early persistent crying with later behaviour problems (Forsyth and Canny 1991) suggests that disturbed relationships may persist. Certainly professional help is needed when crying is combined with other signs of infantile disturbance, when abuse threatens or when parents are distraught. In the two case examples which follow, the extremity of these infants' crying and of its effect on their parents is indicated by the fact that both infants were admitted to hospital for investigations of their distress before they were referred for psychological help. Both families were seen under the auspices of the Under Fives Counselling Service of the Tavistock Clinic, an NHS psychiatric outpatient clinic. The Service aims to offer families an appointment within a week or two of referral. It provides up to five sessions which may take place weekly or be spaced over several months according to need. Audit has shown that the majority of problems improve markedly within five meetings, but in some cases further work is needed.

Case example: Hannah

Hannah was referred by a paediatrician at the age of 6 months. She was said to suffer from persistent crying and would not make eye contact. The paediatrician gave the following history. Hannah had been born to a single schizophrenic mother with whom she had spent her first three days in maternity hospital. She was then transferred to a paediatric ward where she spent a month until her move to a foster home. During that month in hospital she developed a reputation as "a screamer". Her foster parents had two little girls of their own, but in spite of their conflicting demands for attention, the foster mother, Martha, had done her best to try to comfort Hannah, to no avail. When Hannah was still screaming at six months old, Martha persuaded the paediatrician to admit Hannah to hospital to establish whether anything was wrong with her. All tests were negative, but it was noticed that Hannah was hypertonic when held and would not make eye contact either with the nurses or with her foster family. The paediatrician knew that this was characteristic of autism and feared that Hannah might have inherited a psychotic constitution from her mother.

I invited the whole foster family to bring Hannah to meet me, since it is usually valuable to begin by exploring how an infant's problem affects everyone in the family and to observe how each affects the infant. However, only the foster mother, Martha, and her two-year-old daughter, Mary, were able to come with Hannah. Hannah was asleep in her buggy and Mary settled easily to play while Martha eagerly grasped the opportunity to share her distress about the pain of this, her first experience of fostering. She was evidently a warm-hearted woman, who had been extremely distressed by Hannah's screaming, which occurred daily and sometimes persisted for up to four hours at a time. "It's worse than crying. It's piercing screams," she said.

I acknowledged how desperate she must have felt and explored how she had dealt with her own exasperation and anger. This is always a crucial issue for the parents of crying babies. When she hesitated, I acknowledged what any mother might feel in the circumstances and she admitted that she had come close to battering Hannah. She had not been able to tell the social worker this in case she took her away. She had always loved Hannah and wanted to help her become a normal, happy child like her two daughters, but now she felt that the task might be beyond her and that she might have to give Hannah up. Both her husband and her mother had said she would never be able to cope with three little children and she feared they were right. Moreover, her husband disliked the idea of her working for money and had not supported her plan to foster, although he was gradually growing fond of Hannah. Whenever Hannah screamed she worried that he would either insist that she gave up fostering or would divorce her. In view of Hannah's screaming, they were both afraid she would become psychotic like her mother.

At this point in our meeting Hannah awoke with an abrupt startle, which Martha said was how she always awoke. Martha lifted her gently onto her lap while talking kindly to her, and showed me how Hannah sat stiffly, not moulding to Martha's body. Most striking to observe, Hannah held her legs raised above Martha's lap, and Martha explained that Hannah never let her legs rest on Martha's body. Hannah had always rejected cuddling and Martha showed me how Hannah strained away from her chest when she drew her towards her. She told me that holding her when she screamed made her cry more. Babies like this, who seem to need holding but reject it, pose a particular problem that would benefit from a growing literature of case studies.

Next Martha laid Hannah on a rug on the floor and knelt beside her. They played together in a lively way, involving Mary in bringing toys for Hannah. Hannah smiled, vocalised and laughed, especially to Mary, but although her eyes swept across both their faces she never allowed a moment of sustained eye contact.

Martha gave a very good impression as a foster mother, being caring, concerned, sensitive and observant, and having a happy, affectionate relationship with her own attractive little girl. She had observed with pain that Hannah had seemed to prefer the isolation in hospital, had screamed much less there than at home and had drunk more milk from a propped bottle than she did on Martha's lap. She was surprised that Hannah loved the swing on the ward when she had always resisted being rocked in arms.

Together we built up a picture of Hannah as a baby very different from her own: a nervous, hypersensitive baby, who had had a bad start in life, who felt overwhelmed and frightened by people when exposed to face, voice and physical contact all together, but who clearly enjoyed relationships with her family when they were modulated. Martha was pleased that I felt it would be all right to continue the propped bottle, to leave Hannah alone in her cot and not to try to cuddle her when she resisted. She thought she would buy her a rocking chair.

Martha left saying she was much relieved that I had appreciated her efforts and had not blamed her. I was aware that I had also given her permission to take her cues from the baby. We agreed to meet again three weeks later, together with her husband.

A week later Martha 'phoned to say that although she would have liked another appointment, in view of the very difficult journey, she would not come as there was no further need. Hannah had made eye contact both with her and her husband on the day of our consultation, she was continuing to do so and had become more smiley and friendly. She had screamed much less and was not so jumpy, but she still kept her legs lifted off the lap and did not want to be cuddled.

We kept in touch by 'phone until Hannah was 11 months old, when Martha reported that Hannah now enjoyed and initiated cuddles. She had only had one screaming fit in the past month, when a stranger visited and made too rapid overtures; after that she had "screamed all night". Otherwise all was well and Martha was confident that she could help Hannah through any remaining difficulties. I was sorry that Martha felt no further need for contact since Hannah's recent screaming fit alerted me to her persisting vulnerability. There is often a conflict for therapists in infant-parent work between supporting parents' autonomy and self esteem by encouraging them to help their children themselves and the therapist's own wish to be maximally effective. In this fascinating case, I was deprived of first-hand follow-up, but was informed by the family's health visitor that Hannah had indeed made all the beneficial changes which Martha had reported. She thought that without intervention Martha would have abandoned her attempt to foster Hannah.

Hannah's capacity to change was a surprising endorsement of the claim that there is no such thing as individual psychopathology in infancy. Forgetting this, I had supposed, as the referring paediatrician had done, that the presenting problems were best understood as Hannah's. Only when Hannah changed in response to the consultation did it emerge that there had been relationship factors sustaining her problems. The initial causes of Hannah's screaming must remain obscure. Perhaps there were constitutional factors and/or perhaps she had been traumatised. Winnicott believed that when babies appear hypersensitive and paranoid from birth, that environmental factors could be to blame. If this was so, then in Hannah's case, a recovery proved possible through an environmental change. When Martha changed so did Hannah.

What had enabled the foster mother to change? During our meeting Martha had been able to face her underlying anger, guilt and sense of failure and her distress at her husband's and her mother's disapproval of her fostering. She said she had not realised how upset she was until she talked to me. Afterwards, she felt relieved of her emotional burden and less determined to prove that she could cure Hannah. She gave me details of how this change of attitude enabled her to adapt herself to Hannah's needs instead of trying to coax her to become like her own children. Babies who have had a muddled start like Hannah seem to need a period of maximal adaptation before they settle down, but instead, in the kindest possible way, Hannah had found herself required to comply. She could not make eye contact until Martha saw her through more accepting eyes.

Hannah also illustrated the amazing speed and ease with which change can take place in infancy. Selma Fraiberg (1980) was so impressed by this that she wrote, "When a baby is at the centre of treatment something happens which has no parallel in any other form of psychotherapy. It's like having God on your side."

The intervention used by Martha and Hannah would have been classified by Selma Fraiberg as developmental guidance. My second case example concerns a family for whom it was not sufficient to explore the reasons in the present for their mutual distress. They needed the interpretative approach of infant-parent psychotherapy to discover its origins in the past.

Case example: Betty

Betty was referred when eight weeks old by a paediatrician who had admitted her to hospital for a week because her mother could not stand her crying any more. Her first baby had also cried persistently until the age of over a year and the mother felt she could not bear "a repeat performance". She had scarcely visited Betty in hospital where Betty continued to cry persistently.

The family came to see me a week later. Both parents, Tim and Tracey, were accountants. Their son Terry was aged 3 years and Betty was nine weeks old. Betty was crying as they entered and continued to cry throughout, with a steady, protesting cry. Tracey responded by offering her appropriate comfort, cradling, patting and rocking, and occasionally putting her down in the buggy or passing her to Tim, all to no avail. Terry busied himself throughout with a succession of scribble drawings which he took to his mother, with smiles and kisses. This little boy, who was said to have cried for sixteen months, appeared to be becoming a compulsive caregiver and this was confirmed in later meetings.

The parents took the opportunity to have a major row. Tracey accused Tim of not wanting the baby, refusing to help at home and even getting ill himself. She readily agreed with my half-humorous suggestion that she must have wished that the paediatrician had also admitted him to hospital and she spoke bitterly of the need for divorce. Tim accused Tracey of refusing to appreciate everything he *did* do to help, which he listed at length. They both shouted above the baby's cries. I could scarcely think: I wanted to scream too. Naturally, I wondered whether Betty could not be comforted because of the extreme tension in this unhappy household. I acknowledged that they all had a great deal to cry about so it was not surprising that Betty had the same problem. And I asked about sources of support; this is always a crucial issue with young families. Although both parents were English, neither parent had family currently living in England. No grandparents had yet to come to visit the baby. Talking about their shared isolation seemed to bring them somewhat together, and we were then able to give some attention to Betty.

Tracey explained that although she could not stand Betty's crying, she always stayed with her, held her and rocked her, so Betty would know she was trying to help; this meant pacing the floor most of the night. Although she was so exhausted, she felt sure she would not hurt her. It was her husband whom she wanted to attack.

Tim said that Betty *is* sometimes peaceful while awake and that Tracey exaggerated the amount that she cried. Tracey admitted, "She is always crying in my mind." I wondered what this perpetual crying represented. I enquired about the parents' childhoods. Tim knew nothing of his infancy. Tracey knew that she too had been a crying baby and had been left to scream sometimes for hours. I acknowledged that she was determined not to give Betty the same unhappy experience of crying alone. I said that Betty's cries must have evoked painful memories of her own childhood cries which were never comforted. Tracy was pleased to have a plausible explanation of her own distress but she did not respond to this with any depth of feeling and I was not surprised that Betty's crying continued. Perhaps

I had made this intervention too early, before a more solid working alliance with the family had been established. Unfortunately with this family an alliance was slow to form since Tim's work and an illness of Terry's both intervened to postpone what were intended to be weekly appointments.

At our second meeting, three weeks later, when Betty was twelve weeks old, she still cried most of the time. There were undercurrents of hostility between the parents, but no open warfare. During this session, I realised why I had felt uncomfortable about Tracey's relationship with Betty, in spite of her evident concern for her and her appropriate handling: even when Betty was not crying Tracey did not make eye contact with her or talk to her. When I invited her to do so she could not think of anything to say except, "I don't want to see your tonsils". She told me she did not feel rewarded by Betty's smiles, they simply made her feel, "So what." Tim too seemed at a loss to talk to Betty and said that he preferred older children like Terry.

The first session had helped the parents to recognise the possible significance of their own childhoods which they now spontaneously recalled. Tracey was reluctant to blame her own mother, but Tim recounted how Tracey's mother had said she hated small children, had sent Tracey to a day nursery as soon as possible and had determined never to have another child. Tracey explained how her mother had depended upon her emotionally as she grew up. Her parents' marriage was stormy, they divorced when Tracey was thirteen years old and Tracey was left alone with her mother who then suffered a depressive breakdown.

The family seemed calmer, but more storms were to come. It was not until our fourth meeting, when Betty was nearly five months old, that Betty's persistent crying finally stopped. No sooner had the family arrived, than another furious row developed. Tracey was again irate that Tim would not help. She was totally incensed by the fact that he "escaped" from the house every day to go to work and enjoy "one long holiday", while she was trapped with the children. She became irrational to the point of delusional about Tim's daily absences and I feared that this time she, not the baby, would need hospitalization. This reminded me of her own mother's depressive breakdown. I asked whether the present desperate situation reminded Tracey of the terrible time her father had walked out and left her to cope with her mother's tears. Tracey wept as she recalled her own helplessness to comfort her mother. She talked at length about this terrible experience. She had never been able to satisfy her mother's demands and had left home at the age of sixteen. Both she and Tim could recognise the parallels with Tracey's current situation.

This proved to be a turning point in the therapy. As soon as Tracey had finished her recollections, Betty stopped crying and Tracey spontaneously related to her as a person, smiling and talking and asking her how she was. "Do you feel better, Betty? I think you do." It was evident that at least Tracey did. After this session Betty stopped her persistent crying and Tracey dropped her irrational accusations of Tim. At two follow-up meetings during Betty's sixth month, Tracey was happy that she was enjoying Betty at an age when Terry had still been a "tyrant". Although Betty no longer cried and was happily responsive when Tracey initiated conversations with her, I noticed that Betty did not initiate conversations with either of her parents, but instead attempted across the room to initiate smiling and talking with me. Clearly problems remained and I was willing to continue meeting but Tracey vetoed further help. She felt that only her return to full-time work would remove her envy of her husband and so save her sanity.

Discussion

This brief intervention was not a therapeutic miracle. Tracey remained burdened by her unhappy past and still at risk of acting it out with Betty, as she already seemed to be doing in a different way with her son Terry, whose need to look after her probably mirrored her own childhood attempt to care for her own depressed mother. What seemed to have happened is what Cramer and Stern (1988) call "a dynamic disconnection" between Tracey's past and Betty's present. Betty's cries no longer touched off Tracey's childhood anguish – Betty had been unhooked from Tracey's hang-ups; so had Tim, who could now be appreciated for his contribution, instead of being attacked for absconding as Tracey's father had done.

When a dynamic disconnection happens, parental behaviour changes without ever having been a focus of therapy. As long as Betty represented Tracey's own childhood screams and the insatiable demands of her own mother, Tracey could not comfort her or respond to Betty as a separate person in her own right. After Tracey's own cries had been heard, she could feel empathy for Betty instead of hostility, and Betty responded with contentment. As Fraiberg (1980) has said, remembering saves a parent from blind repetition because it enables identification with the injured child. Until Tracey changed, Betty's angry crying had probably indicated her sensitivity to Tracey's hostility, reflected in Tracey's bodily tension and in her failure to engage in social interaction with her daughter. Research has shown that one and two-month-old babies have innate expectations of relationships and that they manifest distress when their mothers unexpectedly ignore them for brief periods (Murray 1991). Their facial expressions show that they attribute meaning to this experience. It seems possible to suppose that babies are liable to respond to prolonged periods of social rejection with distress which they may loudly express in protest as long as active parental involvement keeps their hopes for more social contact alive.

These two contrasting cases of persistent crying illustrate the need for every case to be considered in its own right. However, in spite of many obvious differences, both babies illustrate extreme sensitivity to parental feelings. Both mothers had tried their utmost to comfort their babies, but they could not succeed until their own underlying distress had been heard. Only then could they relinquish their personal preoccupations and respond appropriately to their babies' needs.

Although interpreting infants' behaviour is inevitably highly speculative, I would like to suggest possible meaning for these two infants' cries. It seems that Hannah's need was to have her fears of intimacy accepted and to have her own cues followed. Winnicott (1960b) would have said she needed the recognition of her 'spontaneous gesture'. Until this happened, her withdrawal and her prolonged bouts of screaming indicated that she was in the grip of unthinkable anxieties, such as going to pieces, falling for ever, having no relationship to the body and no orientation. Once she felt herself to be existentially confirmed, through contingent responsiveness to her own cues, she could turn to her foster parents for comfort and her unthinkable anxieties could be mitigated.

As for Betty, it seemed that what she had needed was for her mother to withdraw her hostile projections, to empathise with her and to welcome her socially as a person. Until then her angry protest proclaimed her sense of rejection and her demand for the right attention.

The role of eye contact is of particular interest in both cases. Direct eye contact allows an intimate appreciation of facial expression. Hannah avoided it until Martha ceased to pursue it. As Martha reported on the telephone, "It's funny, but when we stopped worrying about it, she looked at us." Presumably Martha's and her husband's pursuit of eye contact had been felt by Hannah as a persecuting demand. When Hannah felt accepted she could enjoy looking back. And once she had discovered that she could initiate contact on her own terms, her acceptance of physical contact soon followed. What had been developing as an extremely avoidant pattern of attachment (Ainsworth 1985) gave hope of becoming gradually secure.

In Betty's case it was her parents who quite unconsciously avoided eye contact with her, while offering plenty of physical contact. Tracey must have been unable to look Betty in the eye because she feared to see projected there the insatiable demands of her own mother and of her own infant-self. Once she had recalled and contained some of these painful memories she did not need to project them. Betty could then be seen by her as more appealing than demanding.

Counter-Transference

Projections do not pass by magic through the air. They are subtly conveyed to babies by eye contact, facial expression, tone of voice, holding and handling. Video can reveal some of the details which pass too swiftly to observe. However, video cannot adequately convey the emotional impact which we as therapists receive. Our capacity for emotional attunement to details too fine for conscious processing contributes to the counter-transference which informs our thinking. For example, while meeting with Martha and Hannah, I found myself responding with unusual therapeutic zeal to their plight. It was through recognising my sense of effort that I became aware of Martha's effort and so could wonder whether Hannah needed a more accommodating approach. Unfortunately counter-transference can also be a source of difficulty in this work, especially when a therapist's feelings become split between parent and infant. This happened with Betty's family when I found myself exasperated with Tracey and identified with Betty's cries. Tracey was rightly angry with me when I briefly took sides and treated her as the patient. I had to remind myself that one family member can express feelings on behalf of another. Since babies are so palpably open to their parents' feelings this is probably more convincingly apparent in infancy than at any subsequent stage of development.

Fraiberg (1980) observed that, like their babies, parents of infants are particularly flexible in their capacity to change. Perhaps this is because there has been less time to establish a history of antagonism; perhaps also the fresh start, which a baby's new life denotes, inspires determination to make a fresh start in their parents. The capacity of both infants and parents to respond to intervention is naturally rewarding for the therapist, although inevitably some families require much more help than these two convenient examples have provided. The preventive aspects of the work are obvious and early intervention should amply repay the resources given to it.

Note

1 First published in *Psychoanalytic Psychotherapy* 8: 141–152 (1994) and amended for J. Raphael-Leff (ed.) (2003) *Parent-Infant Psychodynamics: wild things, mirrors and ghosts* London: Whurr.

Integrating and exploring Winnicott

Introduction

This group of papers, which explores and integrates Winnicott's ideas, is a very fitting ending to this collection of Juliet Hopkins's papers. These papers consolidate the themes of the previous sections of this book and place them firmly within the Winnicottian tradition.

In this section, Juliet Hopkins's papers bring together her thinking on the benefits and disadvantages of Kleinian and Winnicottian technique; the place of interpretation and of regression in therapy; the value of the experience in the present moment; the positive function of defences in providing secondary security; reconstruction and therapeutic revisiting of infantile experience. In all this, she expresses a view that having faith in the re-establishment, through the therapeutic relationship, of developmental processes which have been interrupted, may provide for the spontaneous dissolution of developmental impasses.

'The dangers and deprivations of too-good mothering' (1996) has become a classic paper, elucidating the rather startling idea that it is possible to be 'too-good' a mother. Juliet Hopkins is clear that she is trying to redress what was, in her view, an over-emphasis at the time of writing the paper on the importance of harmony and attunement between mother and baby. She argues that what is needed for emotional health is a *balance* between the satisfaction and frustration of the baby's needs. This facilitates the development of the 'capacity for concern' (Winnicott 1963c) because of the need to repair a relationship following conflict due to the ordinary frustrations and disillusionments that need to be part of the baby's experience, through what is termed 'interactive repair' (Tronick, Cohn, & Shea 1986).

Using baby observation material, she illustrates how a mother who anticipates all her baby's needs, 'even his need for independence', by fitting herself too closely to the baby's needs for too long, robs or deprives the baby of these important experiences. Winnicott states this powerfully, saying that some overly responsive parents can inadvertently 'worse than castrate' their baby by not appropriately disillusioning the baby, after the first important few months of allowing them the illusion of the world fitting around their needs (Winnicott 1960a: 51). He bluntly argues that in ordinary circumstances the idyll of primary maternal preoccupation has to come to an end and that, if it does not, the consequences are either that the child has to reject the doting parent or become so disempowered as to lack any genuine sense of agency. This is a paper full of startling and interesting ideas, drawing together the consequences of an idea expressed by Winnicott in various papers that Juliet Hopkins refers to, but never explored in its own right.

The second paper in this section, 'From baby games to let's pretend: the achievement of playing', is a delightful description of the ways in which the capacity to play develops. As with many other developmental achievements, it is common to write and talk about playing as if it just suddenly arrives in its full-blown fantasy form, when in fact it transforms and develops within an environment which facilitates and fosters this development from early babyhood onwards. That this process can go awry is only too obvious when faced with a child who cannot play. Being able to discern any small stages that are the stepping stones to full-blooded play is an important part of the repertoire of anyone working closely with children – teachers, nurses and therapists.

Drawing on her experience of having clinical supervision with Winnicott for one of her training cases, Juliet Hopkins shares with the reader her delight in discovering as a trainee, through her patient, that it seemed that 'one form of playing could lead to another'. Her enduring respect for the importance of playing in child mental health is very apparent in this paper and is directly linked with Winnicott's view that 'through playing, therapy of a deep going kind may be done without interpretative work' – hence Winnicott's and Juliet Hopkins's respect for nursery nurses, play therapists and others who use the medium of play in their work.

The final chapter, 'Narcissistic illusions in late adolescence: defensive Kleinian retreats or Winnicottian opportunities?' (1999, 2006), takes the reader into the consulting room to think about a very different kind of patient – a young woman who was eighteen years old at the start of three times weekly treatment and was married by the end of it. The patient was from a privileged, celebrity background and the paper is an object lesson in learning about how the difficulties of human relationships cross all social divides. The detailed account of the intensity of the transference relationship, and how this unhappy and very disturbed young woman managed to come down from the heights of narcissism to the pleasures of being ordinary and recognizing that this helped her to feel happier, is touching.

Juliet Hopkins describes how, within the therapeutic relationship, this patient regressed in a benign way. This required time, so that the patient could 'unfreeze' previous developmental failures, leading to the possibility for there to be a 'spontaneous dissolution' of what had been developmental impasses. This eventually led to a happier ordinariness, despite accompanying fury at no longer being special. She discusses this recovery in terms of Winnicottian 'opportunities' which needed time to be fully experienced within the transference relationship. She contrasts her technique within this treatment with a more Kleinian approach which she could equally well have chosen but which might have missed the opportunity for the patient to experience, within the present relationship with her therapist, more about her early life and family relationships.

True to the spirit of Juliet Hopkins's thinking, the papers in this final section of the book are highly individualistic and independent in their expression, carefully examining theoretical ideas which extend Winnicottian ideas, as well as meticulously exploring the clinical and observational material on which they are based. The pros and cons of differing theoretical approaches are honestly and fairly discussed, and the subtleties that she explores come through to the reader with a clarity that is illuminating and stimulating.

ML

10 The dangers and deprivations of too-good mothering[1]

Summary

The paper explores Winnicott's ideas on the detrimental effects of mothering which is too well adapted to infant needs. Winnicott claimed that such too-good mothering, when pursued beyond the baby's earliest months, led to two possible outcomes: the child would either reject the mother or would remain in a state of arrested development, merged with her. The paper follows the development of a baby girl, observed by the Bick method, and illustrates how her mother's devoted and sensitive care effectively deprived her of the development of some aspects of the sense of self and of possibilities for negotiation, concern and reparation. The baby developed a paranoid orientation and later rejected her mother after the birth of her sister. The paper also mentions the alternative outcome of a persisting state of passive merger with the mother and ends by hoping for further exploration of the means by which some sensitive, responsive parents may inadvertently "worse than castrate" their children by depriving them of an autonomous sense of agency.

Introduction

Winnicott's recognition of the merits of the "ordinary devoted" or "good enough" mother is widely acknowledged. Less often quoted is his recognition of the dangers of the too-good mother, that is, of the mother who remains too well adapted to her infant's needs beyond the first few months. References to the too-good mother are scattered among Winnicott's writings. For example, "A mother who fits in with a baby's desires too well is not a good mother" (1958: 215). "The infant gains from the experience of frustration, since incomplete adaptation to need makes objects real, that is to say hated as well as loved." " exact adaptation resembles magic as the object that behaves perfectly becomes no better than an hallucination" (1958: 238). Such magic can be frightening and the mother who persists in anticipating her baby's needs, before he even recognizes them himself, may be experienced as a witch. But the most devastating allegation made by Winnicott against mothers who "do all the right things at the right moment" is that they do "something worse than castrate the infant" (1965: 51). Winnicott does not satisfactorily explain this dramatic statement. He goes on to say that two possibilities are open to the infant of such a mother: "either being in a permanent state of regression and of being merged with the mother, or else staging a total rejection of the mother, even of the seemingly good mother." Clearly the dangers of too-good mothering are serious. However, they have been given little attention, especially outside psychoanalysis.

Most of recent child development research and child guidance literature has tended to imply or assume that the more sensitive, contingent and emotionally available the mother can be, the better for her infant. The benefits of harmony have been extolled and the benefits of conflict, frustration, anger, and hate have been largely ignored.

It was not only from his observations of the mother-child relationship that Winnicott derived his ideas about the dangers of perfection, but also from his experiences as an analyst who was at times too good. He wrote of the dangers of the analyst's premature understanding that could rob the patient of the capacity to understand himself. "One can say that some patients are lucky when their analysts do not understand too much at the beginning . . . Gradually, they like to be understood, but they may feel cheated if understood so quickly that the analyst seems to be a magician" (1969). More seriously, an analyst who is too understanding can make the patient feel that he is trying to hypnotise him, inviting a severe regression and pulling him back to merging with him (1965: 51). When this happens with a neurotic patient, the patient retains an awareness of his separate status, but develops an egocentric illusion that the analyst shares his feelings and attitudes and that he himself is of particular significance in the analyst's life. A more disturbed patient may develop a delusion of merger in which identities and even body boundaries are affected and the patient may suppose himself, for example, to be merging with the couch. Winnicott must have been referring to these sorts of borderline or narcissistic pathology when he described the outcome of too-good mothering as remaining merged with the mother, unless the child is able to escape by rejecting her completely.

The antithesis of the analyst being too good was for him to make mistakes. Winnicott recognised several potential benefits to the patient of the analyst's mistakes and failures. In particular, he noted that mistakes aroused anger which prevented regression and enabled the patient to free himself from excessive dependence (1958: 298). In this way, Winnicott drew a parallel between the dangers of too-good analysts and too-good mothers and between the benefits of their mistakes.

Winnicott's idea that too-good mothers can arrest their infants in a state of merger rests on his theory that merger is the psychological state in which babies begin. He proposes that babies have a very close emotional identification with their mothers and that the well-mothered baby develops an illusion that his mother's care is a function of himself, a matter of his own creation, a happening under his own control. In Kleinian terms, the baby is living in projective identification with the mother. As long as the mother makes maximal adaptation to the baby's needs, the baby is protected from awareness of them and of his dependence on her to satisfy them. It is crucially with regard to this issue of the provision of maternal care that Winnicott's concept of the illusion of merger applies.

Can Winnicott's views on merger be reconciled with contemporary findings in child development? Recent research has shown that new babies, at least when in the state of alertness necessary for experimental studies, do not confuse their bodies with their mothers' bodies or their sense of agency with hers either (Stern 1985). However, there is no evidence yet on the question of whether babies can reliably make such cognitive distinctions with regard to an experience of care. I find it easy to suppose that at times of excited feeding or of drowsy contentment the baby may lose awareness of the mother's separate existence. It seems likely that in normal development the capacities to experience separateness and merger, which are both features of healthy adult life, co-exist from the start (Lachmann and Beebe 1989).

According to Winnicott, it is the mother's task to disillusion the baby gradually, so that he distinguishes the "not-me" from the "me" and recognises his dependence upon her. This is the task which Winnicott believes the too-responsive mother fails to perform.

Sadly Winnicott does not give details of the clinical outcome when the too-good mother is rejected by her child. I assume that this must lead to an emotional alienation from the mother, an inability to confide in her or to turn to her at times of distress and a character in which opposition and hate defend against a fear of engulfment.

This paper aims to take the first steps in exploring the detrimental effects of too-good mothering by following the development of a baby who rejected her too-good mother and by briefly considering the alternative clinical outcome of a persisting state of merger.

The too-good mother

The too-good mother is not necessarily a mother who aspires to be perfect or considers that she is. She is not the classical 'smothering' mother who believes herself to be devotedly meeting her infant's needs while in fact pursuing her own needs with insensitive disregard of his. Nor is she the 'martyred' mother who resentfully sacrifices herself to her baby's care and who may find that her baby does in fact become the tyrant she had supposed him to be. The too-good mother finds infant care extremely gratifying. She is so closely identified with her infant that in sensitively meeting his needs, she feels that she is meeting her own. She remains in a persisting state of primary maternal preoccupation (Winnicott 1965: 52) which leaves little or no room for conscious resentment. In contrast, the ordinary devoted mother can hate her infant (1958: 201). Her love contains elements of conscious resentment, experienced as "a drat the kid element". As he gets older, she can allow him "some negative care" and "an alive neglect" (1964). And she is not afraid at times to allow him sufficient frustration to hate her.

Too-good mothers are among those mothers whom Raphael-Leff (1991) described as "facilitators", to distinguish them from "regulators" who expect their baby to fit in with them. Facilitators idealise their babies and achieve infantile bliss through vicarious identification with them; they aim to spare their babies all frustration and to be their babies' sole source of goodness. Too-good mothers are those facilitators who have sufficient empathy, sensitivity and skill to be able to achieve this as nearly as possible. Perfection does not exist.

Does there exist a too-good father? Winnicott does not mention this possibility. Perhaps fathers can always avoid an over-close identification with their infants because they never share the same body. Studies show in general that they offer their infants much more dys-synchrony than mothers do (Biringen et al., 1997). This enables them to provide their infants with the necessary difference and dissonance which too-good mothers fail to provide. The detrimental effects of too-good mothering must be inevitably greatest when fathers are absent or fail to perform their usual role, as was the case in the following family.

A too-good mother and her baby: beginnings, the end of merging and self-weaning

My example concerns a mother-baby couple which I had the opportunity to observe by the Bick method (Bick 1964) in their home for an hour each week many years ago. At the time, I was very impressed by this mother's sensitive, loving relationship to her baby and it was only some years later when I learned how the relationship had broken down that I started to try to understand what had gone wrong. Hence the motive for this paper.

Louise was the first child of professional parents. Her mother had gladly given up work in a care-giving profession to become a full-time mother. When I first met Louise at 6 days old, I found a contented, responsive baby and a blissfully happy mother, Mrs. L. Unfortunately, I was only able to meet Mr. L twice. He worked long hours and was often away. Mrs. L's own parents lived abroad.

During the early weeks, mother and baby continued to seem in perfect harmony. Louise was never left to cry for a moment and Mrs. L was always devotedly on hand to comfort, feed or talk to her, alertly sensitive to all her moods. For example, Mrs. L's need to protect Louise from distress was apparent in her decision not to bath her for several weeks after Louise cried loudly during her first experience of being bathed.

There are many mothers, like Mrs. L, who make a maximal adaptation to their babies at the start, though few achieve such immediate harmony, especially with a first baby and with no supportive help. The first requirement for a change in maternal adaptation comes around 3 to 4 months when babies initiate moves towards independence. They begin at times to resist close body contact, to strain away from mother's body and to 'ask' to be put down. They also look increasingly away from their mothers in order to give their attention to toys or to other people.

Winnicott's view was that these first steps towards autonomy signified the end of the period of merging. "As soon as mother and infant are separate from the infant's point of view, then it will be noted that the mother tends to change in her attitude. It is as if she now realises that the infant has a new capacity, that of giving a signal so that she can be guided towards meeting the infant's needs" (1965: 50). Experience shows that ordinary devoted mothers not only begin to allow their babies space to signal their needs, forcefully if necessary, but are usually a little ahead of their babies' moves towards independence, anticipating and encouraging the next forward step. Some mothers cannot manage this transition to autonomy gradually, but respond with a sudden severance of sensitive contact, an instant weaning or an abrupt return to work. Other mothers respond, usually quite unconsciously, with withdrawal or hostility to their babies' budding autonomy, while continuing to be completely tuned to their babies' needs in all other respects. Only too-good mothers continue to make near-perfect adaptation to their babies, including all their babies' moves towards independence.

I first saw Louise indicate her wish to be put down off her mother's lap at 15 weeks. After a contented breast-feed and several minutes of happy conversation on mother's knee, she flung herself backward against mother's arm, stiffened, arched her body and grizzled. "Oh you want to go down on the mat again," said mother and laid her gently down where Louise enjoyed kicking. Mother waited several minutes until Louise looked back at her with a smile before she knelt down beside her to play.

This observation was to prove typical of later interactive sequences in Louise's moves towards independence: Louise led and mother followed. Mother allowed Louise to play alone in her presence, but she always remained alert for the smallest sign that Louise wanted to resume contact with her and was immediately responsive. In other words, she showed no change in her attitude and continued to be as empathic and adapted as before. She seemed to want Louise's life to be an idyll in which there should be no room for conflict, dissatisfaction or anger.

However, Louise was not to be fobbed off. At 18 weeks old, she became impatient with her breast-feeds and would pull angrily away from the breast, "while swearing at me", Mrs. L. said, whenever the let-down reflex was slow to function. Although she never cried by day, she sometimes woke screaming at night and was difficult to comfort. It was perplexing that such a well-mothered baby should wake screaming. This was the first indication of a sense of persecution which became a feature later. In spite of many broken nights, Mrs. L said she never felt resentful because she shared Louise's distress. Amazingly, it was not until Louise was 16 months old that she told me she had resented her for the first time since she was born.

Mrs. L was reluctant to introduce solids. She said she did not want Heinz to come between her and her baby. However, when Louise was 5 months old, she reluctantly responded to advice and found that Louise ate eagerly and wanted to master her own spoon.

At 6 months Mrs. L introduced juice from a beaker, which Louise also welcomed. Following this development, at mid-day feeds Louise refused the breast, but when offered the beaker she drank thirstily. Within a month, she had weaned herself. Mrs. L. was devastated. She wished she had thrown the beaker away; but such an act would have been entirely out of character. She always felt bound to fulfil Louise's wishes.

Louise's motives for self-weaning are a matter for conjecture. Since she had had no practice in tolerating frustration she may have found it unusually hard to bear the pain of breast-feeding at a time that her gums were seen to be inflamed from teething. Perhaps also she may have needed to protect a mother who could not bear to be hated or to protect herself from her mother's too close attentiveness and attunement. Her self-weaning must have introduced a needed dys-synchrony between her own and her mother's feelings.

A baby with the initiative to wean herself does not appear to be "worse than castrated". Louise's frustration of her mother's wish to breast-feed her was probably the first clear sign that her response to too-good mothering would not be passivity and merger but the alternative of rejection.

Of course much must remain unknown and speculative in this method of baby observation. In particular, I learned almost nothing of Mr. L's relationship to Louise. He was said to be delighted with her, but too busy to share her care. This must have suited Mrs. L, who probably did little to encourage him to be involved, just as she did nothing to bring Louise into relationship with me.

Louise and Janet at 50 weeks: sense of urgency and desire

In order to evaluate Louise's ongoing development, I have found it helpful to compare her with another baby girl, Janet, whose mother could simply be considered "good enough". By chance both babies were observed greeting their mothers after brief separations at 50 weeks old.

Louise's mother had gone on a shopping expedition, leaving Louise, which she seldom did, with Granny, who had come on a month's visit. Louise was sitting on the floor, expectantly waiting for Granny to find her another book, when mother returned. Mother beamed at Louise and appeared about to pick her up, but Louise turned her head away and Granny intervened to ask what mother had bought. Mother excitedly produced a new dress and Granny congratulated her with an enthusiastic kiss. Louise had been waiting solemnly and she now began to wail. Mother picked her up instantly and kissed her while Louise cuddled into her for a moment, before turning to point imperiously to a toy on the floor. Mother obligingly picked it up and sat down to play with her.

The observer who visited Janet found her contentedly sitting on the kitchen floor banging and stirring saucepans with a wooden spoon, while her older sister, Anne aged 4 years, watched TV and the au-pair peeled potatoes. When mother entered, burdened with bags from the supermarket, Anne ran to greet her, while Janet with a beaming face crawled across the floor vocalizing loudly. While mother bent to hug Anne, Janet pulled herself to stand against her mother's leg, shouting for attention. When mother picked her up she rewarded mother's hug by pressing her open mouth wetly against mother's cheek. Mother returned the kiss and put Janet down in her high-chair, where she banged her tray with delight.

Of course, not all differences between babies can be attributed to differences in their care, for babies' temperaments play a major part in shaping their care-givers' behaviour, but I think it is possible to associate some of the differences noted between the babies in these two observations to differences in their experiences with their mothers.

Louise's response to her mother's return contrasts with Janet's in its lack of vigour and delight. Janet sustained a strongly positive approach to her mother, in spite of the frustration that her sister got to mother first. In contrast, Louise initially avoided eye contact with her mother and remained passively seated, waiting for mother's initiative. Her immature wail indicated her displeasure that she was excluded from the affection between mother and Granny. Unlike Janet, she had not yet begun to give affection, and it is interesting that although she always enjoyed receiving cuddles, she had still not initiated giving cuddles or kisses when observations ceased at 18 months. I think it could be said that Mrs. L did not leave enough space for Louise to discover her own wish to give. Louise took her mother for granted.

The closeness between Mrs. L and Louise also ensured that Louise did not adopt a soft toy or blanket as a transitional object. It could be said that her mother *was* her transitional object and that she treated her in some ways as an inanimate object, that is, ruthlessly. Janet's attempt at 8 months to adopt a blanket was thwarted by her mother who said she knew what a nuisance a transitional object can be.

Further comparison between the two babies showed that Janet observed her mother's face more closely than Louise observed Mrs. L's. Janet's mother's face reflected a wide range of feelings, including anger, and this must have helped to make Janet observant. By 10 months Janet had already discovered how to melt her mother's frown, while Louise was accustomed to a mother who tried to anticipate and so avoid any potential frown of Louise's.

Janet was a very smiley baby, who had learned to woo her mother. Louise was more sober. Mrs. L's continual availability must have deprived Louise of discovering how to gain and hold her mother's attention by positive means, such as smiles, charm, humour and affection. She had been deprived both of the opportunity to learn how to master distress and of the opportunity to discover, develop and act on positive feelings of desire and longing.

The effects of the deprivation of frustration on the development of a sense of agency have been explored by Demos (1986), a developmental psychologist. Although a baby is born with an initial sense of her own capacity for action, experience plays a major part in developing this aspect of the sense of a core self (Stern 1985). Demos points out that a baby who is comforted at once has no chance to become aware of what has upset her, or of the intention and desire to mend it, and no means to discover how to put it right. As long as negative experiences are not so overwhelming that they lead to disintegration and despair, they enable the infant to discover that she can endure them and attempt an active mastery of the situation; she learns that persistence may be rewarded (Demos 1986). However, a mother like Mrs. L, who makes herself indispensable, teaches her infant to be passive and dependent in response to distress, as Louise was seen to be when Mrs. L came home from shopping. Winnicott was aware that too much gratification fobs off desire and renders an infant incapable. This must be one of the major ways that he considered that too-good mothers could "worse than castrate" their infants.

However, what is considered 'castration' in one culture may be valued in another. Some Asian cultures have a tradition of never letting a baby cry. Demos would expect these babies to be passive in comparison to Western babies, and she has observed that indeed they are (Demos, unpublished talk, 1992). According to Roland (1988), a psychoanalyst with much experience in the East, these babies would grow up to become adults for whom "dependence and inter-dependence are far more valued and cultivated than autonomy and separation." They become members of a culture which values group collaboration and conformity more highly than individual assertion.

Fortunately for Louise there are more ways than through frustration to develop a sense of personal initiative. Other salient experiences mentioned by Winnicott are play and being alone in the presence of mother. Mrs. L provided both these experiences. She responded sensitively to Louise's cues to be left to her own devices and also developed a wide repertoire of games which they greatly enjoyed together. In spite of the many favourable aspects of Louise's development, there were further problems ahead. In her second year she developed a paranoid attitude and a failure, which was confirmed later, to develop a capacity for concern.

Louise 12–18 months: persecution

Even after Louise started to walk on her first birthday, Mrs. L continued to be maximally adaptive and devoted to her daughter. Louise was advanced in her growing vocabulary of single words and her capacity to master posting boxes and puzzles. She was a contented baby and it continued to be a pleasure for me to visit the home.

Mrs. L had created a child-proof environment in which it was intended that 'no' should be unnecessary. This contrasted with the environment in Janet's home, where, from around 10 months, she had been taught 'no' to the TV knobs, to throwing food and to demands for attention at unwelcome moments. Mrs. L was a model of patience, tact and distraction and could almost always find harmonious ways of gaining Louise's collaboration. If Louise was ever cross, as she sometimes was about nappy-changing, mother would playfully disarm her, for example, with a game of lions and tigers. It required some ingenuity for Louise to arrive at an effective way of saying 'no'. This she did at the age of 15 months by refusing for three weeks to eat anything except bananas and milk. Although Mrs. L was concerned, she meekly accepted the dictates of Louise's diet. If Louise had been seeking confrontation, her strategy fell flat.

Following this episode, for several months, Mrs. L reported that Louise would eat nothing that had been on Mrs. L's plate, not even chocolate. Mrs. L observed that Louise was happy to take food from her father's plate and added with some intuition, "She seems to think I'm a witch who's poisoning her." This was not the only way in which Louise manifested a paranoid attitude. Whenever she fell and hurt herself, she cried, not simply with distress, but with outrage, as though the floor had got up and hit her.

Enid Balint (1993: 65) has described how a paranoid attitude can develop in children like Louise, who are reared on a theory that only their own needs matter, that children create the laws and mothers have to obey them. "According to this theory any increase in tension is felt as an injustice and therefore an attack on the individual by the world and intolerable."

Louise's paranoid feelings indicated not only her inordinately high expectation of freedom from frustration, but also her difficulty in integrating her aggression. No doubt this must have reflected Mrs. L's own problems in this area. It appeared that she must have a deep-seated fear of her daughter's potential hatred.

Parents who are as self-effacing and eager to please as Mrs. L must surely have repressed their own hostility. Although I was never aware of any latent hostility on Mrs. L's part, such as is usually detectable in reaction-formation, it may be that Louise's paranoid feelings developed partly in response to some unconscious hostility from her mother. Perhaps she found Mrs. L's very niceness poisonous, since it either fobbed her off or left her always as the only one mean or envious enough to be resentful. Possibly also, the intensity of watchfulness with which such a highly attuned mother must inevitably monitor her child, is experienced as invasive and therefore something to resent. And, last but not least, a mother who provides no easily justifiable reason for her child to hate her must make it hard for the child to take responsibility for doing so and to focus hate where it belongs.

In contrast to Louise, Janet had plenty of ordinary opportunities to experience and master her aggression in confrontation with both mother and sister. She developed both a 'cheeky' and a 'wicked' grin, which gave warning of her intention to defy the ban on the TV knob or to pinch one of Anne's toys. By 18 months, she had discovered how to annoy, how to appease and how to try to make amends. She also showed clear evidence of empathy and concern, for example, when she tried to comfort Anne, who was crying because she'd lost her teddy. "There-there" she said, and offered Anne her own rag doll. How could Louise begin to master any of these achievements when she had not yet been treated as responsible for her own actions or been exposed to any anger or neediness of Mrs. L's? I had to wait until Louise was 6 years old before I learned how she had developed.

Follow-up. Louise at six years old

My observations of Louise ceased at 18 months because the family moved abroad. Mrs. L maintained contact with cards and photos at Christmas time. I learned that Louise had gained a sister when she was rising three years old. It was not until the family came on a visit to London when Louise was aged six that I was able to see them again. The visit was not the happy one I had anticipated. I scarcely saw the children, because Mrs. L wanted to seize the opportunity to talk to me, as a child psychotherapist, about Louise's disturbance.

There had been no major difficulties until Louise's sister was born, when Louise amply confirmed Dunn's finding (Dunn 1984: 143) that "in families with an intense relationship between mother and first-born daughter, the siblings are likely to be hostile". Soon after her sister's arrival she had become extremely oppositional and negativistic. She refused to accept affection from either parent and persistently wished her sister dead. She appeared to have no sense of concern for anyone who was ill or unhappy at home or at school, and she refused to say 'please', 'thank you', 'sorry', 'hello' and 'goodbye'. Worst of all, said Mrs. L, she seemed convinced she was a bad person and was out to prove it. "How can she feel so bad when she was so much loved?" she asked.

Mrs. L.'s account suggested that Louise had fulfilled Winnicott's prediction by rejecting her parents. She was the victim of extreme ambivalence. On the one hand she refused to use words which tacitly acknowledged separateness, dependence, indebtedness and concern. On the other hand she insisted on defining a separate sense of self through opposition and hatred. Most seriously she had not apparently developed a sense of personal agency for love and concern, while her paranoid stance suggested a failure to differentiate a sense of agency with regard to hate.

Since this painful meeting with Mrs. L, I have met with two other families in which an idyllic early relationship between mother and daughter had broken down into hatred and defiance. It was helpful to have learned how this could occur.

The development of concern and security

Parents sometimes wonder whether a child's concern for others will develop naturally in a loving home or whether it needs to be taught. For Louise at least, it seems that a capacity for concern did not develop through identification. When concern does develop spontaneously, as it did for Janet, this must depend on something more than having a parent deeply concerned for the child. Winnicott suggested what this was. He believed that the capacity for concern developed initially within the two-person relationship. He described how guilt is first aroused as the child begins to recognise and accept his ambivalence. However, if the child has adequate opportunities for giving and for making reparation, this guilt becomes modified and can be expressed as concern; as long as the possibility for reparation remains available, the guilt is not felt (Winnicott 1965: 77).

A baby like Louise who has been unable to integrate her aggression will obviously have trouble integrating her ambivalence and reaching the 'phase of concern' (Winnicott 1958: 264). This difficulty must have been increased in her case by having a mother with a powerful wish to give, who never appeared needy and who never made demands, whether for example, to give affection or to tidy up toys. Consequently, Louise was deprived of many ordinary opportunities for reparation. I think that this was possibly the most serious way in which her development was "worse than castrated". Her resulting sense of guilt and badness must have contributed to the later breakdown of her relationship to her parents.

My retrospective assessment of Louise at 18 months is of a baby with delayed and possibly derailed emotional development. Yet, according to attachment theory, a baby whose mother is maximally physically and emotionally available, especially at times of her infant's distress, should develop a secure attachment. This paradox might be resolved by using the research findings of Tronick et al. (1986). Tronick has found another variable besides parental availability which contributes to infant security at a year: it is the capacity of the baby for interactive repair (Tronick cited by Lachmann and Beebe 1989). This is the baby's capacity, within normal playful interaction with mother, to re-establish moments of harmony and synchrony, following moments of disruption and dyssynchrony. The significance of the capacity for interactive repair in contributing to security is that it widens the relevance of infant experience to include the mastery of negative feelings which occur in ordinary dyssynchronous interactions with the mother. The overly attuned mother, with too much need to repair dyssynchrony herself, could partially stifle her infant's capacity for interactive repair and so compromise her infant's security. Certainly, Louise's response to her mother's return at 50 weeks, suggested an insecure attachment; she turned her head away rather than expressing her feelings directly.

The alternative clinical outcome: permanent regression and merger

Winnicott did not specify which variables determine whether the outcome of too-good mothering will be the child's rejection of the mother or "permanent regression and merger" with her. These variables are bound to be complex, involving, as they must, the child's temperament and his relationships with other family members as well as the effects of significant life events. Another relevant variable is likely to be gender. The girl's need to achieve a separate identity from her mother may push her into a rejecting role, while the boy's gender difference may more easily allow him to continue a passive merger role with less fear of engulfment by his mother. Certainly, clinical experience provides many examples of immature boys with over-responsive mothers and of adult men who benignly, but narcissistically, assume that their female partners' needs and wishes coincide with their own.

Immature children, who remain partially arrested in a transitional relationship to their mothers, tend to be slow to speak and to continue to assume, long past the usual age, that their mothers know all about them and are wholly responsible for their lives. They tend to enjoy passive pursuits like TV, reading and computers and do not make close friends. This arrested adjustment can serve as a successful defence against the rage inherent in recognising separateness and against the entry into triangular relationships which separateness involves. It can lead to unreality feelings and may break down in latency and adolescence in ways which bring the child to psychotherapy. Unless a break-through to self- and object-awareness occurs, a particular type of narcissistic outcome ensues: the child has been "worse than castrated" though the failure to discover the self-agency needed for the sustained pursuit of desire and for the constructive use of aggression. This view of Winnicott's has been amplified by Hamilton (1982) but has been disputed by Stern (1985: 218) who argues that the over-attuned mother can delay the infant's move towards independence but cannot interfere with "individuation". The risks inherent in over-responsive mothering have not been widely understood.

Conclusion

Winnicott's view of the dangers of too-good mothering and of the benefits of conflict, anger and hate in infant development are needed to balance the present emphasis in much clinical thinking on the unalloyed benefits of sensitive and responsive maternal care. Winnicott did, of course, recommend complete maternal adaptation to infant needs at the start. His clinical intuition that this was optimal has been supported by the experimental work of Sander (1977) who has shown how consistent, sensitive experiences of mutual regulation with mothers, during the first three months, facilitate the infant's capacity for self-regulation. From then on the mother-infant couple needs to balance the infant's experiences between satisfaction and frustration and between merger and separation. It is experiences of frustration and conflict in concert with their successful repair and resolution which are optimal for development.

Finally, more knowledge is needed of the variety of perplexing ways in which responsive and empathic parents may contribute to their children's pathology. Attention is also needed to the challenging technical problems arising in the therapy of children who have already received too much sensitive attention and have been too well understood.

Acknowledgement

I should like to express my gratitude to Mary Sue Moore Ph.D. for her invaluable comments.

Note

1 *Journal of Child Psychotherapy* 1996 22 (3): 407–422.

11 From baby games to let's pretend

The achievement of playing[1]

I first met Dr Winnicott in 1960 when I had the opportunity to observe him performing 'snack-bar therapy'. This was his name for the provision of the least help needed to release a child from an impasse in development. Winnicott did this work in his role as child psychiatrist at Paddington Green Hospital. On the day that I visited, the last child patient was what was then called 'an illegitimate child', a boy of seven years who was brought by his voluble Irish mother. When the interview with Winnicott was over the boy ran off to the toilet. As he emerged to rejoin his mother I was amazed to see Winnicott stand up and bar his way. I was still more amazed when, in a flash, the boy climbed straight up Winnicott, slithered over his shoulder and ran to his mother's arms. We all laughed and Winnicott said something about the boy's courage standing him in good stead.

Winnicott's playful use of an Oedipal challenge to this fatherless boy was a startling contrast to the exclusively interpretative approach to which I'd been introduced at the Tavistock Clinic. As students of child psychotherapy we were not expected in those days to initiate play with children. Perhaps Winnicott enjoyed having presented an unorthodox challenge to me as well as to his small patient.

A year later I was fortunate to have Winnicott as the supervisor of one of my training cases. As far as I know, no other student child psychotherapist ever shared this good fortune, since doctrinal differences dictated that students should be supervised only by the orthodox. However, the Tavistock training, though Kleinian in orientation, allowed some leeway to its few 'middle-group' students like me to select our own supervisors. I needed my training analyst's insistence to gain courage to approach Winnicott and felt over-awed when he agreed to see me. My anxiety increased when he fixed a regular appointment at lunch-time and sat listening to me with closed eyes. I felt sure he would have preferred an after-dinner nap. However, when he shared his thoughts I found he had not been asleep but had been listening intently. There was nothing doctrinal about his views. He never told me what to do or say. He listened with closed eyes and then shared his thoughts, letting me see how he played freely with alternative ideas and encouraging me to do the same. I had to tolerate much uncertainty.

My intention in this paper is to give a brief account of the therapy which Winnicott enabled me to do with a little boy who could not play. I intend to use the development of this child's capacity to play to illustrate Winnicott's thoughts on playing. In this way I hope to show the sequence of stages through which a child achieves the full capacity for playing and at the same time to recapitulate Winnicott's own original achievement, his revolutionary theory of playing.

My patient was a little boy of three years old called Paddy. He had no speech and was not toilet-trained. His parents reported that he had never shown signs of attachment to them and often wandered off and got lost. He showed no awareness of danger, no response to pain and regularly ate dirt and rubbish. He had never learned to play but simply wandered about 'getting into things'. Paddy's birth and early history had been normal but his development was so slow and so deviant that the referring paediatrician was uncertain whether he was mentally handicapped or psychotic.

Paddy was the only child of a very disturbed and unhappy couple. His mother was a seriously depressed and anxious woman, preoccupied with thoughts of suicide. She suffered from severe eczema and explained that she had always avoided touching or holding Paddy in case his germs infected her skin. Paddy's father was a very eccentric man who read philosophy all day and had never been able to find a job. Neither parent had ever thought of playing with Paddy and they were at a loss as to how to relate to him.

It was arranged that Paddy should come to see me five times a week, the expected frequency for child analysis in those days; weekly casework was provided for his parents. The developments which I shall describe in Paddy were facilitated not only by his own psychotherapy but by beneficial changes which his parents became able to make.

My first encounters with Paddy were utterly bewildering. He wandered cheerfully around the room, clambered over furniture, dropped and threw toys and made a lot of noise by banging and shouting. I found myself entirely unable to think of any of the interpretations I had been learning how to give. Winnicott was later to write 'Interpretation when the patient has no capacity to play is simply not useful or causes confusion' (1971a: 51). In supervision he warmly supported my intuitive response which was simply to verbalise what Paddy was doing and feeling. Winnicott spoke of the importance for children of naming their emotions, intentions and body-parts. Naming, he said, makes shared and therefore socially acceptable what previously was only private fantasy. Putting children's experiences into words gives them greater self-awareness and hence greater control: it allows fantasy to be checked with reality, it increases the capacity to remember and it reduces guilt. So 'naming' was not simply the failure to interpret which I had feared it to be.

Since naming can elucidate latent meaning Winnicott might well have considered it to be a form of interpretation, but, like other child analysts of his time, he reserved the use of the term interpretation for the classical transference interpretation. My Kleinian teachers believed that only transference interpretations could bring about lasting change. However today most Kleinians (e.g. Alvarez 1992) recognise naming as a valued form of interpretation, suited to an immature child's developmental level. Like Winnicott, Anna Freud always recognised the value of 'verbalisation and clarification' (A. Freud 1965: 228), but she saw it primarily as a preparation for analysis proper, rather than recognising its full therapeutic potential.

Fortunately Paddy warmly welcomed my attempts to feed back in words what he was feeling and doing. He began to look eagerly at my face to see my interest in him reflected there. Much later, in a paper on 'The Mirror-role of Mother' (1971: 131), Winnicott described how vital it is for the infant to see his mother's face reflecting and responding to his own state of mind, not frozen or preoccupied. Paddy appreciated that my face and words mirrored his experience and so confirmed his existence. He began to talk, to point to himself when he wanted something and to call himself 'Paddy'. He seemed touchingly overjoyed to discover that he possessed his own thoughts and feelings. He had arrived at feeling 'I am'.

For Paddy, the discovery of 'I am' was accompanied by the parallel exploration of 'We are'. Paddy took great pleasure in having or doing the same as me. He was thrilled to discover that we both had blue sweaters, both had buttons and could both draw circles. He liked to imitate me and be imitated. We 'clapped handies', blew raspberries and made animal noises. Thus we established mother – baby games which normally originate within the first year. These games express a mutual identification in which the infant distinguishes between the 'me' and the 'not-me' while retaining through play the potential for assuming either the mother or the baby role. Winnicott thought that such early playfulness within the holding relationship took place in the transitional space, the overlap between mother and baby at a time when the baby was not yet fully aware of the mother as a separate person upon whom he depended. Certainly at this early stage of his therapy, Paddy had not yet begun to experience me as a separate person whom he missed between sessions or whom he could imagine to have a personal life of my own.

Winnicott had observed that the development of play depends upon trust. Paddy's first venture into play with me must have been based on his growing confidence that I would continue to prove reliably friendly and emotionally available, able to respond to his spontaneous gestures.

I remember asking Winnicott how I could enable Paddy to move on to the next stage of development; surely interpretation was needed now? But no, it seemed that one form of playing could lead spontaneously to another. Playing could be both a reflection of the therapeutic process and a means of bringing it about. Paddy began to pretend. His first pretend play, like that of many babies, took the form of pretending to feed me and inviting me to pretend to feed him. Plasticine and water became 'nanas and mook' (bananas and milk) and part of each daily session became a mutual feast.

Winnicott knew that this new capacity for togetherness was essential for providing the context in which Paddy could risk discriminating and tolerating differences. Paddy started to become interested in observing and exploring my body and focused on differences in our clothing and anatomy instead of on our similarities. All the toys had previously been held in common, but now he selected 'his' cars and bricks and allotted me the others. He would sit surrounded by his chosen toys and indicate that I should not let mine intrude upon his boundaries. The difference between 'me' and 'not-me' was becoming increasingly delineated.

During this period Paddy gradually developed a powerful attachment to me. He greeted me with enthusiasm and felt very rejected when it was time to go. Disillusionment was painful. He was forced to confront my separateness and to face his anger about it. Hide and seek became his favourite game. This allowed him to play out his anxieties about separation and loss of contact and about retaliation and attack. He would jump out of his hiding place to frighten me and liked to kick me on occasion. These games of hide and seek enabled me to verbalise his hopefulness that he would not be forgotten when out of sight and that I would want to find him when he disappeared. I was becoming for him both a mental image which he could recall in my absence and a separate person in the external world who come and went.

During my supervision I gradually realised that Winnicott's approach to children's play was different from Melanie Klein's. Klein used play to understand and interpret children's anxieties. Winnicott did this too, but he was more interested in the way that children themselves use play to reflect and facilitate the development of the self. He decried 'running commentary' analyses which, by verbalising everything, steal the child's experience of his own creativity. For Winnicott, the significant moments in child analysis were not the therapist's interpretations but the child's use of play to surprise himself with new awareness, just as adults make self-discoveries by talking problems through with a friend. Winnicott recognised that, through playing, therapy of a deep-going kind may be done without interpretative work. This enabled him to appreciate fully the work of play therapists (1971a: 51).

Paddy's next forward step was his attempt to integrate his aggression through symbolic play. He intended that we should both enact crocodiles. Instead of the mutual feasting we had enjoyed, we voraciously attempted to eat each other. This play was not playful, but urgent, compulsive and aggressive. Such play is likely to be motivated by the repetition compulsion (Freud 1920) with the aim of mastering unresolved trauma.

It was at this point in Paddy's therapy that interpretation began at last to play a significant part. When repression has rendered conflicts deeply unconscious they cannot be spontaneously resolved through play, which may become unplayful and repetitive as Paddy's play did. Interpretation aims to help children understand what they are worried about so that they can recognise it and work it through.

Paddy's crocodile play could be understood in many ways, but it was particularly meaningful to him when I likened the crocodile's scaly, wounded skin to his mother's eczema, and spoke of his feelings of responsibility for causing this. Klein had taught me that children's imaginary monsters were projections of their own aggression, but Winnicott's view that playing takes place in the overlap of the 'me' and the 'not-me' led me to the realisation that Paddy's crocodiles reflected not only Paddy's own aggression but also the experience which had aroused it (Hopkins 1986); in this case, his mother's physical rejection of him on account of her eczema. Playing out these aggressive themes helped Paddy to separate fantasy from reality, to recognise that wishing to hurt is not the same as doing and that thought is not equivalent to action. But Paddy's feelings of responsibility for his mother's eczema and for her rejection of him ran deep and proved very hard to mitigate.

Interestingly, it was after Paddy had tested my capacity to contain the crocodile's aggression that he ceased to be oblivious to physical pain. Perhaps he now allowed himself to cry when hurt because he could rely on my survival and so on my availability to comfort him (Fraiberg 1982).

After fifteen months of therapy had passed, Paddy was talkative, toilet-trained and no longer eating rubbish. His parents had been greatly reassured by the improvements in his development and he began to develop an affectionate attachment to them both. A nursery school agreed to give him a place and so he gained his first opportunity to play with other children.

One of the benefits of my supervision with Winnicott was the extension of my imagination beyond the range of children's unconscious fantasies as described by Freud and Klein. For example, Winnicott was fascinated by children's response to gravity. He thought of gravity as posing a male quality to be mastered and a female quality of uniting with earth, whether in love or despair.

From early in his therapy Paddy worked at defying gravity by erecting great piles of wobbly furniture. He wanted to put a cushion on top and sit there. Winnicott thought that Paddy was aiming to recreate mother's lap, to climb up into her arms and resist being dumped on account of her depression. Paddy was asserting his determination to keep himself up even if mother let him down. He developed games of climbing round the room without touching the floor. These games were very exciting and here he illustrated Winnicott's thesis (1971a: 52) that playing is inherently exciting and precarious, not on account of instinctive arousal as Klein believed, but on account of the precariousness of the interplay in the child's mind between what is subjective and what is objectively perceived. Paddy was excited by managing the interplay between fantasies of falling and of flying and the reality of his limited powers to master gravity. And, when he mismanaged the interplay, he fell.

I now know that Winnicott's sensitivity to the effect on Paddy of his mother's depression was based on his own experience of a depressed mother (Phillips 1988). His personal mastery of this childhood experience has provided us with some of his most profound insights.

Paddy had yet to achieve the capacity for role-playing. This first began at the age of four and a half years when he called himself 'King of the Castle' and called me 'The dirty rascal'. From there he went on to role-play various admired daddy-figures: the coal man, postman, milkman and dustman. This make-believe led us into themes of Oedipal rivalry and jealousy. Later he risked reversing roles with me, for example saying, 'You be Paddy. I'm you. I go home to my daddy-man and you cry'. This was clearly a means of mastering his jealousy, but it was also the first step towards putting himself in another's shoes, a development which Winnicott later called 'inter-relating in terms of cross-identifications' (1971: 119); this represents the creative aspect of introjective and projective processes.

Paddy's capacity to verbalise his fantasies increased. When I told him of my coming summer holiday he clutched his genitals and told me that his willy was a baby camel with two humps which would feed him in the desert. This symbolism was meaningful to me but Paddy's distress about my holiday ensured that he used the symbolism in a literal way; he could not allow us playful space to think about it. A year later, rising six years old, he remembered this fantasy with much amusement and told me, 'I really believed my willy made milk! Now I pretend my willy makes me fly – but not *really*!' Paddy had now achieved both a sense of humour and a more mature capacity for playing, a capacity which Winnicott distinguished from the physical activity of play. Playing denotes the ability to distinguish reality from fantasy and past from present, while giving playful rein to a creative imagination which is neither delusional nor literal.

Today, the cognitive aspects of this development are being explored by researchers on the 'theory of mind'. Winnicott could have told them, what so far their research has ignored, that the capacity to think flexibly and imaginatively about thinking, to play with reality, depends upon a facilitating environment. In ordinary good-enough homes this capacity develops naturally enough. But in homes where the baby finds no mutuality, where the parent's face does not reflect the baby's experience and where the child's spontaneous gesture is not recognised or appreciated, neither trust in others nor confidence in the self develop and play is stunted. During his therapy Paddy had gained enough trust in me to play and had used his play and my reflection upon it to develop both a capacity for imagination and for self-reflection. He had also developed affectionate attachments, lost his symptoms and become able to prosper in a mainstream school. When therapy ended he was not free from problems but he was able to cope.

In the thirty-three years which have elapsed since then, children's toys and games have changed, but the way in which children use play to find and become a self remains as Winnicott described it. Winnicott was alone among psychoanalysts in recognizing that playing was at the root of our capacity for creative living and for the enjoyment of life. He expanded Freud's view that mental health is reflected by our capacity to love and to work. He saw that our mental health also depends upon the establishment of a transitional realm in which subjective and objective overlap and in which all playing, all culture and all religion belong. He recognised that our mental health depends upon our capacities to love, to work and to play.

Note

1 Originally published in *Journal of the British Association of Psychotherapists* 31(1) part 2 July 1996 pp20–27 and reprinted in Kahr, Brett (ed.) (1996) *The legacy of Winnicott: essays on infant and child mental health* London: Karnac Books.

12 Narcissistic illusions in late adolescence

Defensive Kleinian retreats or Winnicottian opportunities?[1]

This chapter describes the development and gradual dissolution of narcissistic illusions, characterised by idealisation, grandiosity and merger, in the psychotherapy of Roberta, an eighteen year old girl.

Two different traditions regarding the understanding and treatment of narcissism originated in London. Klein and her followers (e.g. Steiner 1993) have understood illusions of self-importance to be defensive retreats from acute ambivalence that require immediate, active interpretation. Winnicott (1952a, 1954) too accepted the defensive aspect of such illusions, but also believed that the regression to a transitional relationship to the therapist which they represented provided a developmental opportunity to 'unfreeze' previous developmental failures. This view, supported by Milner (1955) and Bollas (1987), leads to a more facilitating, less challenging, technical approach. Roberta's therapy was conducted according to the Winnicottian tradition and aims to illustrate its effectiveness.

Referral and background

Roberta was the second of three daughters born to parents who were national celebrities in the world of television. She sought help for depression and for a distressing feeling that she could never be satisfied. I found her to be a beautiful, vivacious adolescent of eighteen, fashionably and seductively dressed. Her account of herself was articulate and sensational and I was surprised to learn that she was training to be nothing more glamorous than a nurse.

Most of the details of Roberta's history emerged during the first year of her therapy. She wanted to achieve a coherent picture of a childhood fraught with conflicting experiences of adoration and rejection and of sexuality and violence.

Roberta had been her mother's favourite, a status which she had enjoyed because it protected her from the worst excesses of mother's violent rages, and which she had regretted because she had had to bear the brunt of mother's cloying need for admiration and caresses. Mother's impatience with her children and her need to pursue her glittering career meant that the children were cared for by a series of live-in nannies and were sent to boarding school from the age of 5 years. Father could be more nurturing than mother but he was very seldom available.

The parents' marriage was always stormy and sometimes violent. Roberta was allowed to sleep between them until she was six. She harboured the fantasy that they would divorce and each marry her. She grew up wanting sexual relationships with both her parents and was surprised to discover that not everybody did. However, she was sure that her main reason to sleep with them had been in order not to be forgotten, since, for both her parents, to be out of sight was to be out of mind.

When Roberta was fifteen her parents each revealed their possession of a lover and decided to get divorced. Roberta had come to believe that she was indispensable to her mother and she was outraged by her betrayal. She moved away to live with her father and his mistress in an extreme of vengeful hatred and vowed never to see her mother again, a vow which she had kept throughout the three years which had since elapsed.

The development of narcissistic illusions

Roberta entered therapy three times a week with excitement. She allowed herself immediately to regress and to experience herself as a small child alone with a perfectly empathic parent. She seemed destined to be an ideal patient. Her material was always presented clearly and helpfully. She accepted deep interpretations and thought between sessions about what I had said. It seemed natural to her to suppose that while I fed her on therapy she was providing me with a delectable meal. From what she told me, as a child, she had worked assiduously to be a devoted carer-giver to both her parents and her decision to become a nurse was an extension of this role. Within the therapeutic setting she clearly aimed to be my perfect daughter, to make me feel well loved as mother and brilliant as a therapist. She did this so successfully that I found myself reciprocating her idealisation. I could not help but find her 'special' and for a while our relationship resembled that between a doting parent and adoring child.

Roberta told me that she had always experienced her mother's kisses and touches as sexual. My words were soon experienced sexually by her too and she declared herself to be "in love". Her initial experience of therapy as mutual feeding became extended to experience it as "marriage" and any threats to its continuation as "divorce". Although she was afraid of being overwhelmed by her homosexual feelings for me and always kept them carefully controlled, she somehow used them to emphasise her love for me rather than to make me feel in danger of being seduced. I supported this intention. For example, when she reported a dream of caressing my breasts, I emphasised her need for maternal care, rather than her wish to excite me. Roberta expressed relief that, unlike her mother, I did not need to be excited. She claimed that when she was with me she felt safer than ever before.

It gradually emerged that Roberta's experience of safety with me was in part related to a grandiose illusion of unwarranted importance in my life. She was convinced that she was my only adult patient and that I could not possibly be married, otherwise I would not be able to give her such devoted attention. She basked in the certainty of our mutual love and assumed that I always felt exactly as she did. She also assumed that I always dressed with her in mind: clothes which she liked were selected to please her while other clothes were selected to stimulate her competitiveness. I later discovered that her grandiosity had reached the point of illusory merger with me when I stumbled across her unquestioned assumption that through therapy she was becoming a therapist; this preconscious conviction conflicted with her actual knowledge of the demands of training.

The start of Roberta's psychotherapy coincided with the start of a relationship with a new boyfriend, Tony, whom she later married. The most striking aspect of Tony's entry into Roberta's life was that I heard astonishingly little about him. Roberta did not believe that she could be special to both of us at once, just as it had seemed impossible to be special to both her parents together. She was convinced that, if she told me about Tony, I would be so overcome with envy and jealousy that I would destroy their relationship. Since I appeared not to mind, she thought I was either hiding my fury, or that I judged the relationship with Tony to be beneath contempt. She was unable to speak of her love for Tony for almost a year. Then I learned that she felt safe with him because he worshipped her and would always put her first in his life. It seemed that she felt that security was only possible through idealisation.

Technique

In the early stages of therapy I did not try to modify Roberta's idealisation of our relationship, as I relied upon time and the disappointments of the analytic relationship to begin this for me. However, I did not always accept her illusions entirely either, but adopted a slightly quizzical approach, intended to help Roberta realize that I did not necessarily take her assumptions for granted.

It seemed that Roberta had been waiting for exactly this opportunity. Winnicott (1954) described this situation when he wrote 'it is as if there is an expectation that favourable conditions may arise justifying regression and offering a new chance for forward development, that which was rendered impossible or difficult initially by environmental failure'. In the same paper he observed that in 'the return to early dependence . . . the patient and the setting merge into the original success situation of primary narcissism'. By this Winnicott meant that the patient returned to the period of development when the infant does not yet reliably distinguish between himself and the environment, that is, between himself and the mother. It became a striking feature of Roberta's therapy that in certain aspects of our relationship, particularly with regard to emotions, she failed to distinguish between us; she developed an illusion of sameness, even of merger, within the transference. Winnicott used the term "transitional" to describe the intermediate state between subjectivity and objectivity in which neither predominates. The illusion of merger could thus be understood as representing a self-created or transitional relationship to me as a subjective object (Winnicott 1969); surprisingly this co-existed with a more objective capacity to perceive me and my work, for at the same time she could show herself aware of some of my actual qualities and be able to make good use of interpretation. For example, she brought the subjective and objective strikingly together when I told her of the first holiday break. 'How can we possibly change from lovers to patient and therapist!' she tearfully exclaimed. At that moment she clearly expressed an awareness of both the illusion and the reality.

The benefits of allowing the development of illusion have been described by Milner (1955) in her account of the analysis of an eleven year-old boy. She describes the benefits of allowing him to use her as a transitional object. She felt that it was necessary for this boy both to experience and to become conscious of the need for fusion with her before he could relinquish this satisfaction and experience the relief of disillusion; this was a necessary therapeutic development because in his infancy he had experienced 'a too sudden breaking in on the illusion of oneness', so that he had had to adapt to the demands of external reality too soon. Her paper implies that it is technically important to allow the patient the unchallenged freedom to create the illusion of oneness, and not to press for acknowledgment of twoness until the patient shows signs of initiating this development himself. The reliable relief provided by the unchallenged illusion of oneness helps to make possible the subsequent toleration of twoness. As Winnicott (1952a: 221) wrote, 'disillusionment implies the successful provision of opportunities for illusion.'

Roberta's spontaneous recovery from one aspect of her illusion of oneness occurred early in the second year of therapy, when the repeated painful experiences of my holidays took its effect. She realized that I might not be single but probably had a family of my own. In the context of this development I felt able to become more active in challenging her illusions and exploring more of their role in her relationships, as the following sections illustrate.

Understanding the narcissistic illusions

Roberta's illusions can be understood paradoxically as having both defensive and developmental functions.

a) Narcissistic illusions as defensive attempts to evade anxiety and to achieve security

Exploration of the function of Roberta's narcissistic illusions revealed that they were both a way of protecting her from the anxieties inherent in two- and three-person relationships and her chief means of ensuring the security of her parents' love. By imagining herself to be in sole possession of my love, Roberta avoided all competition with rivals. By imagining that we were the same, she avoided all rivalry with me. Roberta was very aware of the intense sexual rivalry which she had experienced with her mother and her older sister, and she dreaded repeating it with me. The illusory transference successfully protected her from all the conflicts inherent in the three-person Oedipal situation. It was the anxieties belonging to two-person relationships that became the first focus of our work.

Roberta was easily made aware of how her illusory transference protected her from the anxieties which threatened to ruin her two-person relationships: "either too little or too much". By this Roberta meant the dread, on the one hand, of separation and rejection, and on the other, of exploitation and suffocation.

Roberta's terror of "too little" was extreme. She could not tolerate being alone. In daily life she contrived to prevent this eventuality arising, but when it did she played the radio loudly to fill the void. In her memory, her parents alternately indulged and banished her, treating her at one moment like a princess, and at the next, relegating her to the nursery. The experience of being sent to boarding school at the age of five had been a final confirmation of Roberta's equation of separation with rejection. My holidays repeatedly rearoused in her the desperate sense of being unwanted that she had suffered at boarding school.

It seemed that Roberta had been unable to achieve a normal degree of separation from her parents in childhood because the intense ambivalence which they aroused had prevented her from internalising representations of them as helpful people. She continued to depend for her sense of well-being on the physical availability of a caring adult. However, unlike her parents, I was in touch with her feelings, held her in mind, and gradually achieved with her a coherent picture of her history. As she felt understood and internalised by me, she began to internalise me herself. This meant that she was gradually able to relinquish the need to idealize and merge with me and was able to trust me with her hate. At first she risked hating me only for my absences, then for the inequality of our relationship, and, only when she had discovered that I survived her hatred without retaliation, did she allow herself the extremes of hatred with which therapy was to end.

Roberta's growing ability to internalise me helped to mitigate her fears of "too little". However, there was always a fine balance in the transference between the risks of "too little" and "too much". If I said anything to indicate that her therapy might continue beyond the two years which she had decided to undertake, she was liable to be overcome with a fit of choking. She felt suffocated by my imagined need for her. She compared the ordeal with me to the daily hour she used to spend watching her mother bath before dinner. At these times she felt trapped, exploited and compelled to meet her mother's needs for flattery, caresses and massage. She dared not leave for fear of her mother's fragility and for fear of her violence. It must always have felt dangerous to frustrate the narcissistic needs of a mother whose murderous hatred could break through into violence unless she were charmed into the illusion of mutual adoration on which she fed. Roberta had developed social skills of charm, tact and empathy which enabled her to play her parents' game, to pander to their narcissistic needs and to be rewarded by moments of exclusive intimacy. In therapy her illusory infatuation allowed her to enjoy this security with me when she needed it, while at other times she was available to do interpretative work on the dangers of feeling sufficiently separate from me to risk "too little or too much". Within eighteen months she became able to tolerate being alone at home and lost her symptom of choking in therapy.

The illusion of acquiring my skills as a therapist through merger was found to be a repetition of similar illusions which Roberta had developed with regard to both her parents. She had always thought of her mother as a sister and an equal and it came as a great shock to her to realize that she and I were of different generations. Likewise, she had previously believed that she had acquired her parents' most admired qualities simply through identification with them. It came as another shock to her to realize in therapy that she did not share their fame and status. It was Roberta's illusion that parental qualities could be acquired through merger which seemed to explain her life-long learning difficulties. She had supposed that she could acquire knowledge and success simply by being her parents' child. Consequently, in spite of high intelligence, she had failed to learn to read until the age of eleven years, and she had always done poorly at school. In therapy, Roberta realized with fury that she would have to work to obtain a degree before she could train as a therapist. She said she felt "damned" and "blown to bits". Clearly, her identification with me, as with her parents, had protected her from intense feelings of envy and deprivation.

Not only had Roberta harboured unconscious illusions about sharing her parents' achievements and fame, she had also developed a conscious illusion about possessing her father's penis. Since latency Roberta had been aware of feeling bisexual and had imagined that she could change her sex by changing her clothes. When dressed in slacks she felt male and visualized her father's penis as part of her own body. Then she felt free, confident, outspoken and sexually powerful in ways which matched her childhood picture of her father's vaunted sexuality.

It seemed that father had contributed to this illusion by regarding Roberta in some ways as his only son, named after himself. The illusion may also have developed as a defence against her father's extremely sensuous relationship with her. Even when she was a teenager they still regularly bathed together, "as chaps" father said.

When Roberta described her experience of intercourse her language conveyed that she experienced her lover's genitals as her own. Confrontation with this illusion led Roberta to abandon it. She lost the capacity to feel that she possessed her father's penis and she felt extremely angry with me for depriving her of it. This meant that she could no longer believe that Tony's penis was her own and she was sure that she would never enjoy sex so much again. But in spite of discovering intense penis envy, she gradually found that there were also rewards in making love as a woman.

At the end of her first year of therapy Roberta became aware of further aspects of the illusion of merger when for the first time she experienced Tony's kisses as coming from him and expressing his love. She then realized that she had previously experienced his kisses as if Tony were giving her own love back to her, just as during sex she had always felt she gave herself her own orgasm. This development followed work in the transference which had revealed that she experienced my love exclusively as a response to her own. She clearly had had no belief in the existence of her mother's spontaneous affection for her, but had always felt that she herself had had to initiate it. She once described her mother as a bottomless jug which she had had to fill up continuously in order to be sure that there would be just enough left inside for herself. By endlessly providing her mother with love in order to gain some for herself, she maintained the illusion of omnipotent control and evaded dependency while also eliciting her mother's love.

Throughout this period of work the needs of Roberta's parents for her collusion with their illusions was supported by numerous anecdotes. Both parents emerged as fragile people who depended upon their celebrity status for their self-esteem. Their ostentatious lifestyle featured in the media and they regarded themselves and their daughters as extremely special people. Roberta seems to have discovered that the only way of holding their benevolent attention was to share their illusions; there was security in unity, even if illusory.

In the course of therapy Roberta was surprised to discover that I did not need to be idealized and that I could reliably maintain contact with her through a range of moods. Envy, jealousy and hatred were particularly hard for her to share since she could not expect a parent-figure to tolerate the expression of such feelings towards themselves. Without the protection of mutual idealization Roberta lamented that she felt "abandoned" and "orphaned" in the transference and fearful that I would end her therapy. Such anxieties are usual when patients are threatened with the loss of familiar, though pathological, means of feeling safely in contact with parents. Attachment theory explains why it can feel so dangerous to relinquish such 'secondary security' (Main 1995) which developed in childhood because actual security with emotionally available parents was unavailable. For a small child loss of emotional contact with parents is felt to threaten survival. Roberta's dreams at this time were full of life-threatening disasters.

b) Narcissistic illusions with gratifying and developmental functions

When Winnicott (1954) wrote of the regressed patient's capacity to return to the original success situation of primary narcissism, he emphasised the gratification which derived from the patient's capacity to recapture the early satisfaction of feeling at one with the environment.

Roberta's great pleasure in her use of me certainly led me to believe that she must have found much satisfaction in her earliest relationship to her mother. She had apparently felt herself to be adored and had also had much physical satisfaction from cuddling and caresses.

Winnicott described how regression is used, not only to return to pregenital success situations, but also to return to developmental impasse which occurred because of environmental failure. Such failures can result in a "freezing of the failure situation" until a new environment gives hope that the original experience may be repeated "in an environment which is making adequate adaptation". I believe that Roberta used her regression with me in an attempt to deconstruct or "unfreeze" her paranoid, vengeful relationship to her mother. In the transference she re-entered the transitional relationship in order to enjoy for the first time, without the intrusion of her mother's demands for excitement and admiration, the close support which she had experienced only episodically in childhood. While she loyally repeated the mutual idealization which had been the only means she knew to maintain contact with both her parents, she was simultaneously excited by her awareness of my difference from her parents – by my reliability, my respect for honesty and my capacity to hold her in mind. She was able to use interpretation to feel deeply cared about and understood in a way that for a while at least, she experienced as genuinely ideal (Alvarez 1992).

When a patient uses a therapist as a transitional object it is interesting to know what sort of transitional object, if any, the patient had employed in infancy. Roberta had no knowledge of having used any special object in babyhood, but from very early in childhood she remembered 'being addicted to' her mother's empty scent bottle. She comforted herself by holding it to her nose. She had taken this uncuddly object with her to boarding school 'to keep the glamour alive'. Through its faint trace of smell, the scent bottle must have allowed Roberta to feel merged with her mother, which protected her from any awareness of the hatred associated with her mother's glamorous life through which she repeatedly abandoned and neglected her children. Instead of being able to pass through the transitional phase to establish a life which was increasingly independent of her mother, she had remained fixated on an idealized, glamorous, empty relationship. The therapeutic relationship provided her with a renewed opportunity to use dependence in order to move into independence.

Balint (1968) has made a valuable distinction between benign and malignant uses of regression in psychoanalysis. He considered a patient's use of regression to be benign when it was used for purposes of recognition; that is, for enabling the analyst to recognise and verbalise significant aspects of the patient's internal problems. This enabled the patient to make a 'new beginning' and to recover. However, a patient's use of regression was considered to be malignant when its prime aim was to seek gratification. Such use was, in general, associated with demands for gratification by external action, with the development of addiction-like states and with signs of severe hysteria.

There is no doubt that, in Balint's terms, Roberta's use of regression was predominantly benign. She used it not only for the recognition of internal conflicts but also for the recognition of certain 'self-states' (Bollas 1987) which her parents had apparently ignored or denied. In particular, she had no experience of sharing calm and peaceful states of mind, whether of satisfaction or of boredom. 'Togetherness' in her family had always been associated with intimacy, excitement, drama and violence. In particular, as therapy progressed, she liked to share with me an unintegrated state which she called 'feeling scattered'. This involved lying silent for long periods while she enjoyed feeling held and letting her mind wander. Typically the silence ended in the emergence of a memory, often of some childhood contact with her mother's body. Apart from discovering the benefits of allowing herself the freedom to feel scattered, Roberta also discovered that it was possible to feel fully alive in my presence without feeling excited. In her family, she claimed, being alive and being excited had always been synonymous. She found it a great relief to discover that this need not be so. In this way she supported Bollas' (1987) finding that 'regression to dependence allows a person to form important insights from within the self via fundamentally intra-subjective means'.

While Roberta used me as an ideal mother she experienced her relationship to her own estranged mother as increasingly persecuting; she felt herself to be continuously contaminated and tortured by her preoccupation with her. As Searles (1956) described, intense vengefulness can actually be a means of keeping a relationship alive. Slowly, Roberta began to mourn both for the loved aspects of her mother whom she had lost, and for what her mother had never been able to give her; she relinquished much of her vengeance. She became aware of wanting to see her mother again and a reconciliation took place. Roberta was pleased to discover that she could use her attachment to Tony to create and maintain a necessary distance from her mother, while remaining on friendly terms. In this and other ways to be described, Roberta successfully justified the optimism which her idealization had conveyed.

Further aspects of disillusionment: towards becoming a separate person

As therapy progressed into its second year, Roberta's need to feel merged with me lessened. She began to imagine me with a family and to notice more about me. These changes made me feel able to confront her more directly. For example, I questioned her assumption that I always felt the same as she did. Roberta agreed that I might not do so, but was panic-stricken to realise that she actually did not know what I felt. A few sessions later she had reverted to the comfort of her earlier assumption.

None of her illusions was surrendered easily. Each one was reinstated and had to be confronted again and again. Each confrontation led Roberta to express hatred towards me for humiliating her and to renewed attempts to create idealization by other means. When she failed to produce the tranquillising security of mutual idealisation, then Roberta resorted to the drama and excitement associated with disaster or violence. She was aware that such excitement provided a "fix" and was better than the boredom and frustration associated with disillusionment. She began to assault Tony and to bring me sensational accounts of her cruelty to him. I understood this as an attempt both to excite me into violence towards her, and to expose me to her own childhood experience of being the passive witness of terrifying scenes of violence. Roberta was horrified to discover her sadism but experienced her destructiveness as her most authentic emotion.

Disillusionment was not only furthered by confrontation through interpretation. There were many other ways in which Roberta's illusions were shattered.

My holidays have already been mentioned. In anticipation of each holiday Roberta was tearful and worried how she would cope, feeling as though once again she was being forced to live a separate existence at boarding school. During my absence she suffered from fears and nightmares, particularly of my death. On my return she experienced acute ambivalence, which often left her trembling. She was simultaneously delighted to be back, reassured by physical contact with the couch, bitterly tearful, longing to punch me and furious that it was necessary to tell me what had happened in my absence because I did not know. Her responses to reunion provide a classic example of the 'anxious ambivalent' type of attachment, observed by Ainsworth (1983) in infants as young as twelve months of age. Such infants had had highly inconsistent mothering. Subsequently Main and Hesse (1990) have shown that when an infant's experience of mothering has been not only very inconsistent but also frightening, the infant at twelve months shows features of extreme disorganisation under stress. As development proceeds, the child is liable to react by becoming controlling of the parent, either in a care-giving or in a coercive, punitive way. Roberta had mastered both these techniques. The tender care-giving of her early response to me was supplemented by coercive threats to punish and abandon me during the last year of her therapy. Main's find-ings suggest that it was an underlying terror of disorganisation or disintegration which maintained Roberta's pursuit of intimacy.

Apart from my holidays which temporarily forced Roberta to become fully aware of my separate existence, Roberta was also very disillusioned by having flu and discovering that I did not come to nurse her. On another occasion she was shocked to realise that I must have colleagues who might be more important to me than she. But the deepest blow to Roberta's narcissism was experienced in the second year of therapy when I refused to come to her wedding.

The prospect of marriage had been used by her in therapy as an alternative exclusive relationship and an ever-ready means of escape, since Tony opposed her treatment. Roberta was adamant that I should come to the wedding cer-emony to give her emotional support. She found it utterly unbelievable that I should refuse to attend this high society event which she had intended to "enrich and enliven my life". When at last it was clear that I would not move from my professional role, she lamented tearfully that she would never be able to feel loved by me again.

Roberta planned all the details of her wedding herself. While listening to her elaborate plans I told her that I felt like an onlooker of a game of "Let's pretend". This made her shocked to realize that the wedding was actually going to hap-pen. She recognised that her plans felt exactly like the dolls-house games about an ideal family which she had played with her sisters in childhood. It seemed likely that Roberta had kept alive her capacity to enjoy transitional experiences in her play with her sisters to whom she had felt very close in her parents' many absences. When arranging the wedding Roberta tried once again to make her imaginary world triumph over the vagaries of her family, and she was repeatedly disillusioned when they would not play the parts which she allotted to them. The disadvantages of illusion became painfully clear to her.

After her honeymoon Roberta constantly lamented that she had become "noth-ing but a patient" and could not be "my daughter" any more. Her hatred and anger towards me increased steadily during the last fifteen months of treatment. She had finally realized that the overall effect of therapy was to make her feel increasingly ordinary, when she had intended that it would make her feel increasingly special. She was appalled that I had appeared to offer her both a psychotherapy training and an exclusive intimate relationship, but instead had relegated her to the mere rank of patient. She suspected that I took pleasure in destroying her grandios-ity, and felt that I would rejoice to hear that she was overcome with humiliation when she realized for the first time, on boarding a bus, that she was as ordinary as everyone else on board. She also finally realized that I did not dress for her and accepted that I did not necessarily feel the same as she did about everything she told me. These disillusionments made her feel that "all the shine" had gone out of our relationship and that I had made her feel perpetually "scratchy and itchy". These adjectives suggested that we were now experienced as separate but still touching, in a hostile way.

Now that Roberta was convinced that I had lured her into therapy on false pretences, she assumed that after seducing her I would abandon her as her mother had done. If we were entirely separate then rejection must surely follow. She threatened to leave first, but then resorted to another ploy in her attempt to re-establish the illusion of intimacy to which she was still partly addicted. She took a job which necessitated appointments after work. It emerged that she was sure that I would meet this need by seeing her in my home where she felt sure I must have a consulting room. A dream revealed that she intended moving into my bed, just as she had done between her parents. However in order to meet her demands for new times I reduced her sessions temporarily to twice a week. Roberta threatened to terminate immediately, but she reluctantly decided to continue for another six months. Although so furious, she felt terrified of managing without me.

Throughout the remaining period of therapy Roberta recurrently insisted that she was leaving me because I would not see her in my home; it was clearly up to me to accommodate her if I wanted to keep her. Although Roberta's demands for intimacy within the transference had seemed like the need of a deprived child for a period of indulgence, Roberta's demands for the intimacy of my home became a most intrusive imposition and an example of the malignant use of regression that Balint described. Roberta herself recognised these demands as a sign of her own intrusiveness, insatiability, and addiction to exclusive relationships. Perhaps they can also be seen as her means of stage-managing her move to freedom by giving herself sufficient reason to hate me.

After she found that I would not see her in my home, Roberta made no further attempts to re-establish her narcissistic illusions. She was surprised to discover that it was possible to sustain moments of what she called "authentic intimacy" in which she experienced close rapport while yet acknowledging herself to be a patient among other patients. However, such moments were rare, for her anger with me predominated. Termination was experienced as a mutual rejection and as a sign of our mutual hatred. She accused me of having seduced her and masturbated her but never having loved her. Leaving was a way of protecting me from her murderous hatred, but also a way of depriving me of the satisfaction of having a long-term patient. She experienced her termination as abortion and knew that she wished to destroy my work and to triumph over me. At last her sexual rivalry was flagrantly displayed.

The positive function of this phase of destructive attack on the analyst has been described by Winnicott (1969). He believed that it was the patient's destructiveness, combined with the analyst's capacity to survive it, which enabled the patient to relinquish the analyst as a transitional object and to use him constructively as a separate person in shared reality. The changes which she made do indicate that she had achieved this.

In spite of her hatred, destructiveness and despair, Roberta continued to retain a positive picture of what had been achieved. She had believed it to be impossible to feel both happy and ordinary, but now, both in her marriage and at work, she found that this was so. She became able to tolerate being separate from Tony, was much less dominating towards him and sometimes allowed him to take control in intercourse. More important, she had lost her perpetual sense of dissatisfaction. This, as she said, was nothing to do with sexual fulfilment, but with the capacity to be separate, to tolerate being alone and to feel free from the pressure to create idealised relationships. The depression, which had dogged her whenever idealisation failed, had gone. In spite of all her fury and disappointment, I was surprised to find that Roberta continued to feel grateful for what I had helped her to achieve.

Roberta opened her last session with a gift of flowers and ended it with a wish to vomit to ruin my room for other patients. Her farewell openly displayed the intense ambivalence from which her narcissism had protected her. She had relinquished her initial need of me as a transitional object and had allowed a genuine encounter which had enabled her to recognise and accept her separate existence, to sustain it outside the context of our immediate relationship and so to achieve the possibility of feeling satisfied.

Conclusion

The course of Roberta's treatment bears out the belief of both Kleinians and Winnicottians that narcissistic illusions serve as a defence against ambivalence; as Roberta's illusions diminished so her ambivalence in the transference increased. Naturally, it is impossible to know whether a Kleinian technique, involving immediate interpretation of the narcissistic transference, would have been therapeutically more effective. I have simply aimed to illustrate the value of Winnicott's approach. It seems to have been important to allow the narcissistic transference to flourish long enough to begin its own spontaneous dissolution since this approach provided time in which to explore the source of the transference in family relationships and to utilize its optimism to revitalize development. Immediate interpretation of its defensive aspects would have spared Roberta the repetition of the experience of seduction at the cost of failing to understand her apparent initial seduction by her parents and the role which her attachment to them as internal representations still played in perpetuating the need for her illusions. Perhaps Roberta's impressive capacity to use therapy may also have been in part a repetition: the repetition of relationships with certain nannies whom Roberta at first discounted (as her parents had done) but whom she acknowledged had enabled her to recognise some of her parents' failings and had shown a respect for reality which her parents appear to have lacked.

Acknowledgement

I am much indebted to Christopher Bollas for his illuminating supervision of my work with Roberta.

Note

1 Published in *Psychoanalytic Inquiry* 19: 229–242 (1999) and as chapter 10 in M Lany-ado & A Horne (2006) *A Question of Technique: Independent Psychoanalytic Approaches with Children and Adolescents* Hove & New York: Routledge.

References

Ainsworth, M.D.S. et al. (1971) Individual differences in strange situation behaviour of one-year-olds. In H.R. Schaffer (ed.), *The Origins of Human Social Relations*. London: Academic Press.

Ainsworth, M.D.S. et al. (1974) Infant-mother attachment and social development. In M.P.M. Richards (ed.), *The Integration of a Child Into a Social World* (pp. 99–135). Cambridge: Cambridge University Press.

Ainsworth, M.D.S., Blehar, M.C., Waters, E. & Wall, S. (1978) *Patterns of Attachment: A Psychological Study of the Strange Situation*. Hillsdale, NJ: Lawrence Erlbaum Associates.

Ainsworth, M.D.S. (1982) Attachment: retrospect and prospect. Chapter 1 in C.M. Parkes & J. Stevenson-Hinde (eds), *The Place of Attachment in Human Behaviour*. London: Tavistock Publications.

Ainsworth, M. (1983) Patterns of infant-mother attachment as related to maternal care. In D. Magnusson & V. Allen (eds), *Human Development: An Interactional Perspective* (pp. 35–55). New York: Academic Press.

Ainsworth, M.D.S. (1985) Patterns of infant-mother attachment: antecedents and effects on development. *Bulletin of New York Academy of Medicine* 61: 771–791.

Alvarez A. (1992) *Live Company. Psychoanalytic Psychotherapy With Autistic, Borderline, Deprived and Abused Children*. London: Routledge.

Bain, A. & Barnett, L. (1980) *The design of a day care system in a nursery setting for children under five* (Tavistock Institute Occasional Paper No. 8). London: Tavistock Institute of Human Relations.

Balint, E. (1993) *Before I Was I. Psychoanalysis and the Imagination*. London: Free Association Books.

Balint, M. (1959) *Thrills and Regressions*. London: Hogarth Press.

Balint, M. (1968) *The Basic Fault: Therapeutic Aspects of Regression*. London: Tavistock.

Balint, M. (1969) Trauma and object relationship. *International Journal of Psychoanalysis* 50: 429–435.

Baradon, T., Broughton, C., Gibbs, I., James, J., Joyce, A., & Woodhead, J. (2005) *The Practice of Psychoanalytical Parent-Infant Psychotherapy: Claiming the Baby*. New York: Routledge.

Barrows, P. (2003) Change in parent-infant psychotherapy. *Journal of Child Psychotherapy* 29(3): 283–301.

Barrows, P. (ed.). (2004) *Key Papers From the Journal of Child Psychotherapy*. Hove: Routledge.

Beebe, B. & Lachman, F.M. (2002) *Infant Research and Adult Treatment. Co-constructing Interactions.* Hillsdale, NJ: Analytic Press.

Bick, E. (1964) Notes on infant observation in psychoanalytic training. *International Journal of Psychoanalysis* 45: 558–566.

Bick, E. (1969) The experience of skin in early object relations. *International Journal of Psychoanalysis* 49: 484–486.

Bion, W.R. (1962) *Learning From Experience.* London: Heinemann.

Biringen, Z., Emde, R.N. & Pipp-Siegel, S. (1997) Dyssynchrony, conflict and resolution: positive contributions to infant development. *American Journal of Orthopsychiatry* 67 (1): 4–19.

Bollas, C. (1987) *The Shadow of the Object: Psychoanalysis of the Unthought Known.* London: Free Association Books.

Boston, M. & Szur, R. (eds) (1983) *Psychotherapy With Severely Deprived Children.* London: Routledge & Kegan Paul.

Bowlby, J. (1951) *Maternal care and mental health.* World Health Organization Monograph.

Bowlby, J. (1958) The nature of the child's tie to his mother. *International Journal of Psycho-Analysis* 41: 89–113.

Bowlby, J. (1982) *Attachment and Loss, Vol. 1: Attachment.* London: Hogarth Press. (Original work published 1969)

Bowlby, J. (1973) *Attachment and Loss, Vol. 2: Separation.* London: Hogarth Press.

Bowlby, J. (1979) On knowing what you are not supposed to know and feeling what you are not supposed to feel. *Canadian Journal of Psychiatry* 24: 403–408. (Reprinted as Chapter 6 in *A Secure Base: Clinical Applications of Attachment Theory*, 1988, London: Routledge)

Bowlby, J. (1980) *Attachment and Loss, Vol. 3: Loss, Sadness and Depression.* London: Hogarth Press.

Bowlby, J. (1985) The role of childhood experience in cognitive disturbance. Chapter 6 in M.J. Mahoney & A. Freeman (eds), *Cognition and Psychotherapy.* New York: Plenum.

Bowlby, J. (1988) *A Secure Base: Clinical Applications of Attachment Theory.* London: Routledge.

Bowlby, J., Figlio, K. & Young, R.M. (1986) An interview with John Bowlby on the origins and reception of his work. *Free Associations* 1: 36–64.

Brazelton, T.B. (1985) Application of cry research for clinical perspectives. In B.M. Lester & C.F.Z. Boukydis (eds), *Infant Crying.* New York: Plenum.

Bretherton, J. (1987) New perspectives in attachment relations. In J. Osofsky (ed.), *Handbook of Infant Development* (2nd ed.). New York: Wiley.

Byng-Hall, J. (1995) *Rewriting Family Scripts: Improvisation and Systems Change.* New York: Guilford Press.

Byng-Hall, J. & Stevenson-Hinde, J. (1991) Attachment relationships within a family system. *Infant Mental Health Journal* 12: 187–200.

Canham, H. (1999) The development of the concept of time in fostered and adopted children. *Psychoanalytic Inquiry* 19: 160–171.

Coser, R.L. (1963) Alienation and the social structure: case analysis of a hospital. In E. Freidson (ed.), *The Hospital in Modern Society* (pp. 231–262). New York: Free Press.

Cramer, B. & Stern, D. (1988) Evaluation of changes in mother-infant brief psychotherapy. *Infant Mental Health Journal* 9: 20–45.

Cramer, B., Stern, D. et al. (1990) Outcome evaluation in brief mother-infant psychotherapy: a preliminary report. *Infant Mental Health Journal* 11: 278–300.

Daws, D. (1989) *Through the Night: Helping Parents and Sleepless Infants.* London: Free Association Books.

Delozier, P. (1982) Attachment theory and abuse. In C.M. Parkes et al. (eds), *The Place of Attachment in Human Behaviour* (pp. 95–117). London: Basic Books.

Demos, V. (1986) Crying in early infancy. In T.B. Brazelton & M.W. Yogman (eds), *Affective Development in Infancy*. Norwood, NJ: Ablex.

Dickes, R. (1978) Parents, transitional objects and childhood fetishes. In A. Grolnick & L. Barkin (eds), *Between Reality and Fantasy* (pp. 307–319), New York: Jason Aronson.

Dunn, J. (1984) *Sisters and Brothers*. London: Fontana.

Emanuel, R. (1984) Primary disappointment. *Journal of Child Psychotherapy* 10: 71–88.

Emde, R. (1988) Reflections on mothering and on re-experiencing the early relationship experiences. *Infant Mental Health Journal* 9: 1–9.

Fairbairn, W.R.D. (1952) *An Object Relations Theory of the Personality*. New York: Basic Books.

Fonagy, P. (2001) *Attachment Theory and Psychoanalysis*. New York: Other Press.

Forsyth, B.W.C. & Canny, P. (1991) Perceptions of vulnerability 3 1/2 years after problems of feeding and crying behaviour in early infants. *Journal of Pediatrics* 88: 757–763.

Fraiberg, S. (1980) *Clinical Studies in Infant Mental Health: The First Year of Life*. London: Tavistock.

Fraiberg, S. (1982) Pathological defences in infancy. *Psychoanalytic Quarterly* 51: 612–635.

Fraiberg, S., Adelson E. & Shapiro, V. (1975) Ghosts in the nursery: a psychoanalytic approach to impaired infant-mother relationships. In S. Fraiberg (ed.), *Clinical Studies in Infant Mental Health* (1980, pp. 164–196). London: Tavistock.

Freud, A. (1936) *The Ego and the Mechanisms of Defence*. London: Hogarth Press.

Freud, A. (1952) The role of bodily illness in the mental life of children. *Psychoanalytic Study of the Child* 7: 69–81.

Freud, A. (1965) Normality and pathology in childhood: assessments of development. *The Writings of Anna Freud*, Vol. 6. New York: International Universities Press.

Freud, A. (1967) Comments on trauma. In S. Furst (ed.), *Psychic Trauma*. New York: Basic Books.

Freud, A. (1974) *Infants without families*. London: Hogarth Press.

Freud, S. (1909) Analysis of a phobia in a five-year-old boy. *SE* 10: 122. London: Hogarth Press.

Freud, S. (1915a) Thoughts for the time on war and death. *SE* 14: 275–302. London: Hogarth Press.

Freud, S. (1915b) Some character types met with in psychoanalytic work. *SE* 14: 311–333. London: Hogarth Press.

Freud, S (1915c) Observations on transference-love. *SE* 12: 159–171. London: Hogarth Press.

Freud, S. (1920) Beyond the pleasure principle. *SE* 18. London: Hogarth Press.

Freud, S. (1924) The economic problem of masochism. *SE* 19. London: Hogarth Press.

Freud, S. (1926) Inhibitions, symptoms and anxiety. *SE* 20. London: Hogarth Press.

Freud, S. (1937) Constructions in analysis. *SE* 23, London: Hogarth Press

Freud, S. (1938a) An outline of psychoanalysis. *SE* 23: 144–207. Hogarth Press.

Freud, S. (1938b) Splitting of the ego in the process of defence. *SE* 23: 275–278. London: Hogarth Press.

Glenn, J. (1984) Psychic trauma and masochism. *Journal of American Psychoanalytical Association* 32: 2.

Greenacre, P. (1953a) *Trauma, growth and personality*. London: Hogarth.

Greenacre, P. (1953b) Certain relationships between fetishism and the faulty development of the body image. *Psychoanalytic Study of the Child* 8: 79–98.

Greenacre, P. (1968) Perversions. General considerations regarding their genetic and dynamic background. *Psychoanalytic Study of the Child* 23: 47–62.

Greenacre, P. (1979) Fetishism. In I. Rosen (ed.), *Sexual Deviation* (2nd ed., pp. 79–108). Oxford: Oxford University Press.

Hamilton, V. (1982) *Narcissus and Oedipus. The Children of Psychoanalysis*. London: Routledge and Kegan Paul.

Hamilton, V. (1985) John Bowlby: an ethological basis for psychoanalysis. In J. Reppen (ed.), *Beyond Freud: A Study of Modern Psychoanalytic Theorists* (pp. 1–28). New York: Analytic Press.

Hamilton, V. (1987) Some problems in the clinical application of attachment theory. *Psychoanalytic Psychotherapy* 3: 67–83.

Heimann, P. (1950) On counter-transference. *International Journal of Psychoanalysis* 31.

Hesse, E. & Main, M. (1999) Second generation effects of unresolved trauma in non-maltreating parents: dissociated, frightening and threatening parental behaviour. *Psychoanalytic Inquiry* 19: 481–540.

Hopkins, J. (1969) Children in hospital. *Far Eastern Medical Journal* 5: 279–284.

Hopkins, J. (1977) Living under the threat of death. The impact of a congenital illness on an eight-year-old boy. *Journal of Child Psychotherapy* 4: 5–24.

Hopkins, J. (1984) The probable role of trauma in a case of foot and shoe fetishism: aspects of the psychotherapy of a six-year-old girl. *International Review of Psychoanalysis* 11: 79–91.

Hopkins. J. (1986) Solving the mystery of monsters: steps towards the recovery from trauma. *Journal of Child Psychotherapy* 13: 61–72.

Hopkins, J. (1989) Ways of seeing 4. *Journal of Child Psychotherapy* 15: 33–39.

Hopkins, J. (1992) Infant-parent psychotherapy. *Journal of Child Psychotherapy* 18: 5–18.

Hopkins, J. (1998) *Introduction: academic and professional context* (Unpublished paper accompanying doctoral submission). UEL/Tavistock.

Hopkins, J. (2010, October) *Dual heritage in 50 years of work as a child psychotherapist.* Unpublished talk given at a memorial conference for Dr Brian Lake, 'Is attachment theory attached to psychoanalysis?' Leeds, UK.

Hurry, A. (ed.). (1998) *Psychoanalysis and Developmental Therapy.* Psychoanalytic Monographs No. 3. London: Karnac Books.

Hurry, A. & Sandler, J. (1971) Coping with reality: the child's defences against the external world. *British Journal of Medical Psychology* 44: 379.

Jacobson, E. (1959) The exceptions. *Psychoanalytic Study of the Child* 14: 135–154.

Katan, A. (1973) Children who were raped. *Psychoanalytic Study of the Child* 28: 208–224.

Kennedy, H. (1972) Problems in reconstruction in child analysis. *Psychoanalytic Study of the Child* 26: 386–402.

Khan, M.M.R. (1972) Exorcism of intrusive ego-alien factors in the analytic situation and process. In *The Privacy of the Self* (1974, pp. 280–293). London: Hogarth Press.

Lachmann, F.M. & Beebe, B. (1989) Oneness fantasies revisited. *Psychoanalytic Psychology* 6: 137–149.

Lieberman, A.F. & Zeanah, C.H. (1999) Contributions of attachment theory to infant-parent psychotherapy. In J. Cassidy & P.R. Shaver (eds), *Handbook of Attachment: Theory, Research and Clinical Applications* (pp. 555–574). New York: Guilford Press.

Lussier, A. (1960) The analysis of a boy with a congenital deformity. *Psychoanalytic Study of the Child* 15: 430–453.

Lyons-Ruth, K. & Jacobovitz, D. (1999) Attachment disorganisation: unresolved loss, relational violence and lapses in behavioral and attentional strategies. In J. Cassidy & P.R. Shaver (eds), *Handbook of Attachment*. New York: Guilford Press.

Lyons-Ruth, K., Bronfman, E. & Atwood, G. (2000) A relational diathesis model of hostile-helpless states of mind. In J. Solomon & C. George (eds), *Attachment Disorganisation*. New York: Guilford Press.

Lyons-Ruth, K. (2003) Attachment research and dissociation. *Journal of the American Psychoanalytic Association* 51(3).

Main, M. (1977) Analysis of a peculiar form of reunion behaviour seen in some day care children: its history and sequelae in children who are home-reared. Chapter 2 in R.A. Webb (ed.), *Social Development in Childhood: Day-Care Programs and Research*. Baltimore: Johns Hopkins University Press.

Main, M. (1990) Parental aversion to physical contact with the infant: stability, consequences and reasons. In T.B. Brazelton & K. Barnard (eds), *Touch*. New York: International Universities Press.

Main, M. (1995) Recent studies in attachment: overview with selected implication for clinical work. In S. Goldberg, R. Muir & J. Kerr (eds), *Attachment Theory: Social, Developmental and Clinical Perspectives*. Hillsdale, NJ: Analytic Press.

Main, M., Kaplan, N. & Cassidy, J. (1985) Security in infancy, childhood and adulthood: a move to the level of representation. In I. Bretherton & E. Waters (eds), *Growing Points of Attachment Theory and Research* (Monograph 50 of the Society for Research in Child Development, pp. 66–104). Chicago: University of Chicago Press.

Main, M. & Stadtman, J. (1981) Infant response to rejection of physical contact by mother: aggression, avoidance and conflict. *Journal of American Academy of Child Psychiatry* 20: 292–307.

Main, M. & Weston, D. (1981) The quality of toddlers' relationship to mother and to father. *Child Development* 52: 932–940.

Main, M. & Weston, D. (1982) Avoidance of the attachment figure in infancy: descriptions and interpretations. Chapter 2 in C.M. Parkes & J. Stevenson-Hinde (eds), *The Place of Attachment in Human Behaviour*. London: Tavistock.

Main, M. & Goldwyn, R. (1986) Predicting rejection of her infant from mother's representation of her own experiences. *International Journal of Child Abuse and Neglect* 8: 203–217.

Main, M. & Solomon, J. (1986) Discovery of an insecure-disorganised/disoriented attachment pattern. Chapter 6 in T.B. Brazelton & H. Yogman (eds), *Affective Development in Infancy*. Norwood, NJ: Ablex.

Main, M. & Cassidy, J. (1988) Categories of response to reunion with the parent at age six. *Developmental Psychology* 24: 415–426.

Main, M. & Hesse, E. (1990) Parents' unresolved traumatic experiences are related to infant disorganised attachment status: is frightened and/or frightening parental behaviour the linking mechanism? In M.T. Greenberg, D. Cicchetti & E.M. Cummings (eds), *Attachment in the Preschool Years* (pp. 161–182). Chicago: University of Chicago Press.

Marshall, T. (1982) Infant care: a day nursery under the microscope. *Social Work Service* 32: 15–32.

McGuire, J. & Richman, N. (1986) The prevalence of behavioural problems in three types of preschool group. *Journal of Child Psychology and Psychiatry* 27: 455–472.

McKenna, J. (1986) An anthropological perspective on the sudden infant death syndrome. *Journal of Medical Anthropology* 10(1): 9–92.

Menzies, I.E.P. (1960) A case-study in the functioning of social systems as a defence against anxiety. *Human Relations* 13: 95–121 and Pamphlet No. 3. London: Tavistock Institute of Human Relations.

Menzies Lyth, I. (1959) The functioning of social systems as a defense against anxiety. In I. Menzies Lyth (ed.) (1988), *Containing Anxiety in Institutions: Selected Essays Vol. 1*. London: Free Association Books.

Menzies Lyth, I. (1982) *The psychological welfare of children making long stays in hospital: an experience in the art of the possible* (Tavistock Institute Occasional Paper No. 3). London: Tavistock Institute of Human Relations.

Miller, L. (1992) The relation of infant observation to clinical practice in an under fives counselling service. *Journal of Child Psychotherapy* 18: 19–32.

Milner, M. (1952) Aspects of symbolism in the comprehension of the not-self. *International Journal of Psychoanalysis* 33: 181–195.

Milner, M. (1955) The role of illusion in symbol formation. Chapter 5 in M. Klein et al. (eds), *New Directions in Psycho-analysis*. London: Tavistock.

Murray, L. (1991) Intersubjectivity, object relations theory and empirical evidence from mother-infant interactions. *Infant Mental Health Journal* 12: 219–232.

Perry, B.D., Pollard, R.A., Blakeley, T.L., Baker, W.L. & Vigilante, D. (1995) Childhood trauma, the neurobiology of adaptation and 'use-dependent' development of the brain: how 'states' become 'traits'. *Infant Mental Health Journal* 16: 271–291.

Phillips, A. (1988) *Winnicott* (Fontana Modern Masters). London: Fontana Press.

Phillipson, H. & Hopkins, J. (1964) Personality and perception. *British Journal of Medical Psychology* 37: 1–15.

Prior, J. & Glaser, D. (2006) *Understanding Attachment and Attachment Disorders* (Child and Adult Mental Health Series). London: Jessica Kingsley.

Provence, S. & Lipton, R.C. (1962) *Infant in Institutions*. New York: International Universities Press.

Raphael-Leff, J. (1991) *Psychological Processes of Childbearing*. London: Chapman and Hall.

Renvoize, J. (1982) *Incest. A Family Pattern*. London: Routledge & Kegan Paul.

Rodrigue, E. (1968) Severe bodily illness in childhood. *International Journal of Psychoanalysis* 49: 290–293.

Roland, A. (1988) *In Search of Self in India and Japan: Toward a Cross-Cultural Psychology*. Princeton, NJ: Princeton University Press.

Rosen, V.H. (1955) The reconstruction of a traumatic childhood event in a case of derealization. *Journal of American Psychoanalytical Association* 3: 211–221.

Rosenfeld, S. (1975) Some reflections arising from the treatment of a traumatised child. In *Hampstead Clinic Studies in Child Psychoanalysis* (20th Anniversary Proceedings, pp. 47–63). New Haven, CT: Yale University Press.

Sameroff, A.J. & Emde, R.N. (eds) (1989) *Relationship Disturbances in Early Childhood: A Developmental Approach*. New York: Basic Books.

Sandler, J. (1959) The background of safety. In *From Safety to Superego* (1987). London: Karnac Books.

Sander, L. (1977) The regulation of exchange in the infant-caretaker system and some aspects of the context-content relationship. In M. Lewis and L. Rosenblum (eds), *Interaction, Conversation and the Development of Language*. New York: Wiley.

Searles, H (1956) The psychodynamics of vengefulness. In *Collected Papers on Schizophrenia and Related Subjects* (pp. 171–191). New York: International Universities Press.

Senn, M. (2007) John Bowlby interview with Milton Senn MD in October 1977. *Beyond the Couch: The Online Journal of the American Association for Psychoanalysis in Clinical Social Work* 2.

Sroufe, L.A. (1983) Infant caregiver attachment and problems of adaptation in preschool: the roots of maladaptation and competence. In M. Perlmutter (ed.), *Minnesota Symposia in Child Psychology* (Vol. 16, pp. 41–83). Hillsdale, NJ: Erlbaum.

Steiner, J. (1993) *Psychic Retreats* (The New Library of Psychoanalysis 19). London: Routledge.

Stern, D. (1985) *The Interpersonal World of the Infant: A View from Psychoanalysis and Developmental Psychology*. New York: Basic Books.

Stern, D. (1995) *The Motherhood Constellation: A Unified View of Parent-Infant Psychotherapy*. New York: Basic Books.

St James-Roberts, I. (1991) Persistent infant crying. *Archives of Disease in Childhood* 66: 653–655.

Stoller, R.J. (1975) *Perversion. The Erotic Form of Hatred*. New York: Delta.

Stroh, G. (1974) Psychotic children. In P. Barker (ed.), *The Residential Psychiatric Treatment of Children* (pp. 175–190). London: Crosby.

Tizard, J. & Tizard, B. (1971) The social development of two-year-old children in residential nurseries. In H.R. Schaffer (ed.), *The Origins of Human Social Relations*. London: Academic Press.

Tonnesmann, M. (1980) Adolescent re-enactment, trauma and reconstruction. *Journal of Child Psychotherapy* 6: 23–44.

Tronick, E., Cohn, J.F. & Shea, E. (1986) The transfer of affect between mothers and infants. In T.B. Brazelton & M.W. Yogman (eds), *Affective Development in Infancy*. Norwood, NJ: Ablex.

Tustin, F. (1972) *Autism and Childhood Psychosis*. London: Hogarth Press.

Tustin, F. (1986) *Autistic Barriers in Neurotic Patients*. London: Karnac Books.

Winnicott, D.W. (1941) Observations of infants in a set situation. In *Collected Papers. Through Paediatrics to Psychoanalysis* (1958). London: Tavistock.

Winnicott, D.W. (1952) Anxiety associated with insecurity. In *Collected Papers: Through Paediatrics to Psychoanalysis* (1958). London: Tavistock.

Winnicott, D.W. (1952a) Psychoses and childcare. In *Collected Papers: Through Paediatrics to Psychoanalysis* (1958). London: Tavistock.

Winnicott, D.W. (1954) Metapsychological and clinical aspects of regression within the psychoanalytic set-up. In *Collected Papers: Through Paediatrics to Psychoanalysis* (1958). London: Tavistock.

Winnicott, D.W. (1956) Primary maternal preoccupation. In *Collected Papers: Through Paediatrics to Psychoanalysis* (1958). London: Tavistock.

Winnicott, D.W. (1957) On the contribution of direct child observation to psychoanalysis. In *The Maturational Processes and the Facilitating Environment* (1965). London: Hogarth Press.

Winnicott, D.W. (1958) *Collected Papers: Through Paediatrics to Psychoanalysis*. London: Tavistock.

Winnicott, D.W. (1960a) The theory of the parent-infant relationship. In *The Maturational Processes and the Facilitating Environment* (1965). London: Hogarth Press.

Winnicott, D.W. (1960b) Ego distortion in terms of true and false self. In *The Maturational Processes and the Facilitating Environment* (1965). London: Hogarth Press.

Winnicott, D.W. (1963a) Psychiatric disorder in terms of infantile maturational processes. In *The Maturational Processes and the Facilitating Environment* (1965). London: Hogarth Press.

Winnicott, D.W. (1963b) From dependence towards independence in the development of the individual. In *The Maturational Processes and the Facilitating Environment* (1965). London: Hogarth Press.

Winnicott, D.W. (1963c) The development of the capacity for concern. In D.W. Winnicott, *The Maturational Processes and the Facilitating Environment* (1965). London: Hogarth Press.

Winnicott, D.W. (1964) *The Child, the Family and the Outside World*. London: Penguin Books.

Winnicott, D.W. (1965) *The Maturational Processes and the Facilitating Environment.* London: Hogarth Press.

Winnicott, D.W. (1967a) DWW on DWW. In C. Winnicott, R. Shepherd & M. Davis (eds), *Psychoanalytic Explorations* (1989). London: Karnac Books.

Winnicott, D.W. (1967b) Mirror-role of mother and family in child development. In *Playing and Reality* (1971). Harmondsworth: Pelican Books.

Winnicott, D.W. (1969) The use of an object and relating through identification. *International Journal of Psychoanalysis* 50: 711–716.

Winnicott, D.W. (1969) Preface. In J. McDougal & S. Lebovici, *Dialogue with Sammy: a psychoanalytic contribution to the understanding of childhood psychosis*. London: Hogarth Press.

Winnicott, D.W. (1970a) Residential care as therapy. In C. Winnicott, R. Shepherd & M. Davis (eds), *Deprivation and Delinquency*. London: Tavistock.

Winnicott, D.W. (1970b) The mother-infant experience of mutuality. In E.J. Anthony & T. Benedek (eds), *Parenthood: Its Psychology and Psychopathology*. London: J.A. Churchill.

Winnicott, D.W. (1970c) On the basis for self in body. In C. Winnicott, R. Shepherd & M. Davis (eds), *Psychoanalytic Explorations* (1989). London: Karnac Books.

Winnicott, D.W. (1971) *Playing and Reality*. London: Tavistock.

Winnicott, D.W. (1971a) Playing. A theoretical statement. In *Playing and Reality*. London: Tavistock.

Zavitzianos, G. (1971) Fetishism and exhibitionism in the female and their relationship to psychopathy and kleptomania. *International Journal of Psychoanalysis* 52: 297–305.

Appendix
Publications

1964 Phillipson, H. & Hopkins, J. 'Personality and Perception' *British Journal of Medical Psychology* 37(1): 1–15.

1969 'Children in Hospital' *Far Eastern Medical Journal* 5: 279–284.

1977 'Living under the Threat of Death' *Journal of Child Psychotherapy* 4: 5–24.

1983 'Problems of Preparing Young Children for Unplanned Hospital Admissions' in *Paediatric Projects*. Monograph No. 1 *Preparation of Young Healthy Children for Possible Hospitalization: the issues*.

1983 'Mastering the experience of hospitalization: the emotional task facing young children and their parents' *Nursing Times*, Oct. 19.

1984 'The Probable Role of Trauma in a Case of Foot and Shoe Fetishism' *International Review of Psychoanalysis* 11: 79–91.

1986 'Solving the mystery of monsters: steps towards the recovery from trauma' *Journal of Child Psychotherapy* 12: 61–71.

1987 'Failure of the Holding Relationship: Some Effects of Physical Rejection on the Child's Attachment and on his Inner Experience' *Journal of Child Psychotherapy* 13; 5–18, and in C.M. Parkes, J .S Hinde, & P. Morris (eds) (1991), *Attachment Across the Life Cycle*. London: Routledge.

1988 'Facilitating the Development of Intimacy between Nurses and Infants in Day Nurseries' *Early Child Development and Care* 33: 99–111, and in A.S. Honig (ed.) (1990), *Optimising Early Childcare and Education*. New York: Gordon and Breach.

1989 'Ways of Seeing 4' *Journal of Child Psychotherapy* 15: 33–39.

1990 'The Observed Infant of Attachment Theory' *British Journal of Psychotherapy* 6: 460–470.

1992 'Infant-Parent Psychotherapy' *Journal of Child Psychotherapy* 18: 5–17.

1993 'The Meaning of Monsters in Repetitive Play' *Educational Therapy and Therapeutic Teaching* 1: 52–56.

1994 'Therapeutic interventions in infancy: two contrasting cases of persistent crying' *Psychoanalytic Psychotherapy* 8: 141–152, and in J Raphael-Leff (ed.) (2003), *Parent-Infant Psychodynamics: Wild Things, Mirrors and Ghosts*. London: Whurr.

1996   'The dangers and deprivations of too-good mothering' *Journal of Child Psychotherapy* 22: 407–422.

1996   'From baby games to let's pretend: the achievement of playing' *Journal of the British Association of Psychotherapists* 31: 20–28.

1999   'Narcissistic illusions in late adolescence' *Psychoanalytic Inquiry* 19: 229–242, and in A. Horne & M. Lanyado (eds.) (2009), *Through Assessment to Consultation.* Hove & New York: Routledge 2009.

1999   'The family context'. In M. Lanyado & A. Horne (eds.), *The Handbook of Child and Adolescent Psychotherapy.* London & New York: Routledge.

1999   'The contribution of attachment theory'. In M. Lanyado & A. Horne (eds.), *The Handbook of Child and Adolescent Psychotherapy.* London & New York: Routledge.

2000   'Overcoming a child's resistance to late adoption: how one new attachment can facilitate another' *Journal of Child Psychotherapy* 26: 335–347.

2006   'Individual psychotherapy for late-adopted children: how one new attachment can facilitate another'. In J. Kenrick, L. Tollemache & C. Lindsay, *Creating New Families: Therapeutic Approaches to Fostering, Adoption and Kinship Care.* London: Karnac Books.

2008   'Infant-parent psychotherapy: Selma Freiberg's contribution to understanding the past in the present'. In L. Emanuel & E. Bradley, *What can the matter be? Therapeutic Interventions with Parents, Infants and Young Children.* London: Karnac Books.

Index